EDWARD VI

Also in the Yale English Monarchs series

EDWARD VI

Jennifer Loach

Edited by George Bernard and Penry Williams

YALE UNIVERSITY PRESS
NEW HAVEN AND LONDON

Set in New Baskerville by Fakenham Photosetting, Norfolk
Printed in Great Britain by St Edmundsbury Press

Library of Congress Cataloging-in-Publication Data

Loach, Jennifer.
Edward VI / Jennifer Loach: edited by George Bernard and Penry Williams
(Yale English monarchs)
Includes bibliographical references and index.
ISBN 0–300–07992–3 (cloth: alk. paper)
1. Edward VI. King of England, 1537–1553. 2. Great Britain—History—Edward
VI, 1547–1553. 3. Great Britain—Kings and rulers Biography. I. Bernard, G.W.
II. Williams, Penry. III. Title. IV. Series.
DA345.L63 1999
942.05′3′092—dc21
[B] 99–35554
CIP

A catalogue record for this book is available from the British Library.

10 9 8 7 6 5 4 3 2 1

CONTENTS

ILLUSTRATIONS

PREFACE

Jennifer Loach, who succumbed to cancer on 29 April 1995 only a week short of her fiftieth birthday, which she was intending to celebrate in Prague, made a remarkable impact on those who knew her. A striking figure – in the words of the *Times* obituarist 'she was a captivating woman, memorably well-dressed, the coils of dark honey-coloured hair, looped and piled, always about to but never quite escaping'[1] – she combined a rapier-sharp mind with thorough and rigorous scholarship. Educated at King Edward VI School for Girls, Birmingham, she was awarded an Open Scholarship to St Hilda's College, Oxford, where she became President of the Junior Common Room, won the H.W.C. Davis Prize, and in 1967 took the best First of her year in Modern History. After a year as a senior scholar at St Hugh's College, she moved to Somerville College, where she was to serve for the rest of her life, first as a junior research fellow, then as a lecturer and finally, from 1974, as a Fellow and Tutor in Modern History.

Jennifer took her teaching very seriously and was devoted to her pupils. George Bernard, who was one of her first, testifies to her command of her subject (she was formidably well read in European, not just English, history) and to her generosity with her time. She was immensely stimulating on the history, excellent in sparking off ideas by asking deceptively simple questions, never imposing her superior knowledge, just as effective on the practicalities of essay writing and examination technique, but accepting no laxness. Following Menna Prestwich, her tutor at St Hilda's, she was quick to probe the material dimensions of political and religious figures and institutions, but she did not underplay the role of ideas and rejected crude material explanations. 'The material difficulties of the church can be estimated by the historian with far more exactitude than can its spiritual appeal,' she once wrote.[2] If she accepted the necessity of government and realistically assessed the ways it was conducted, brisk moral judgments – for example in her description of Lord

[1] *The Times*, 5 May 1995 (the obituarist was T.C. Barnard).
[2] *EHR*, xcvi (1981), 867.

Burghley's secretary Michael Hickes as 'in his public life little more than a rapacious weevil in the rotten wood of the court' – reflected her Quaker upbringing.[3]

Later she supervised a number of graduate students, many of whom had first come to know her as undergraduates – Angela Britton (whose thesis on the early Stuart House of Lords was deemed publishable as it stood by the external examiner), Philippa Tudor (whose thesis on early Tudor devotional writing anticipates many of the arguments of Eamon Duffy's *The Stripping of the Altars*, 1992), Gary Hill (on the Howard dukes of Norfolk), Alun Fellows (on the judiciary) – though partly through personal choice, and partly because of the dearth of academic posts in the 1980s, none of them went on to become history lecturers.

Jennifer became a prominent figure in the Oxford History Faculty and from 1989 served as an elected member of Hebdomadal Council, the executive cabinet of the university. At one point, though still young for such a post, she was actively considered when another college was electing its head of house. She lectured frequently to schools and at sixth-form conferences. Jennifer's standing and reputation as an Oxford college tutor was high and well known.

What of her as an historian? It would be fair to acknowledge that she had not made quite the impact on the scholarly world that those who knew her work best thought she ought to have done. Her doctoral research, begun in 1967, on parliaments in the reign of Queen Mary, was original and brilliant. She chose to work in what was a little-explored area for which the sources were scanty and often tantalizingly obscure in meaning. Quickly she transformed the subject, handling the material with a scrupulousness and independence of mind that allowed her to question the assumptions with which she had begun. Accepted opinion saw parliament as essentially engaged in conflict with the crown, ultimately leading to the Civil War of the 1640s: Mary's parliaments, as portrayed for example by Sir John Neale, appeared as troublesome precursors, though not yet grown to full maturity, in that epic account of English history. It is hard to convey now, after a generation of 'revisionist' scholarship, how radical and how fresh Jennifer's questioning of such assumptions was. She saw the ruling classes represented in parliaments as engaged in a kind of 'joint-stock' enterprise in which the monarch, as manag-

[3] Ibid., xcii (1978), 442.

ing director, and the MPs, as shareholders, worked in partnership, however much they might on occasions disagree on details, towards a common end. And, she insisted, parliaments could not be properly understood unless the continuing importance of the nobility in the House of Lords and in society more widely was fully recognized. Jennifer's thesis, itself delayed by the demands of teaching, was completed in 1974.[4] If it had been swiftly published as a book – something impossible in the desperate state of academic publishing in the mid-1970s – or if Jennifer had at once summarized its conclusions in an article, then she would have been recognized more widely for what she was: a pioneer in the wave of 'revisionist' writing on parliaments in politics in Tudor and Stuart England. By an independent route, Jennifer reached conclusions about parliaments similar to those of Sir Geoffrey Elton, first voiced in his Royal Historical Society lecture of 1973, Conrad Russell, in a paper published in February 1976, and Kevin Sharpe in his D.Phil. thesis on Sir Robert Cotton in 1975 and in his introduction to *Faction and Parliament* (1978).[5] The origin of 'revisionism' is one of the remarkable features of writing on early modern English history in the 1970s that still awaits an intellectual explanation.[6] Jennifer Loach deserves recognition in that context, especially since by the time that her thesis was published in 1986,[7] and a splendid general survey of parliament under the Tudors appeared in 1991,[8] those who then encountered her work for the first time would not have seen it as original as it undoubtedly was when its claims were first staked out in her thesis. These general ideas, especially in relation to Tudor parliaments, had become familiar through the energetic

[4] J. Loach, 'Opposition to the Crown in Parliament, 1553–1558', University of Oxford D.Phil. thesis, 1974.

[5] G.R. Elton, 'Tudor Government: the Points of Contact: I Parliament', *Transactions of the Royal Historical Society*, 5th series, xxiv (1974), 183–200 (reprinted in *Studies in Tudor and Stuart Politics and Government*, Cambridge, 4 vols, 1974–83, iii, 3–21; C. Russell, 'Parliamentary History in Perspective 1604–29', *History*, lxi (1976), 1–27; K.M. Sharpe, 'The Intellectual and Political Activities of Sir Robert Cotton', University of Oxford D.Phil. thesis, 1975 (published as *Sir Robert Cotton 1586–1631: History and Politics in Early Modern England*, Oxford, 1979); K. Sharpe, 'Introduction: Parliamentary History 1603–1629: in or out of Perspective?', in K. Sharpe, ed., *Faction and Parliament* (Oxford, 1978), 1–42.

[6] See R. Hutton, 'Revisionism in Britain' in M. Bentley, ed., *Companion to Historiography* (London, 1997), 377–91.

[7] J. Loach, *Parliament and the Crown in the Reign of Mary Tudor* (Oxford, 1986).

[8] J. Loach, *Parliament under the Tudors* (Oxford, 1991).

lecturing and publishing of Sir Geoffrey Elton above all. Jennifer's researches on Mary's reign had also led her to question the traditional view that the queen was a bigot who imposed her faith on an unwilling because by now largely Protestant populace: instead Jennifer emphasized the limited extent of sympathy for reformed religion and the willing participation of the ruling classes in the restoration of Catholicism. Here again Jennifer's conclusions place her among that pioneering group of historians who in the 1970s were revising the orthodox Protestant grand narrative of the successful, speedy and inevitable progress of the English Reformation. But it was not until the last year of her life that she published a spirited essay defending Mary's religious policies as far more positive and more welcome than the caricature in John Foxe's *Acts and Monuments*.[9] Jennifer's scholarly rigour and perfectionism no doubt contributed to a certain diffidence in publishing; and she viewed polemic and academic self-promotion with distaste. Expressing measured sceptical dissent in reviews in a learned journal[10] appealed to her temperament in a way that the thunder of academic controversy did not. And commitment to her college, her pupils, and above all to her husband Alan (pursuing his own demanding career as a consultant anaesthetist) and young family (Hannah and Oliver were born in these years), held up the business of revising the thesis for publication. Jennifer would not have wanted it any other way, but privately she remarked on the difficulties encountered by women developing their careers in an academic world increasingly dominated by demands for speedy publication in time for the next Research Assessment Exercise. The situation is certainly worse now than it was then.

If Jennifer began as an historian of parliament, she soon widened her fields of activity and broadened her consideration of Marian parliaments to encompass the mid-Tudor period in general. With Robert Tittler, she put together a seminal collection of essays, *The Mid-Tudor Polity*, published in 1980, which showed that the reigns of Edward VI and Mary should not be seen as an interval of crisis and sterility between the longer and more glamorous reigns of Henry VIII and Elizabeth. In 1992 she published a pamphlet on the mid-

[9] 'Mary Tudor and the Recatholicisation of England', *History Today* (Nov. 1994), 16–22.
[10] For example *English Historical Review*, xcvi (1981), 866–9, xcviii (1983), 623–5.

Tudor crisis that must have moulded a thousand undergraduate essays. A love of architecture – she taught on the Oxford special subject 'Wren to Hawksmoor' – led her to treat ceremonial seriously, as is shown by a remarkable paper on the funerals of Henry VII and Henry VIII.[11]

Jennifer's work reflected a firm, austere scholarship, a deep respect for the evidence and for traditional historical scholarship, combined with an unwavering commitment to the lucid and economical presentation of her conclusions. A good deal of her writing was focused on others' suggestions and interpretations: these are succinctly described, scrutinized, and usually qualified or rejected. She would often include for such treatment historians of a previous generation, even making them her starting point: this sometimes led her to tilt at opinions that were no longer widely held. Perhaps that gave some of her work a negative air. But above all it reflected the challenges of teaching – the challenge of teaching potentially good students who needed, however, to be stretched. Confronting them with conventional views, asking probing questions – and showing them with the apt detail that careful reading could yield that the pious orthodoxies did not work very well – was at the heart of her method of encouraging the young to develop questioning minds of their own. She succeeded to a remarkable degree.

Jennifer's principal interest in her last years was this book, a political biography of Edward VI, which she was commissioned to write in 1988. Historical writing on that reign was dominated in the first half of the twentieth century by A.F. Pollard's *England under Protector Somerset* (London, 1900). Somerset was the hero of the story: he was the 'good duke', with 'no mean or selfish motives' and 'aims that were essentially noble'. He attempted to cure the ills of the commonwealth and especially the sufferings of the poor, but was brought down by his fellow nobles and councillors, who resented attempts to curb their greed. A harsh regime then followed under John Dudley, elevated as duke of Northumberland, who ruled only in the interests of the landowners and sacrificed the well-being of the country to his own ambitions. The young King Edward played only a limited role in events. In general, the reign of Edward, together, indeed, with that of his sister Mary, was presented as amounting to no more than an insignificant and turbulent inter-

[11] J. Loach, 'The Function of Ceremonial in the Reign of Henry VIII', *Past and Present*, cxlii (1994), 43–68.

lude between the glowing and creative reigns of Henry VIII and Elizabeth.

Such an approach to the middle years of the sixteenth century was largely echoed in G.R. Elton's *England under the Tudors* (London, 1955), by far the most popular and influential textbook for several decades. For Elton, the period from the death of Thomas Cromwell in 1540 to the accession of Elizabeth in 1558 was one of 'somewhat purposeless turmoil'. The reigns of Edward and Mary 'well-nigh ruined the achievement of the first Tudors. Disorder at the top was again threatening the stability of the realm.' Elton did, however, reverse Pollard's judgments on Somerset and Northumberland. Accepting that Somerset was 'noble-minded and generous', he considered him 'high-handed and incompetent', thoroughly deserving his own overthrow: nobility of character was never, for Elton, as valuable in a ruler as ruthless competence. Admitting that 'no one has ever had a good word' for Northumberland, Elton claimed, with some reason, that he showed 'skill and penetration in public affairs'; but 'his party's selfish greed' brought him down in the end. About Edward, Elton was very brief.[12]

In the first biography of Edward to be published for fifty years, *The Last Tudor King. A Study of Edward VI* (Bath, 1958), Hester Chapman had more to say. She presented Edward as an intelligent and vigorous boy rather than a pallid and sickly child. Her work is lively and colourful, sometimes more like the prose of a novelist than an historian. Understandably, in a book intended for the general public, she concentrated upon the personal side of the story rather than on political or social analysis; consequently the biography had little impact upon the historiography of the reign.

In the 1960s Wilbur K. Jordan attempted a serious and large-scale study. In two volumes amounting to 1,096 pages, Jordan produced a minutely detailed, and sometimes indigestible, survey.[13] Although the book was more an history of the reign than a biography of the king, Edward VI was brought very much to the fore. He was, Jordan claimed, no religious bigot, but certainly a firm Protestant. Above all, he promised in the last two or three years of his life to develop into an outstanding monarch. Yet while Jordan gave a new slant to

---

[12] G.R. Elton, *England under the Tudors* (1955), 193, 222, 209–10.
[13] W.K. Jordan, *Edward VI: the Young King* (London, 1968); *Edward VI: The Threshold of Power* (London, 1970).

the study of Edward himself, his interpretation of the two men who ruled in the king's name differed little from that of Pollard. Somerset was presented as 'a very great man whose magnanimity was never to be forgotten as Englishmen spoke in quiet corners ... of the age of the "Good Duke" '.[14] Northumberland remained the villain, almost at times the pantomime villain, in Jordan's melodramatic prose: he had a 'dark and possibly twisted mind'; he was 'almost pathological in his fear of plots', and displayed an 'almost psychotic mood of reaction'.[15]

The view of the mid-Tudor years as a period of turmoil, an unhappy and uncreative interlude between the two great reigns of Henry VIII and his younger daughter Elizabeth, was summed up, without much qualification, in W.R.D. Whitney Jones's *The Mid-Tudor Crisis 1539–1563* (London, 1973). For Whitney Jones, England then underwent a serious crisis: economic, social, administrative and religious. The succession of a boy and then of a woman threatened the stability of the monarchy and encouraged the return of over-mighty subjects. But if Whitney Jones did pay full attention to the period he treated, his work rested on assumptions that were increasingly being questioned.

Doubts had been expressed on specific points of this overarching interpretation. C.S.L. Davies, studying the Vagrancy Act of 1547 which imposed slavery as a punishment for refusal to work, argued that 'sheer impracticality' and 'sheer incompetence' characterized Somerset's social policies: Somerset's standing as a reformer was called into question.[16] M.L. Bush's *The Government Policy of Protector Somerset* (London, 1975) questioned both Somerset's ideals and his competence. Arguing that the Protector was more interested in the conquest and domination of Scotland than in social policy, he rejected almost entirely the Pollard thesis of the 'good duke'. D.E. Hoak, in *The King's Council in the Reign of Edward VI* (Cambridge, 1976) offered a serious examination of the workings of government under Edward. Somerset emerged as an autocratic as well as an incompetent politician whose fall was the result of misgovernment rather than high ideals. Northumberland received more favourable treatment from Hoak than he had before. Hoak summarized and

[14] Jordan, *Edward VI: the Young King*, 523.
[15] Jordan, *Edward VI: the Threshold of Power*, 54, 67, 76.
[16] C.S.L. Davies, 'Slavery and Protector Somerset: the Vagrancy Act of 1547', *Economic History Review*, 2nd series, xix (1966), 533–49.

extended his claims in an essay on Northumberland in the 1980 collection that Jennifer Loach and Robert Tittler edited.[17]

In the nearly two decades since then, there have been many specialist studies of particular aspects of the reign of Edward, but there has been no recent attempt to offer a fresh vision and an overall summing-up based on substantial archival research. It is this that Jennifer Loach embarked upon when she accepted the invitation to write this book for the English Monarchs series. Jennifer recognized that writing a life of a king who died in his sixteenth year posed unusual challenges for a political historian. Should the book concentrate on the biographical details of a boy and his upbringing? Or should the scope be widened to included assessment of the activities of those who ruled in the king's name? Jennifer chose the second course, discussing the issue with each of us independently, before we knew what lay in the future for her, and we were both convinced that this was the right approach. In editing the book we have accordingly been inclusive rather than exclusive in setting the boundaries. None the less one of the book's strengths does lie in its examination of Edward's upbringing, courtly activities and health, on which matters Jennifer has important new perspectives to offer.

It remains to explain the circumstances in which we have completed Jennifer's text. In June 1996 Alan Loach passed on to us Jennifer's disks (it was impossible to obtain anything from the hard disk on her computer, but virtually all the disks had last been updated within weeks of her death). Two months later Penry Williams had sight of Jennifer's notes and papers and in September 1997 Alan Loach brought them to George Bernard in Southampton. It is from what we found that we have put together this book. At first it seemed that what survived was disparate material from which a number of articles might emerge; but on closer analysis, and assisted by an early manifesto that Jennifer had drawn up for the book, we felt that we could see a way of arranging the material that would turn it into a coherent study of the reign of Edward VI. Overwhelmingly what is published here is Jennifer's work in her own words. Her draft sections were very polished, mostly fully referenced, if often unfinished. But some references had to be corrected or supplied (we are grateful to Graeme Smith for early assistance

[17] D. Hoak, 'Rehabilitating the Duke of Northumberland: Politics and Political Control, 1549–1553', in J. Loach and R. Tittler, eds, *The Mid-Tudor Polity* (London and Basingstoke, 1980), 74-93.

here). In places we needed to complete or to write linking passages between chapters or sections of chapters. There was little published before Jennifer's death that she had not taken account of. But we have tried to update her text in the light of any substantial subsequent scholarship. Many sections were largely finished, but inevitably there were some gaps in what Jennifer left behind. Here we have supplemented Jennifer's disks with unpublished lectures found in her papers, and by drawing on some previously published work, the details of which we acknowledge elsewhere. For the final chapter, we have used drafts of her general lectures on the reign of Edward VI, but here we have had to go beyond Jennifer's words, and possibly thoughts, on occasion. Our most difficult task was treating the ascendancy of Northumberland, and in particular religious change under Northumberland: here we have assembled material from diverse places, including draft lectures and previously published papers, and added an outline of matters that Jennifer had not yet treated. Throughout we have had two objectives, first, to make the book as readable and useful as possible, and secondly, to preserve, as far as we can, the scholarly integrity of Jennifer's interpretations. Sometimes we have allowed to stand arguments that we might ourselves wish to qualify. Inevitably too we are aware of tensions, on a few occasions, in the argument, and while we have done our best to resolve them, we have sometimes left them largely untouched. At other times we have put the interests of the reader, as we see them, above absolute fidelity to the drafts and notes. The exercise has raised intriguing questions about the nature of 'authorship'. Essentially this is Jennifer's book; but, had she lived to complete it, undoubtedly it would have been different. Just how Jennifer would have felt about its appearance in this form is impossible to say. We can do no more than hope that she would have been satisfied with what we have done. But we are confident that the book as published will make a major contribution to Tudor historiography and trust that it will be seen as a fitting tribute to Jennifer's memory.

George Bernard and Penry Williams

ACKNOWLEDGEMENTS

On behalf of Jennifer Loach we should wish to thank the following archives, record offices, libraries and institutions for permission to cite manuscripts in their possession, and their staff for their assistance: the Public Record Office, London; the British Library, London; the Bodleian Library, Oxford; the Inner Temple Library, London; the Society of Antiquaries, London; the Bibliothèque Nationale, Paris; the College of Arms, London (especially John Brooke-Little and Dr Robert Yorke); the History of Parliament Trust, London; The Queen's College, Oxford; Guildford Museum and Record Office.

Jennifer Loach would have wished to thank Barbara Harvey, Alastair Parker and Paul Slack for their comments and advice; Fiona Kisby and John N. King for references and for sharing unpublished material; her graduate students Dakota Hamilton and Philippa Tudor; Trevor Hughes and Paul Beeson for advice on medical matters; the British Academy for the award of a Senior Fellowship; Somerville College, Oxford, for sabbatical leave and for general support.

The publishers wish to thank those who have allowed the editors to draw on previously published material: Judith Loades of Headstart History (for Chapter 5, which is based upon Jennifer Loach's *Protector Somerset: A Reassessment*, Bangor, 1994); Oxford University Press (for Chapter 13, which uses material from Dr Loach's *Parliament and the Crown in the Reign of Mary Tudor*, Oxford, 1986).

We should wish to thank John Cooper for lending us his notes of Jennifer Loach's last lectures; Graeme Smith; Ralph Houlbrooke, Diarmaid MacCulloch and Jack Scarisbrick for their helpful scrutiny of the text; and Robert Baldock, Alex Nesbit and Tom Buhler of Yale University Press for their encouragement and assistance.

George Bernard and Penry Williams
July 1999

ABBREVIATIONS

Add.	Additional
APC	*The Acts of the Privy Council of England*, ed. J.R. Dasent (46 vols, London, 1890–1964)
BL	British Library
BN	Bibliothèque Nationale
Cal. Pat. Rolls	*Calendar of the Patent Rolls*, ed. R.H. Brodie (5 vols, London, 1924–9)
CSP Dom	*Calendar of State Papers, Domestic, 1547–1590*, ed. R. Lemon (2 vols, London, 1856–72)
CSP Foreign	*Calendar of State Papers, Foreign, Edward VI and Mary*, ed. W.B. Turnbull (2 vols, London, 1861)
CSP Spanish	*Calendar of State Papers, Spanish*, vols ix (*1547–1549*), x (*1550–1552*), xi (*1553*) ed. M.A.S. Hume and R. Tyler (London, 1912, 1914)
CSP Venetian	*Calendar of State Papers . . . Venice*, vol. v (*1534–1554*), ed. R. Brown (London, 1873)
Edward VI, Chronicle	*The Chronicle and Political Papers of King Edward VI*, ed. W.K. Jordan (London, 1966)
EHR	*English Historical Review*
Foxe	J. Foxe, *The Acts and Monuments*, ed. J. Pratt (8 vols, London, 1870)
HMC	*Historical Manuscripts Commission*
HMC, Salisbury	*Historical Manuscripts Commission, Calendar of the Manuscripts of the Marquis of Salisbury at Hatfield House* (24 vols, London, 1883–1976)
Hughes and Larkin	P.L. Hughes and T.F. Larkin, *Tudor Royal Proclamations* (3 vols, New Haven and London, 1964, 1969), vol i
LP	*Letters and Papers, Foreign and Domestic, of the Reign of Henry VIII*, ed. J.S. Brewer, J. Gairdner and R.H. Brodie (23 vols in 38 parts, London, 1862–1932)
Lisle Letters	*The Lisle Letters*, ed. M.StC. Byrne (6 vols, Chicago, 1980)
NPG	National Portrait Gallery

Nichols,   J.G. Nichols, *The Literary Remains of King Edward VI* (2
   Literary   vols, London, 1857)
   Remains
PRO   Public Record Office
PRO SP 10   Public Record Office, State Papers Domestic,
                Edward VI
RSTC   *A Short Title Catalogue, of Books printed ... 1475–1640*,
                ed. A.W. Pollard and G.R. Redgrave, revised by W.A.
                Jackson, F.S. Ferguson and K.F. Pantzer (3 vols,
                London, 1976–91)
Scépeaux,   *Mémoires de la vie de François de Scépeaux, sire de*
   Mémoires   *Vieilleville*, in *Collection complète de mémoires relatif à*
                l'histoire de France, ed. C.-B. Petitot (Paris, 1822), vols
                xxvi–xxvii
State Papers *State Papers ... King Henry VIII* (5 parts in 11 vols,
                London, 1830–52)
Wriothesley,   C. Wriothesley, *A Chronicle of England*, ed. W.D.
   Chronicle   Hamilton (2 vols, London, Camden Society new
                series, xi, parts i and ii, 1875, 1877)

Chapter 1

THE BIRTH OF EDWARD VI

Early in September 1535 Henry VIII and his second wife, Anne Boleyn, spent a few days at the Wiltshire home of a loyal but undistinguished courtier, Sir John Seymour. Wolf Hall was a pleasant, old-fashioned house, filled with Sir John's numerous, and ambitious progeny: Edward, Sir John's eldest son, was already part of the royal household, as was his sister, Jane, who was one of the queen's ladies-in-waiting. The visit to Wolf Hall was a success, and Edward Seymour was rewarded accordingly by promotion to a position of influence close to the king as a gentleman of the privy chamber.

Jane Seymour was probably not present at the king's visit, but fairly soon afterwards she appears to have caught Henry's eye. In January 1536 Anne Boleyn suffered a miscarriage, and her weakened health or depressed spirits seem to have prompted Henry to embark on a series of rather public flirtations with other women. Precisely when Jane's quiet charms attracted the attention of the king is not clear, and we do not know how she felt about his approaches. Her cautious – and public – response to a purse full of sovereigns was a declaration that she would accept money from the king only when God sent her 'quelque bon party de mariage',[1] presumably meaning that she would accept a gift from the monarch as a wedding present and not otherwise. Her response may suggest that she felt no enthusiasm for the role of royal plaything. Equally, she may have been encouraged by Edward Seymour in the belief that holding the king at bay might be a way of playing for the highest possible stakes.[2]

Throughout most of April 1536 all seemed to be well with Henry's marriage to Anne. On 18 April the imperial ambassador, Eustace Chapuys, was invited by Henry to kiss Anne's hand, a sign

[1] *CSP, Spanish*, v (part ii), no. 43, 84.
[2] E.W. Ives, *Anne Boleyn* (Oxford 1986), 247; G.W. Bernard, 'The Fall of Anne Boleyn' *EHR*, cvi (1991), 584–610, esp. 588–9.

that she was still in favour; and although he avoided doing so, he did publicly recognize her for the first time.[3] On 24 April the first indications of an alteration appeared, with the issue of a special judicial commission, the instrument that was to destroy Anne and her friends. On 27 April the writs for a new parliament were issued. Since the Reformation Parliament had been dissolved only a few weeks before, this suggests that new and unforeseen political circumstances had arisen. Then, on Sunday 30 April a court musician, Mark Smeton, was arrested and interrogated under pressure, possibly under torture. He confessed to adultery with Anne. Next day, at the end of the May Day tournament at Greenwich, Henry left suddenly for Whitehall with only six attendants, leaving Anne behind. By the morning Anne herself, her brother Lord Rochford and three gentlemen of the privy chamber, Henry Norris, William Brereton and Francis Weston, were lodged in the Tower with Smeton. Evidence was rapidly and extensively gathered and on 12 May Norris, Brereton and Weston were arraigned and found guilty of treason. Three days later Anne and Rochford were charged with incest, adultery and treason. They were sentenced to die; on 17 May the marriage of Anne to Henry was dissolved; and on 19 May she was dead.

Whether Anne was actually guilty of some at least of the offences with which she was charged or whether Henry's mind was poisoned against her by political opponents, including Thomas Cromwell, it is impossible to determine with certainty, given the incomplete and conflicting evidence. It does, however, seem sure that Henry was deeply shaken and shocked by the reports presented to him of her misconduct and was not seeking a way to dispose of a wife of whom he had tired.[4]

However that may be, on 30 May 1536, only eleven days after the queen's death, Henry and Jane Seymour were married in the queen's closet at York Place.[5] There is little in Jane's pale and puffy appearance, as depicted by Holbein, or in her few recorded utterances, that explains how she came to captivate the king. Indeed, so lacking in force is her image that some historians have depicted her as no more than a tool in the hands of a faction that wished only to

---

[3] *CSP, Spanish*, v (ii), no. 43a, 91–3; cf. Bernard, 'Fall of Anne Boleyn', 589–90.
[4] For the recent debates see Ives, *Anne Boleyn*, Bernard, 'The Fall of Anne Boleyn', and in *EHR*, cvii (1992), 651–74.
[5] M.St C. Byrne, ed., *The Lisle Letters* (Chicago, 6 vols, 1981), iv, 52 (no. 848a).

destroy Anne Boleyn, and, with her, the minister who had smoothed her passage to the crown, Thomas Cromwell. However, it has proved difficult to find evidence to support the existence of such a faction. Whilst Agnes Strickland's portrait of Jane as a shameless schemer, giving 'her hand to the regal ruffian before his wife's corpse was cold',[6] is undoubtedly overdrawn, the surviving evidence suggests that Jane Seymour enjoyed being queen. Moreover, Jane's instructions about suitable clothing to Lady Lisle, whose young daughter wished to join her household, suggest a certain brisk realism – and it is also interesting that Jane expressly prohibited the French headdresses that were so closely associated with her predecessor. It is therefore not unthinkable that she may herself have been an active participant in the events that made her queen.[7]

Whatever the nature of Jane's hold over the king, Henry clearly enjoyed showing off his young wife before his people and his court:[8] he may indeed have felt, in Sir John Russell's words, that he had 'come out of hell into heaven'.[9] He showered Jane with expensive gifts,[10] replaced Anne's badge of the leopard by Seymour panthers,[11] and embarked on extensive developments at Hampton Court meant to provide her with new lodgings and a fashionable long gallery.[12]

The king intended his new wife to be crowned in the autumn of 1536, but plague in London caused a postponement.[13] In the aftermath of the Pilgrimage of Grace, Henry told the rebel leader, Robert Aske, and a Yorkshire gentleman, Sir Oswald Wolsthrop,

[6] A. Strickland, *Lives of the Queens of England from the Norman Conquest* (8 vols, 1851), iii, 2.

[7] *Lisle Letters*, iv, 151–2 (no. 887), 161–5 (nos 894–5).

[8] C. Wriothesley, *A Chronicle of England*, ed. W.D. Hamilton (2 vols, Camden Society, 1875 and 1877), i, 43–9; *Lisle Letters*, iii, 396 (no. 713), 419 (no. 722), 576 (no. 813).

[9] *Lisle Letters*, iii, 396 (no. 713).

[10] See, for example, the 'Seymour cup', designed by Holbein: D. Starkey, ed., *Henry VIII. A European Court in England* (London, 1991), plate IX: 14, 127.

[11] H.M. Colvin, ed., *The History of the King's Works, Vol. IV 1485–1660 (Part II)* (London, 1982), 26.

[12] Simon Thurley, 'Henry VIII and the Building of Hampton Court: a Reconstruction of the Tudor Palace', *Architectural History* (1988), 1–51, esp. 29–37.

[13] The general view seems to have been that the event would take place on 29 October, the Sunday before All Hallows (*Lisle Letters*, iii, 489 (no. 769)). The sum of £320 had already been spent when the preparations were halted (Colvin, *King's Works*, iv, 291). For the postponement see *LP*, XI, 501, 528.

that he intended to have Jane crowned at York when parliament was held there.[14] But since the offer of a parliament at York had been a concession made to the rebels under duress by the king's commanders and since no such parliament was ever held, it is unlikely that Henry ever seriously intended to have Jane crowned at York. But in any case the queen's pregnancy, announced by a *Te Deum* at St Paul's on Trinity Sunday, 27 May 1537, prompted the king to postpone plans for the coronation.[15] The king was clearly delighted about the impending birth, and added a nursery to the building works at Hampton Court;[16] the new rooms were just finished when Jane went into labour on 11 October.[17] In the early hours of the following day, the eve of St Edward's Day, a baby boy was delivered.

Later, it would be claimed that Edward was born by Caesarean section. The earliest occasion is in the explanation that one Richard Swann of Hounslow gave in November 1538 of a prophecy 'that he should be killed that never was born'. This supposedly referred to the prince, since a lady had told the king at the time of Edward's birth 'that one of the two must die': Henry had accordingly ordered the child to be saved by being 'cut out of his mother's womb'.[18] A document in the Vatican Library states that Henry caused Jane's death 'when she was in severe labour in a difficult child-birth, by having all her limbs stretched for the purpose of making a passage for the child, or (as others stated) having the womb cut before she was dead'. The story was later repeated by Catholic propagandists under Elizabeth, in a campaign to blacken the reputation of the king who removed England from Roman obedience. Nicholas Sanders, for example, wrote in 1581 that Henry, asked by the doctors whether the mother or the child should be saved, answered that it should be the boy, 'because he [Henry] could easily provide himself with other wives'.[19]

---

[14] *LP*, XII, i 43, 44, 45, 137, 201, 202.

[15] Wriothesley, *Chronicle*, i, 64.

[16] Thurley, 'Henry VIII and the Building of Hampton Court', 29–37.

[17] Wriothesley, *Chronicle*, i, 65–6.

[18] G.R. Elton, *Policy and Police* (Cambridge, 1972), 59, citing PRO, E36/120, fo. 58. In June 1539 one John Ryan, keeper of a lodging house at Tower Hill, allegedly said that it was prophesied that the prince should be as great a murderer as his father, and that he must be a murderer by kind, for he murdered his mother in his birth, which reveals rather different gossip (*LP*, XIV, ii 11, 73).

[19] R.L. de Molen, 'The Birth of Edward VI and the Death of Queen Jane: the Arguments for and against Caesarean Section', *Renaissance Studies*, iv (1990), 359–91.

A weakness of Sanders's story is, of course, that the sex of the child could not have been known until after the birth. Since no woman was expected to survive a Caesarean, the operation was normally used only when the mother was already dead or expected to die. But there is no evidence that Jane was thought to be in danger of death at the time. No immediately contemporary source suggests that, or mentions any Caesarean. Jane did not die immediately after giving birth, but lived for another twelve days, which in itself casts doubt on the likelihood of resort to Caesarean section. She was generally thought to have come through the ordeal of childbirth rather well: some commentators looked forward to a succession of children.[20] Moreover Jane was well enough for her baby to be brought to her chamber immediately after the service of christening.[21] Whilst the possibility of a Caesarean section cannot totally be eliminated, given the uncertainties of the evidence, it does seem very implausible.[22]

Edward's birth was marked by the customary celebration. *Te Deum* was sung in all London parish churches at eight that morning, and there was a solemn procession at St Paul's in the presence of, amongst others, the French ambassador. The bells rang in the city until ten in the evening, there were bonfires, 'fruites and wyne', and 'their was shott at the Tower that night above two thousand gonnes'.[23] The German merchants of the Steel Yard were particularly prominent in these festivities, distributing a hogshead of wine and two barrels of beer to the poor.

On 15 October the baby was christened in the royal chapel at Hampton Court, a highly decorated building recently embellished by the king.[24] Archbishop Cranmer and the duke of Norfolk stood as godfathers, and the Princess Mary, who had appeared at court much more regularly since her father's third marriage, as godmother;[25] Charles Brandon, first duke of Suffolk, served as godfather at the confirmation that followed immediately upon the christening. The baby's other half-sister, the four-year-old Elizabeth,

---

[20] John Husee, writing to Lord Lisle on 16 October about the christening from an eyewitness account, said, 'I pray Jesu send his Grace long to prosper and live, and the King's Highness many more sons' (*Lisle Letters*, iv, no. 1024, p. 425).

[21] *LP*, XII, ii, 911 (p. 320).

[22] I am grateful to Trevor Hughes for advice on Jane's pregnancy.

[23] Wriothesley, *Chronicle*, i, 66–7.

[24] Simon Thurley, *The Royal Palaces of Tudor England* (New Haven and London, 1993), 201–2. See Plate 1.

[25] This account is taken from College of Arms MS M6, fos 23–26v.

carried the baptismal chrism, and was herself carried by Edward Seymour, the queen's brother.

Edward was taken from his 'home' to the chapel and back by Gertrude Courtenay, marchioness of Exeter, with the duke of Norfolk 'staying his head, as she bare him', and the duke of Suffolk at his feet.[26] The journey led through the council chamber, the king's great chamber, the hall and 'second court'. Edward was robed, according to a sixteenth-century drawing, in an elaborate white gown, the train of which was carried by William Fitzalan, eleventh earl of Arundel and Lord William Howard, half-brother to the duke of Norfolk and later created Baron Howard of Effingham. A nurse and a midwife were on hand to provide practical assistance, and elaborate precautions were taken to shield the baby from draughts as he was carried through the open courts of the palace.

At the chapel, a rich porch had been erected, hung with cloth of gold and arras: the floor was boarded and laid with carpets. Inside, an eight-sided platform, again covered with cloth of gold, had been constructed to hold the silver-gilt font, over which was erected a canopy.[27] Amidst the cloth of gold, the rich gifts of plate given by the sponsors, and the twenty-four trumpeters, some thought had also been given to the baby's needs. To the south of the font was a curtained enclosure 'for makyng redy the prince', containing 'a fyer pan of colys with a good perfume', and silver-gilt basins of water 'to wash the prynce if nede be'.

After the service, from which, as was usual, both his parents were absent, Edward was taken to his mother's chamber, where the king also waited. Here he received his parents' formal blessing, as well as that of the Virgin and St George. At the christening he had been proclaimed duke of Cornwall, a dignity to which he had become entitled at birth.[28] Henry was beside himself with pleasure. The christening was marked by further celebrations in London and at court. The king created six new knights, and raised his eldest brother-in-law to the earldom of Hertford.[29]

However, on 23 October the queen became ill. There had been no earlier sign of weakness, and the king had been planning to leave her and resume his progress when she fell prey to 'an naturall

[26] Wriothesley, *Chronicle*, i, 68. The second male attendant was the marquess of Exeter (College of Arms MS M6, fo. 25).
[27] College of Arms MS M6, fo. 82v. See Plate 2.
[28] *LP*, XII, ii, 911.
[29] Ibid., 911, 923.

laxe'.[30] She rapidly worsened, and died during the night of Wednesday, 24 October. Thomas Cromwell later commented that Jane had died as a consequence of 'the faulte of them that were about her, whiche suffred her to take greate cold and to eate such thinges that her fantazie in syknes called for',[31] but it is difficult to fit this description to any condition known to modern medicine. Perhaps the queen succumbed to a puerperal infection, but the fact that she seems to have been reasonably well for some ten days, along with the rapid progress of her illness, argues against even a fulminating puerperal fever. It is possible that the queen's illness was sparsely recorded amid the jubilation celebrating the birth of a male heir, but against that, there is no mention of fever – which would have undoubtedly been a feature of any progressive puerperal infection leading to a general septicaemia. The queen's death occured twelve days after a labour in which no serious difficulty was reported. Her terminal illness was so rapid that after just one day she was dead, having suffered what was termed 'an naturall laxe', in other words heavy bleeding. Although puerperal infection is not entirely to be ruled out, at least as a contributory factor, a more likely explanation of Jane's death is the retention in her womb of parts of the placenta. That led to a catastrophic haemorrhage several days after labour. An experienced midwife would routinely check the afterbirth to make sure that it had been completely extruded, but Jane was cared for by the royal doctors – distinguished academics whose practical experience was very small. A lesser woman might have received better treatment.[32]

Poor Jane: her period of splendour had been short. Her jewels were soon given away, and her jointure reclaimed; even the glass panes put into the windows of her new lodgings only a few weeks earlier were removed so that 'the ayar myght have recourse' to the corpse.[33] On Monday, 12 November her coffin, surmounted by 'a picture' or effigy richly apparelled and wearing a gold crown, with four great white silk banners telling the life of the Virgin Mary around it, left Hampton Court for Windsor, where Jane was buried the next day.[34]

---

[30] Ibid., 970.
[31] *State Papers*, viii, no. ccclxxviii, p. 1 (*LP*, XII, ii, 1004).
[32] I am grateful to Trevor Hughes for these suggestions on the causes of Jane's death.
[33] Thurley, 'Henry VIII and the Building of Hampton Court', 36.
[34] College of Arms MS M6, fos 1–13; Wriothesley, *Chronicle*, i, 70–1.

But her baby thrived: indeed, even before his mother's death he was described as sucking well, 'like a child of his puissance'.[35] In February Henry invited various ambassadors to go to see him, which they did,[36] for they were anxious to set eyes on a child whose hand in marriage they already sought.[37] In May Henry spent the day with his son, 'dallying with him in his arms ... and so holding him in a window to the sight and great comfort of all the people'.[38] At much the same time Margaret Bryan,[39] who had been appointed 'lady mistress' of the prince's household, reported that Edward was in 'good health and merry', with three teeth and another on the way.[40] When Thomas, Lord Audley, the Lord Chancellor, went to see the prince in September 1538, he reported that the child was merry and pleasant; thinner than he had been, 'yet he shotyth owt in length, and wexith ferme and stiff, and can stedfastly stond, and wold avaunce hym self to move and go, if they wold suffir hym'.[41] This growing maturity was reflected in the appointment the next month of a 'dry nurse', Sybil Penne;[42] Edward's personal needs had until then been looked after by wet-nurses and various 'rockers'.[43]

[35] *LP*, XII, ii, 1004.

[36] Ibid., XIII, i, 323, 338, 402.

[37] Ibid., 255, 281, 329, etc.

[38] Ibid., 1011.

[39] Margaret Bouchier, daughter of Humphrey, Lord Berners, and wife of Sir Thomas Bryan.

[40] *LP*, XIII, i, 1290, 1538.

[41] *State Papers*, i no. cxiv p. 586 (LP, XIII, ii, 306).

[42] *LP*, XIII, ii, 524. She was the daughter of Sir Hugh Pagenham, and the wife of John Penne, a groom of the chamber and barber-surgeon to Henry VIII. She was still alive in 1562.

[43] In 1552 one of these women, Jane Russell, was still in receipt of a pension (W.C. Richardson, *The Report of the Royal Commission of 1552*, West Virginia, 1974, 83)

Chapter 2

EDWARD'S UPBRINGING AND EDUCATION

In March 1538 a formal household was set up for the prince. Sir William Sidney, father of Henry Sidney and grandfather of Philip, was appointed chamberlain, Richard Cox, later to be Edward's principal tutor, almoner, and Sir John Cornwallis, of Brome Hall, Suffolk, steward.[1] Strict instructions were issued to the household about keeping the prince's lodgings well aired, and members were told not to visit London during periods when contagious diseases were rife. The household was also told to keep those seeking alms well away from the gates.[2] In 1544 Sidney was succeeded by Sir Richard Page, the stepfather of Anne Stanhope, Edward Seymour's wife: Page was later described by the king's other uncle, Thomas Seymour, as a 'drunken soul'.[3] In 1541 Thomas Wroth, of Enfield, Middlesex, a close friend of the prince, became one of Edward's gentlemen ushers, and by 1547 his chamber included several young noblemen, only a little older than himself, such as Henry Brandon, second duke of Suffolk; Henry Stanley, Lord Strange, heir to the earl of Derby; and Thomas Butler, earl of Ormonde, head of a major Anglo-Irish dynasty and the first of his family to become a Protestant.[4] Edward was also provided with a troupe of players for his amusement.[5]

Improvements were soon made to the prince's lodgings at Hampton Court; these included the addition of a 'wasshing howse', a 'jakes', and a kitchen.[6] Edward also had a set of 'public' rooms,

---

[1] *The Lisle Letters*, v, 79 (no. 1130).
[2] BL, Cotton MS, Vitellius C. x, fo. 65.
[3] PRO, SP10/6, no. 13.
[4] PRO, LC 2/2, fos 53r–v.
[5] *LP*, XIII, ii, 1280.
[6] Simon Thurley, 'Henry VIII and the Building of Hampton Court': a Reconstruction of the Tudor Palace', *Architectural History* (1988), 1–51, 31. In December 1537 curtains were provided for an 18-foot travers in the nursery.

including a chamber of presence. However, much of his first few months seems to have been passed not at Hampton Court but at Havering, a house in Essex that had been part of his mother's jointure.[7] Lord Audley commented that this residence, although much improved by Henry, was nice in the summer, but less attractive in the winter.[8]

There is still extant one list of the gifts given to the two-year-old prince on New Year's Day 1539.[9] Most of the presents were items of plate, such as the king's gilt standing-cup with 'antique woorks with a man on the topp', or Cromwell's gilt cup garnished with antiques, and with dragon feet. Henry Bourchier, earl of Essex, seems to have had a better idea of what would please the child, for he gave him 'a belle of golde with a whisell'.[10]

Judging by all these early reports, Edward was a contented child, and visitors frequently stressed his merriness.[11] He danced around happily when the minstrel played, and was, according to Lady Bryan, 'as full of pretty toys as ever I saw child in my life'.[12] The imperial ambassador described the prince as 'the prettiest child you ever saw'.[13] However, he did sometimes behave badly. Stephen Gardiner, bishop of Winchester, later recalled that the baby prince had burst into tears when visited by the ambassadors of Saxony and Hesse; despite all the 'chering, dandelyng and flatering' of his nurse and Lady Bryan he 'ever cryed and turned awaye his face'. This was despite the efforts of the earl of Essex 'to accustume him to a sterne countenaunce and rowe gret berd' by playing with him and putting his own beard near the prince's face, which made him laugh. (Gardiner believed that the prince's dislike of the Protestant ambassadors proved the child's godliness.)[14]

[7] Simon Thurley, *The Royal Palaces of Tudor England* (New Haven and London, 1993), p. 78.

[8] *LP*, XIII, ii, 306.

[9] BL, Royal MS App. 89, fo. 41.

[10] Ibid.

[11] See, for example, Audley in *LP*, XIII, ii, 306.

[12] *LP*, XIV, ii app. 9; M.A.E. Wood, *Letters of Royal and Illustrious Ladies of Great Britain* (3 vols, London, 1846), iii, 112.

[13] *LP*, XIII, ii, 232.

[14] J.A. Muller, ed., *The Letters of Stephen Gardiner* (Cambridge, 1933), 161–2; S.J. Gunn, 'Henry Bourchier, earl of Essex (1472–1540)', in G.W. Bernard, ed., *The Tudor Nobility* (Manchester, 1992), 141. The incident must have occurred before 1540 and the death of the 'olde' earl of Essex, Henry Bourchier, on 13 March 1540.

The boy's health, like his temper, was good: in October 1541 the French ambassador, Marillac, reported that the prince was 'beau et bien nourry et merveilleusement grand pour son aaige'.[15] But, in the autumn of that same year the prince contracted what was described as 'a quartan fever',[16] something which was always dangerous in a child. Henry summoned 'tous les medecins du pays', but for perhaps ten days Edward's life seemed in danger, one of the doctors telling Marillac that 'sans cet accident ledit prince luy semble estre de composition si grosse, si chérnue et mal saine, qu'il ne peult penser, par ce que présentement il en voit, qu'il soit pour la faire longue'.[17]

The boy recovered, but the incident, coming as it did at the same time as the breakdown of Henry VIII's fifth marriage, to Catherine Howard, was a sharp reminder of how many hopes rested on the four-year-old's shoulders; in April 1542 a doctor told Marillac that he did not predict a long life for the boy – this despite the fact that he had thrown off an infection at that time with much greater ease than did his sister, Mary.[18]

Until the age of six Edward lived, as he later put it, 'among the women'.[19] Then he was handed over to two of the best young humanists that Cambridge could provide – Richard Cox and John Cheke. Cox, a graduate of King's, had been one of the first fellows of Wolsey's new foundation in Oxford, before becoming headmaster of Eton. During the 1530s he served as chaplain to Goodrich, bishop of Ely, and to Cranmer. In 1538 he was appointed Edward's almoner, and two years later he was named as the prince's tutor. However, in 1546 Cox became dean of Christ Church, and chancellor of the university of Oxford the following year: his role, then, at least in the latter years of Edward's education, must have been that of 'director of studies', rather than daily schoolmaster.[20] It was

---

[15] J. Kaulek, ed., *Correspondance politique de MM de Castillon et de Marillac* (Paris, 1885), 302. (The prince was 'handsome, well-fed and remarkably tall for his age'.)

[16] *LP*, XVI, 1297.

[17] Kaulek, *Correspondance politique*, 350–4. ('All the doctors in the country' were consulted, one of whom declared that 'this chance aside, the prince seemed to him so gross and unhealthy that he could not believe, judging from what he could see now, that he would live long'.)

[18] Ibid., 408–10.

[19] Edward VI, *Chronicle*, 3.

[20] *Dictionary of National Biography*, *sub* Cox, Richard (1500–81).

probably Cheke, a graduate of St John's and Regius professor of Greek in Cambridge, who first guided the prince's hand, being appointed in 1544 'as a supplement to Mr Cox'.[21] Roger Ascham, Elizabeth's tutor, also became involved in Edward's education, being 'many times ... with Mr Cheke's means ... called to teach [Edward] to write, in his privy chamber'.[22]

Edward learned fast, and by December 1544 Cox thought him ready to begin reading Cato and Aesop in Latin: in January 1546 he informed Archbishop Cranmer that the young prince had learned almost four books of Cato, some of Aesop's fables, biblical texts and Vives's *Satellitium*.[23] The prince's education was similar to that of his siblings – Mary, Henry's illegitimate son, Henry Fitzroy, and Elizabeth – in its concentration on the classics, and, to a lesser extent, the Scriptures. (Indeed, *Satellitium* had been written for Mary.) The texts Edward read were, in general, the standard ones of the time: Erasmus's *Colloquies*, Cicero, Pliny the Younger, Herodotus, Plutarch and Thucydides.[24]

It is possible that Edward had young colleagues in his school-room, for Cheke's appointment mentions the 'instruccion of the Prince, and the diligent teaching of suche children as be appointed to attende uppon him': certainly his studies after his accession were shared with some other young nobles, including Henry Brandon, duke of Suffolk, who was to die of the sweat in 1551, and Barnaby Fitzpatrick, who became the king's closest friend.[25]

How able was Edward? He began to learn French in late 1546, when Cox told William Paget that he was about to start.[26] By December Edward had advanced enough to write a letter to Elizabeth in French.[27] But when he met the new French ambassador, de Selve, in February 1547, it was in Latin that they conversed,

[21] *LP*, XIX, i, 864.
[22] In 1545 Ascham had presented Edward with a copy of his *Toxophilus* (his treatise on archery), which is now in the Pierrepont Morgan Library, New York. See L.V. Ryan, *Roger Ascham*, (Stanford, 1963), 303. William Grindal, Walter Haddon and Sir Antony Cooke may also have been involved in Edward's education. See M. Dowling, *Humanism in the Age of Henry VIII* (Beckenham, 1986), 212, 218 (n.62).
[23] Dowling, *Humanism in the Age of Henry VIII*, 214.
[24] T.W. Baldwin, *William Shakespeare's Smalle Latine and Lesse Greeke* (2 vols, Urbana, IL, 1944), i, 200–56; Dowling, *Humanism in the Age of Henry VIII*, 31.
[25] On this, see Dowling, *Humanism in the Age of Henry VIII*, 212–13.
[26] Ibid.
[27] *LP*, XXI, ii, 571.

and not French, 'pour ce qu'il n'entend encores bien francoys et ne faict que commencer a l'apprendre'.[28] He was subsequently taught by a native, Jean Belmain, who later dedicated to him a manuscript translation into French of the 1552 Book of Common Prayer.[29] Later gifts, such as Sir William Pickering's present of Meigret's *Grammaire française*, published in Paris in 1550, which included pages of musical notation,[30] the Anglo-French dialogues presented by Pierre du Ploiche,[31] and Acasse d'Albiac's translation into French verse of the Book of Job[32] suggest that Edward did learn to read the language fluently. A French visitor to the court, François de Scépeaux, reported in 1550 that the king spoke 'en bon langaige françois', as well as Spanish and Italian.[33]

Scépeaux went on to claim that Edward 'parloit semblablement fort bon latin, et avoit très beau commencement aux lettres grecques'.[34] Edward's first extant exercise in Greek in fact dates from March 1551. Whether he ever used the Greek grammar presented by David Tolley (or Tavalegus) in 1547 we do not know,[35] but Louis le Roy, in a letter of thanks to the king, referring back to his presentation of manuscript translations of Isocrates[36] and Xenophon as a writing-book, claimed that Edward had 'read and approved my little books'.[37] (Le Roy was rewarded with the large sum of £50.)[38]

Given later events, it is unfortunate that we know so little about the prince's 'religious education'. All his main tutors – Cox, Cheke

[28] G. Lefèvre-Pontalis, ed., *Correspondance politique de Odet de Selve, ambassadeur de France en Angleterre (1546–1549)*, (Paris, 1888), 105 (no. 121).
[29] Belmain was described as of Edward's chamber by the time of Henry's death (PRO, LC2/2, fo. 53). The dedication is in BL, Royal MS 20 A. xiv, fos 1–2.
[30] L. Meigret, *Le Tretté de la grammere francoeze* (Paris, 1550).
[31] P. du Ploiche, *A Treatise in English and French* (1553); K. Lambley, *The Teaching and Cultivation of French during Tudor and Stuart Times* (Manchester, 1920), 129–33; T.A. Birrell, *English Monarchs and Their Books from Henry VIII to Charles II* (London, 1987), 14.
[32] BL, MS 690, a.6; Birrell, *English Monarchs*, p. 15.
[33] Scépeaux, *Mémoires*, i, 339. The English ambassador to France, Pickering, bought for Edward a popular Spanish bedside book, Pedro Mexia's *Sylva de Varia Lecion* (Valladolid, 1550), so the king may have known a little Spanish, or intended to learn some.
[34] Scépeaux, *Mémoires*, i, 341.
[35] 'Progymnasmata grammatice Graece', BL, C.28, a.14.
[36] BL, Royal MS 16 E. xxxii.
[37] W.L. Gundesheimer, *Life and Works of Louis le Roy*, (Geneva, 1966), 13.
[38] PRO, E101/426/8.

and Ascham – were later to be convinced Protestants; both Cox and
Cheke were Marian exiles. However, it would be unwise to argue
from this that they were more than 'reformed' Catholics or
Erasmians in the 1540s. Obviously, the prince's religious establishment, which in 1547 included John Pilkington, Anthony Otway,
Giles Eyre and Roger Tonge,[39] had been chosen for him, most probably by Cranmer. Whoever instructed Edward, he was clearly a keen
pupil, for by the time that Peter Martyr's *De sacramento eucharistiae*
entered his library in 1549, the young king appears, from his manuscript notes, to have been 'quite capable of following the theological controversies that were raging around him'.[40] And Edward
wrote a long and competent treatise in his own hand on the pope as
Antichrist.[41]

Edward's education was not entirely literary. In 1551 Cheke
designed for him an astronomical quadrant[42] engraved by a
Protestant refugee, Thomas Geminus,[43] and also bought Robert
Recorde's *Pathway to Knowledge . . . First Principles of Geometrie*.[44] In his
father's residences Edward was 'almost permanently surrounded' by
maps and globes,[45] and around 1549 he himself seems to have
ordered the hanging in the privy gallery at Whitehall of a new woodcut world map, designed by Sebastian Cabot and cut by Clement
Adams, schoolmaster of the henchmen at Greenwich; this map
showed the North-West Passage.[46] His study of geography probably

---

[39] PRO, LC2/2 fos 51–51v. By 1547 the king's chaplains included Lawrence
Taylor (PRO, SP10/2, no. 74) and by 1552 John Harley, William Bill, Robert
Horne, Andrew Perne, Edmund Grindal and John Knox (PRO, SP10/15, no.
28). Horne, who in 1551 became dean of Durham, was later a Marian exile. So
was Grindal.

[40] Birrell, *English Monarchs* 16.

[41] The draft manuscript with tutor's corrections is BL, Add. MS 5464; a fair
copy is Cambridge University Library, MS Dd 12.59. The editors are grateful to
Professor D. MacCulloch for this information.

[42] Now in Gallery 46, Department of Antiquities, British Library (BL, M & LA
58, 8–211).

[43] Geminus was a Protestant refugee from Liège living in Blackfriars: Birrell,
English Monarchs, 15.

[44] Birrell, ibid., points out that the plainness of the binding suggests clearly
that the volume was 'for use and not for ornament'.

[45] For this, see the 1547 inventories (BL, Harleian MS 1419 A, fos 133–5); P.
Barber, 'England I: Pageantry, Defense, and Government: Maps at Court to
1550', in D. Buisseret, ed., *Monarchs, Ministers and Maps* (Chicago and London,
1992), 42, 55 and n.135 (see also W. Brenchley, ed., *England as Seen by
Foreigners in the Days of Elizabeth and James*, 1865, pp. 159–62).

[46] Barber 'England I', 44.

went much further than merely looking at maps, for in the new library at Whitehall were numerous relevant documents: 'despatches from overseas, acts of parliament, treatises etc from Wolsey' (whose London home it had been), and 'a black coffer ... full of plattes', a drawer of maps, and two shelves of 'paternes for Castles and engynes of warre'.[47] William Thomas, the clerk to the Privy Council, also presented to the king, probably at New Year 1551, his manuscript translation of 'Travels to Tana and Persia', by Giosafat Barbaro, printed in Venice in 1543.[48]

Edward was also taught music. Like Henry, he could play the lute, and perhaps other instruments. Early in his reign Edward used some of the extra pocket money given him by Thomas Seymour to reward 'john Aysshley at sundry tymes when he taught [him] to play on the virginalles'.[49] Two later gifts of viols may imply some familiarity with that instrument.[50] In 1551 the French envoy, having dined with the king, heard him play on the lute,[51] and Christopher Tye dedicated his 1553 Actes of the Apostles ... to the king with the wish

> That suche good thinges, your grace might moue
> Your lute when ye assaye:
> In stede of songes of wanton loue
> These stories then to playe.[52]

Edward was probably taught by one of Henry's most favoured musicians, the Netherlandish lutenist, Philip van der Wilder, who was a member of Edward's privy chamber, and 'Master of his Highnes Singinge Children';[53] late in the reign van der Wilder was rewarded for 'Ribbing and for Lymnyng' the king's lute cases.[54] Certainly, a very considerable number of privy purse payments were to musicians, such as the £10 given in 1550–52 to 'master hobbyes man that played on the lute before his maiestie'.[55]

---

[47] BL, Harleian MS 1419 A, fos 186–8.
[48] BL, Royal MS 17 C. x: text printed by the Hakluyt Society (1873).
[49] BL, Harleian MS 249, fo. 31v. Was this John Ashley at this time a gentleman waiter in Edward's household?
[50] PRO, E101/426/8, fo. 66; APC, iii. 160.
[51] Edward VI, Chronicle, 73.
[52] RSTC 2983.8 sig. A 3 v.
[53] APC, iii. 126.
[54] PRO, E101/426/8.
[55] Ibid., 37.

The foremost historian of the Tudor coinage, C.E. Challis, has argued convincingly that Edward must have been highly intelligent and well trained to be able, as he clearly was, to understand matters as complex as the coinage. Writing in his *Chronicle*, Edward later showed a clear grasp of monetary affairs. In 1550 he gave a full and accurate exposition of a complex agreement between the crown and one of the masters of the Mint; and in the following year he demonstrated a good understanding of the proposals for debasement of the coinage and the profit to be gained from it – no easy matter.[56]

Despite the priggishness of the admonishment that the eight-year-old Edward offered to his half-sister, Mary, for her liking of 'foreign dances and merriments which do not become a Christian princess',[57] the prince seems to have enjoyed life at court. In 1546, for example, he played his part in the reception of Claude d'Annebaut, the lord admiral of France, when he came on a peace mission; the prince rode at at the head of a retinue of lords and gentlemen 'in velvett cotes on horsebacke', accompanied by a thousand yeomen horse, to greet the admiral outside Hampton Court.[58]

[56] C.E. Challis, *The Tudor Coinage* (Manchester, 1978), 107–8; Challis, 'Presidential Address', *British Numismatic Journal*, lxiii (1993), 174; Edward VI, *Chronicle*, 80.
[57] *LP*, XXI, i, 802; Nichols, *Literary Remains*, i. 9.
[58] Wriothesley, *Chronicle*, i, 173. See also *LP*, XXI, i, 1384.

Chapter 3

THE DEATH OF HENRY VIII: THE KING'S WILL AND THE ESTABLISHMENT OF THE PROTECTORSHIP

Henry VIII died on 28 January 1547, leaving his kingdom in the hands of his nine-year-old son, Edward. Intelligent and well educated though the child was, real power would obviously have to be exercised elsewhere. By whom, and with what constraints?

The 1536 Succession Act empowered the king, by his will, to appoint guardians in case his heir was a minor.[1] Henry in his last will, dated 30 December 1546, named sixteen executors, who were also to form his son's Privy Council and have 'the Gouvernment' of his son and his realms and of all public and private affairs until Edward reached the age of eighteen, together with a further twelve men who were to be of the council and to assist the executor-councillors whenever called upon to do. Most (but not all) of the executor-councillors were members of Henry's existing Privy Council and held important offices of state: Thomas Cranmer, archbishop of Canterbury; Thomas Wriothesley, Lord Chancellor; Sir William Paulet, Lord St John, great master of the household; Edward Seymour, Edward's uncle; John, Lord Russell, long-serving diplomat; John Dudley, Viscount Lisle, Lord Admiral; Bishop Tunstall of Durham; Sir Edward North, chancellor of the court of augmentations; Sir William Paget, the king's chief secretary; Sir Anthony Browne, master of the horse. Two were judges, Sir Edward Montagu, chief justice of the Common Pleas, and Justice Thomas Bromley, king's serjeant; two were the Wotton brothers, career diplomats who were, in the event, abroad at the time of Henry's death, Sir Edward, treasurer of Calais, and Dr Nicholas, dean of Canterbury and ambassador in France; and two were members of

---

[1] *Statutes of the Realm*, iii. 655 (28 Henry VIII c. 7).

17

Henry's privy chamber, Sir Anthony Denny and Sir William Herbert.[2]

Can significance be read into the composition of this proposed council? The supposedly radical religious leanings of these last two, Denny and Herbert, have been held to give the list a less balanced and uncommitted tone than might have been expected of a body nominated by the supposedly cautious and conservative Henry – the more so because some of the councillors not included in the list of executors were, like Stephen Gardiner, bishop of Winchester, religious conservatives.[3] Was this apparent radical bias something on which Henry had consciously decided, thus suggesting that he was prepared to envisage further religious change? Or was Henry rather determined to defend what he saw as his achievement in establishing the royal supremacy from possible subversion by conservatives? Or was Henry in the last months of his life a puppet of powerful men who scarcely knew what was being done in his name by some faction? Or was the composition of the list the result of a series of unrelated accidents?[4]

To answer these questions we need to understand something of the situation at court in the last years of Henry's reign, years in which no one minister predominated. Henry governed in these years with the assistance of the Privy Council, which numbered about twenty. The most frequently present, and therefore almost certainly pre-eminent amongst the councillors, had been Hertford, Russell, Lord St John, Sir Thomas Wriothesley, Stephen Gardiner, Sir John Gage, comptroller of the household and chancellor of the duchy of Lancaster, Sir Anthony Wingfield, captain of the guard and vice-chamberlain, and Sir Wiliam Paget.[5] But the king took advice from others besides his council, most notably, it is claimed, from those physically close to him, the staff of the privy chamber.

---

[2] PRO, E23/4/1, printed in T. Rymer, *Foedera* (3rd edn 1741), vi (iii), 142–5, summarized in *LP*, XXI, ii, 634; cf. D. Hoak, *The King's Council in the Reign of Edward VI* (Cambridge, 1976), 34–46.

[3] D. Starkey, *The Reign of Henry VIII: Personalities and Politics* (London, 1985), 160–2.

[4] The most recent discussion is E.W. Ives, 'Henry VIII's Will: a Forensic Conundrum', *Historical Journal*, xxxv (1992), 779–804; R.A. Houlbrooke, 'Henry VIII's Wills: a Comment', *Historical Journal*, xxxvii (1994), 891–9, and Ives, 'The Protectorate Provisions of 1546–7', ibid., 901–14.

[5] J. Guy, *Tudor England* (Oxford, 1988), 189, 480. Sir John Gage, comptroller of the household, and Sir Anthony Wingfield, vice-chamberlain, were among a dozen men named in the king's will as 'of counsail' to assist the sixteen executor-councillors already named whenever called upon to do so (Rymer, *Foedera*, vi (iii), 145).

David Starkey in particular has made claims for the increasing importance of the privy chamber under Henry – the social upgrading of its personnel, and its growth in size; by 1540 there were sixteen gentlemen of the chamber, together with two gentlemen ushers, three grooms and two barbers. These men helped the king to wash and dress, to eat and sleep, and to fill his idle moments by, for example, playing cards. They paid for the king's pleasures and minor expenses, controlling in the process considerable sums of money – between 1540 and 1544 Sir Anthony Denny, one of the two chief gentlemen, dispensed £250,000, using the money for military expenses and for palace building, as well as for 'pocket money'. Denny also controlled the 'dry stamp', a means of securing a facsimile of the king's signature by inking in an impression produced by a sort of template, a procedure which was increasingly employed in the king's later years, with obvious opportunities for misuse.[6]

Because of their proximity to the king, the privy chamber gentlemen had considerable powers of patronage, and this power increased as the ageing monarch became physically more dependent on them; indeed, Starkey has claimed that by the end of 1546 Henry was more or less cut off from contact with anyone other than the staff of the chamber.[7] If this were so, then it would surely be correct to attach great significance to changes in the personnel of the privy chamber. Starkey has drawn attention to the fact that, in October 1546, three months before Henry's death, one of the two chief gentlemen of the privy chamber, Thomas Heneage, was abruptly dismissed, to be replaced by Sir William Herbert. The significance of this change is thought to be the greater because Heneage was a religious conservative, and Herbert, married to Queen Catherine Parr's sister Anne, is often described as a radical.[8]

Two other shifts in the balance of power around the king took place at this time, which some historians, including Starkey, have seen as part of the same process of replacing conservatives by radicals. First, Stephen Gardiner quarrelled with the king over some

[6] D. Starkey, 'Representation through Intimacy: a Study in the Symbolism of Monarchy and Court Office in England', in I.M. Lewis, ed., *Symbols and Sentiments* (London and New York, 1977), 187–224; Starkey, 'Court and Government', in C. Coleman and D. Starkey, eds, *Revolution Reassessed* (Oxford, 1986), 29–58; Starkey, 'Intimacy and Innovation: the Rise of the Privy Chamber, 1485–1547', in D. Starkey, ed., *The English Court* (London, 1987), 100, 115–17.
[7] Starkey, *Reign of Henry VIII*, 164.
[8] Ibid., 156–7.

lands of his bishopric upon which the king was casting an acquisitive
eye. When Gardiner asked, in early December, for a personal audience with the king to discuss the matter, permission was refused –
significantly, by means of a letter sealed with the dry stamp, the seal
controlled by Denny. Was Gardiner the victim of a plot by those
opposed to him on religious grounds? Gardiner was not present at
many of the meetings of the Privy Council that took place in the crucial last weeks of Henry's life.

Secondly, England's premier duke, Norfolk, and his son and heir,
Henry Howard, earl of Surrey, were accused and found guilty of
treason. On 2 December, Sir Richard Southwell, a former Howard
servant, told the Privy Council that Surrey had been plotting against
the crown. Surrey was arrested, and so, on 12 December, was
Norfolk. Investigations revealed Surrey's use of the royal insignia,
his blatant assertions of aristocratic privilege, and his somewhat
incompetent plotting against various members of the council.
Surrey was tried for treason on 13 January 1547, convicted, and
executed. The day before the trial, Norfolk formally admitted his
own guilt in concealing his son's treasonable activity. Both men
were attainted by a statute to which Henry gave his assent the day
before his death; all the considerable Howard land-holding thereby
came into the king's hands. It was a hoard upon which many greedy
eyes were fixed.[9]

So the final shaping of the list of executors came about at a time
when Gardiner and Norfolk were both in disgrace. The exact details
are difficult to establish, for the whole history of the making of the
will is tortuous and controversial. The first clear date that we can fix
upon is 26 December, on which day, Paget later testified, Henry,
having been very sick, asked to see the 1544 will again. Discovering
that Gardiner's name was listed amongst those of the executors, he
asked for it to be struck out.[10] This meant that in the king's last will,
which ends with his declaration that 'we have signed it with our
hand, in our palays of Westminster the thirty day of Decembre, in
the yere of our Lord God a thousand fyve hundred fourty and six',
the list of executors lacked the balance that Gardiner and Norfolk

[9] For the argument that the fall of the Howards was 'a put-up job' and that
they were the victims of a faction led by Hertford, Lisle and Cranmer, see Ives,
'Henry VIII's Will', 783, 795; for a counter, see Houlbrooke, 'Henry VIII's
Wills', 892.
[10] Foxe, vi, 163.

would have provided.[11] But was the will 'signed', and was it finalized, on 30 December 1546, or are appearances deceptive?

The clerk of the privy seal, Wiliam Clerk, carefully recorded that the king himself handed the will over to one of those present, the earl of Hertford, 'in our sightes with your own hande', and that this was witnessed by ten persons: six members of the privy chamber, including Sir John Gates and Sir Henry Neville, the physicians Robert Huick, Thomas Wendy and George Owen, and Clerk himself.[12] According to the 1536 Act, Henry should have signed the will with his own hand, but it appears that he was too ill to do that, sanctioning instead the use of the dry stamp.[13] Each month a 'bridgment' of everything stamped in this way was prepared by a secretary, at this time William Clerk. But the king's will was not included in the list of documents signed by stamp for the month of December 1546, as ought to have been done; instead it appeared in the list for January 1547, when it is the penultimate item, followed by the commission to give the royal assent to the Howards' attainder, a bill passed in both houses of parliament on 24 January.[14]

A further reason for suspicion lies in the presence of a clause in the will – known to historians as the 'unfulfilled gifts' clause – directing that any promises made by Henry of grants of honours and lands should be fulfilled after his death. In particular, this would have involved grants of the newly confiscated Howard lands.[15] This has suggested to some historians that the will may have been fraudulently tampered with. They argue that either the document we now have was altered and the unfulfilled gifts clause inserted in it or that this document is not the one supposedly signed with the dry stamp on 30 December, but another drawn up later, in January, and substituted for it when the situation about the Howard lands became clear.[16] The evidence is complex, detailed and in many respects ambiguous. It is enough here to say that the physical structure of the will is such that it could not have been tampered with after Henry had approved it on 30 December. In particular, it would not have

[11] See note 2 above for will; cf. Starkey, *Reign of Henry VIII*, pp. 160–2.
[12] *State Papers, Henry VIII*, i, no. cclxvi, pp. 897–8 (*LP*, XXI, ii, 770).
[13] *Statutes of the Realm*, iii, 655 (28 Henry VIII c. 7).
[14] *State Papers*, i, no. cclxvi, pp. 897–8 (*LP*, XXI, ii, 770).
[15] H. Miller, 'Henry VIII's Unwritten Will: Grants of Lands and Honours in 1547', in E.W. Ives, R.J. Knecht and J.J. Scarisbrick, eds, *Wealth and Power in Tudor England: Essays Presented to S.T. Bindoff* (London, 1978), 87–106.
[16] Houlbrooke, 'Henry VIII's Wills', 894–5.

been possible to insert an additional clause in the body of the document. Furthermore, it is highly probable that the will we now have is indeed the original approved by Henry.[17] It is, however, plain that the 'unfulfilled gifts' clause provided the legal authorization for a generous distribution of lands and honours to Edward Seymour, some of the other councillors and certain members of the court, either to reward them for their loyalty to Seymour so far, or to ensure their support for his elevation to the protectorship after Henry's death, or to bind them all in gratitude to Edward during his minority.[18]

If, then, the balance of argument would suggest that the king's will was not tampered with in the interests of political faction, it is nevertheless incontestable that there was a marked change in the balance of power at court in the last weeks of 1546, with the fall of the Howards and the loss of favour of Gardiner. Is it correct to see this change, as so many historians do, as religiously motivated? That Gardiner was a religious conservative is undeniable, given his actions in Edward's reign, but his religious views may not have been the reason for his fall, which can more plausibly be explained, as Glyn Redworth has suggested, by his own stubbornness and miscalculations than by the deliberate machinations of his religious opponents.[19] Henry had been personally and fixedly hostile to Gardiner throughout at least the second half of 1546; Foxe tells us that even before his last illness the king would not grant Gardiner an audience when he appeared with the other councillors.[20] When Sir Anthony Browne, one of the gentlemen of the chamber, heard that Henry had struck Gardiner's name from the list of executors of his will, he went to the king and – disingenuously? – suggested that the omission was surely a scribal error. Henry said firmly that he had deliberately left out the bishop, claiming that he was a 'troublesome' man, and 'a wilful man, and not meet to be about his son'. He 'could use him and rule him', the king said, but others would not be able to do so. Browne tried again later, only to be told that if he persisted Henry would also strike him from the list of executors.

[17] Ives, 'Henry VIII's Will', 779–804; Ives 'The Protectorate Provisions', 901–14.

[18] Miller, 'Henry VIII's Unwritten Will'; Houlbrooke, 'Henry VIII's Wills'.

[19] G. Redworth, *In Defence of the Church Catholic: the Life of Stephen Gardiner* (Oxford, 1990), 231–47; for the suggestion that Gardiner was attacked by 'the Seymour/Paget faction', see Ives, 'Henry VIII's Will', 795–9.

[20] Foxe, v, 691–2.

Browne, who was, as Foxe points out, of Gardiner's camp in religious affairs, immediately went to report his failure to Archbishop Cranmer.[21] If there was a radical plot to do down the religious conservatives, and if the radicals wanted to exclude Gardiner, it is extremely odd that Cranmer was so anxious about his fellow bishop's position. Moreover, according to Paget's later account, he and the councillors also tried to dissuade the king.[22] It is difficult to envisage why Paget should have lied about this, but also very difficult to fit his story into any concept of a crypto-Protestant plot.

Equally, is it really possible to identify the Howards firmly with Catholicism?[23] Norfolk was certainly conservative, as befitted a man in his seventies, but two decades earlier he had been a strong opponent of that Catholic heroine, Catherine of Aragon, and a great critic of churchmen: in 1540 he publicly thanked God that he had never read Scripture, and never would. In 1546, however, he did buy an edition of a Church Father, describing the writer as one, 'who doth declare most of any books that I have read how the bishop of Rome from time to time hath usurped his power against all princes, by their unwise suffrance'.[24] Norfolk's eldest son, the earl of Surrey, appears to have been equally free from religious preoccupations. Although he is sometimes described as Protestant-inclined because he got into trouble in 1543 for eating meat in Lent, his main offence then was in fact 'a lewde and unseemly manner of walking in the night aboute the streets and breaking with stone bows of certain windows'. Recklessness characterizes his behaviour much better than any evangelism. And even Susan Brigden, who advances a case for Surrey's evangelical commitment based on a reading of his often obscurely written poems, concedes that by 1546 he had become increasingly estranged from his supposed former evangelical friends.[25]

Another of the Howards, Lord Thomas Howard, *did* indeed get into trouble at this period about religion, but on the reformed side;

[21] Ibid., and vi, 163–4.

[22] Ibid., 164.

[23] 'The Howards ... represented "the old" – in tradition and in religion': Ives, 'Henry VIII's Will', 783. But contrast Houlbrooke, 'Henry VIII's Wills', 892.

[24] *LP*, XVI, 101; M. Dowling, *Humanism in the Age of Henry VIII* (Beckenham, 1986), 205, citing G. Brennan and E.P. Statham, eds, *The House of Howard* (2 vols, London, 1907), i, 439.

[25] *LP*, XVIII, i, 327; *APC*, i, 104–5; *pace* S. Brigden, 'Henry Howard, Earl of Surrey, and the "Conjured League"', *Historical Journal*, xxxvii (1994), 507–37, esp. 519, 522.

in 1546 he was accused, with various other young men, of 'indiscreet meddling in Scripture things'.[26] Norfolk's daughter, Surrey's sister, the duchess of Richmond, was in Edward's reign to be a great patron of Protestants: she protected John Bale and appointed the future martyrologist, John Foxe, as tutor to the children of her executed brother.[27]

Is it even the case that the list of executors had a radical bias?[28] It is possible that Sir Anthony Denny had advanced religious views, but much of the evidence usually cited actually stems from the interest taken in religious matters by his wife.[29] Starkey makes much of the appointment to the privy chamber in late 1546 of Sir William Herbert, later Lord Herbert and earl of Pembroke. Like Denny, Herbert appears to be radical only in his associations, and as the brother-in-law of a queen sometimes described as the furtherer of Protestantism. His claims to be a religious radical were slight; and Pembroke's later career in the reigns of Mary and Elizabeth makes his alleged radicalism, if it ever existed, short-lived.[30] Archbishop Cranmer was, obviously, of a reforming disposition, but he was balanced by the much more traditionalist Tunstal, bishop of Durham, who was deprived later in Edward's reign. William Paulet, Lord St John, was later to be notorious for his willingness to bend with the

[26] APC, i, 408.

[27] J.N. King, English Reformation Literature (Princeton, 1982), 106.

[28] Cf. Ives, 'Henry VIII's Will', 792–3.

[29] Lady Denny was one of the ladies whose name was mentioned in the interrogation of Anne Askew (Foxe, v, 547). P.C. Swensen, 'Patronage from the Privy Chamber: Sir Anthony Denny and Religious Reform', Journal of British Studies, xxvii (1988), 25–44, claims Denny as 'a sincere supporter of religious reform, even of the Rhineland reformers', but admits that 'he was discreet and judicious in this support' (p. 26); argues that he promoted clergy 'who had embraced reformed thought' (p. 34), but concedes that 'such activity must often be inferred rather than directly cited' – 'most of the business that passed under the dry stamp was exactly that – licenses, debts, and so on, with no discernible indication that religious views were involved' (pp. 34–5; cf. doubts at top of p. 38); and, after surveying appointments in which Denny allegedly played a part, he recognizes that 'these incidences of patronage and support do not by any means always involve decisively protestant figures' (p.39). By contrast N.P. Sil, 'Sir Anthony Denny: a Tudor Servant in Office', Renaissance and Reformation, new series, viii (1984), 190–201, emphasizes how 'as a royal servant he always supported the King's Reformation'; even if his 'moderate' religious views were 'not as conservative' as those of the king (p. 191), he 'scrupulously avoided any extreme religious or political group and gave his loyalty to none other than the king' (p. 196).

[30] Starkey, Reign of Henry VIII, 156–7, 163–4.

wind. One of the judges, Montagu, seems from his conduct at the beginning of Mary's reign to have been, by then at least, a Protestant, but the other, Sir Thomas Bromley, was probably a Catholic. Most of the remainder of the guardians could, like William Paget, be described as religious 'neuters'.

If the list is carefully examined, then, it does not seem fundamentally out of character with Henry's known religious inclinations, or, perhaps more important, with his judgement on the administrative and political skills of those who served him.[31] Henry appears to have been capable of major and personal decisions until very near the end of his life, and the exclusion of Gardiner seems to have been a personal whim. If Professor Ives is indeed correct to argue that in its general outlines the will did indeed 'spell out the king's intentions ... for the government of the country during the minority of his son',[32] he is less persuasive in his claim that it reflects how 'in December 1546 the king turned his back decisively on religious conservatism'.[33]

In any case, the will was of short-lived effect, for only three days after Henry's death, on 31 January 1547, the executors elected one of their number, Hertford, as protector of the realm. This change was formalized on 4 February when the young king and thirteen of the executors of Henry's will signed a commission giving sovereign authority to Hertford until Edward reached the age of eighteen, and again by letters-patent granted to Somerset on 12 March. On 1 March a new council of twenty-six members was established: however, on 6 March one of those councillors, the chancellor, Thomas Wriothesley, newly created earl of Southampton, was struck off. The reason given publicly for his dismissal was a complaint laid against him by some common lawyers, but a number of contemporary sources claim that the real reason why he lost office was because he was 'sore against' the establishment of the protectorate;[34] as Dale Hoak puts it, Southampton was forced out 'not because the earl had remained a Henrician catholic or because the common lawyers may have opposed his practices, but because [he] had from the very beginning opposed [Hertford]'s creation as

[31] As Houlbrooke has argued, 'the safety of Edward and the stability of his government were the old king's overriding concerns during the last weeks of his life' ('Henry VIII's Wills', 893).

[32] Ives, 'Henry VIII's Will', 797.

[33] Ibid., 797–9; contrast Houlbrooke, 'Henry VIII's Wills', 893.

[34] BL, Add. MS 48126, fo. 15.

Protector'.[35] (Hoak suggests that Southampton may have refused to affix the great seal to letters confirming Somerset's elevation.)[36] Southampton makes an unconvincing religious conservative. He was zealous in exposing idolatry and superstition in the late 1530s, especially in the dismantling of pilgrimage shrines in 1538. When he silenced Dr Crome's attack on the mass as sacrifice in spring 1546 he was simply doing so on royal orders and enforcing what was orthodoxy in late Henrician England. He would be prominent in suppressing Catholic dissidents in Hampshire in 1549. His last will was not conspicuously traditional and he appointed the radical Bishop Hooper to preach at his funeral.[37]

The exact process by which Edward Seymour came to be chosen as protector is difficult to discern, for statements made later, at the time of his fall, have to be treated with some scepticism. But two things are certain, and a third probable. The first is that William Paget acted, in a sense, as Hertford's agent; later he was to remind the protector of what he had promised him in the gallery at Westminster 'before the breath was out' of Henry's body.[38] Secondly, although the executors were undoubtedly within their rights in choosing to hand over power to the young king's uncle – Henry's will had provided that a majority of them could 'devyse and ordeyn' whatever they thought best for the government of the king and of the realm – there can be little doubt that their willingness to do so was encouraged by a promise of a substantial distribution of titles and lands. A few days after the decision to make Hertford protector, Paget, Denny and Herbert formally recorded for the council what they 'remembered' of things that Henry had intended to put into his will but had somehow forgotten to do. These memories resulted in the elevation of Hertford to the dukedom of Somerset, of William Parr to the marquisate of Northampton, of Lisle to the earldom of Warwick, and of Thomas Wriothesley to the earldom of Southampton. Four new barons were created. Crown land worth well over £3,200 a year, most of it

---

[35] Hoak, *King's Council in the Reign of Edward VI*, 43–5, 231–9; A.J. Slavin, 'The Fall of Lord Chancellor Wriothesley: a Study in the Politics of Conspiracy', *Albion*, vii (1975), 265–86, esp. 276–86.

[36] Hoak, *King's Council in the Reign of Edward VI*, 235–7.

[37] Slavin, 'The Fall of Lord Chancellor Wriothesley', esp. 265–76.

[38] J.Strype, *Ecclesiastical Memorials; Relating Chiefly to Religion and the Reformation* (3 vols in 6 parts, Oxford, 1822), II, ii, 430.

previously belonging to the Howards, was distributed. Almost all the executors received hand-outs.[39]

The third point about the process by which Edward Seymour became protector is that his younger brother was far from happy about events, and needed to be bought off. Although Thomas Seymour had been named by Henry only as one of the assistants to his executors,[40] he received land worth £500 per annum from the king's 'unwritten' will;[41] he also, at the very beginning of February 1547, became a privy councillor, and soon after was appointed lord admiral. Some accounts suggest that John Dudley, already plotting to seize power from his rival, the newly installed protector, encouraged Thomas Seymour in his anger against his elder brother.[42] This may be so, but, as we shall see, Seymour's subsequent behaviour also suggests that he was a vain and impetuous man who would readily feel aggrieved without the need for intervention by a third party.[43]

The probability that a certain amount of plotting and bribery surrounded Hertford's elevation should not obscure the fact that the elevation was a sensible and entirely traditional move. Sixteenth-century government was only with difficulty run by committees, and the conduct of warfare, in particular, was extremely cumbersome without a sole directing hand. A regency, in some shape or form, was a well-established solution to the accession of a minor. The obvious person to be regent was the monarch's mother or his paternal uncle. But Edward's mother had died soon after giving birth to him, and he had no paternal uncles. The choice therefore fell, logically enough, upon his maternal uncle. Indeed, far from laying down a rigidly fixed council to govern in the minority of his son, as Ives has argued,[44] Henry may have had in mind the idea that Hertford would take charge: according to William Clerk, clerk of the privy seal, it

---

[39] Miller, 'Henry VIII's Unwritten Will', 87–106. For the suggestion that Henry himself was planning to advance several of his councillors and servants, and that the request in his will that his executors should implement his plans is by no means unbelievable, and thus not good evidence that the king's will was tampered with, see Ives, 'Henry VIII's Will', 790–1.

[40] Rymer, *Foedera*, vi (iii), 145.

[41] Miller, 'Henry VIII's Unwritten Will', 102.

[42] BL, Add. MS 48023, fo. 350; 48126, fos 6–6v. Cf. Hoak, *King's Council in the Reign of Edward VI*, 232–3, using the latter.

[43] See below, 55–7.

[44] Ives, 'Henry VIII's Will', 799–802. On this point Houlbrooke agrees with Ives, 'Henry VIII's Wills', 899.

was to Hertford that Henry, too ill to sign his will, entrusted the document on 30 December as a token of assent and in the presence of witnesses. Hertford kept the will till the king died. He was being endowed with special status by the king.[45]

[45] *State Papers of Henry VIII*, i, no. cclxvi, 897–8. Ives half recognizes the point, 'Henry VIII's Will', 802.

Chapter 4

EDWARD'S CORONATION

Edward, then living at Hertford, was of course much too young to take an independently active part in these events. He appears to have been told the news of his father's death by the earl of Hertford and Sir Anthony Browne early on 29 January. They took the boy to Enfield, Princess Elizabeth's residence, and then, on 31 January, by horse to London, where the news of Henry's death had just been made public. To salutes from cannons on land and on the river, the young king was escorted to the Tower.

There was much to be done. Henry's body had to be embalmed and properly arrayed before the coffin, covered with a cloth of gold, was laid in the privy chamber, to be watched over by chaplains and gentlemen of the chamber.[1] Meanwhile, the chapel was prepared, and the nobles sought out their mourning habits.

On 1 February the nobility assembled in the king's presence chamber, where the king sat in a chair of state.[2] Kneeling, they kissed the king's hands, saying as they did so, 'God save your grace.' Then Henry's will was read out, and the executors announced that they had chosen Hertford to serve as protector. Hertford made a short formal speech, saying that he would try to do things to the 'contentacion' of those present, and asking for their assistance. With one voice, they agreed. Finally, those present shouted 'God save the king', and Edward, in recognition, doffed his cap.

Meanwhile, the funeral ceremonial took its leisurely course. On 3 February the mourners assembled in twos 'in order after their degrees' to hear requiem mass. The chief mourner was Henry Grey, marquess of Dorset: Edward appears to have played no part in these ceremonies. When, on 14 February, the coffin was conveyed with

---

[1] J. Strype, ed., *Ecclesiastical Memorials* (3 vols in 6 parts, Oxford, 1822), II, i, 17.
[2] College of Arms MS I.7, fos 29v–30; Society of Antiquaries MS 123, fos 317–18.

great solemnity from London to Windsor, Edward was again absent, although Queen Catherine was in the chapel when the cortège arrived at Windsor after an overnight stop at Syon. Edward also missed the funeral itself, on 16 February.

A contemporary account of the funeral notes that afterwards 'the lords disserved themselves, and taking their horses, hasted them al to London that night'.[3] The haste was understandable, for Edward's ceremonial entry into London was to take place on Saturday, 19 February, and the coronation itself was scheduled for the next day. A list drawn up for the council at this time mentions not only the choice of various officers for the coronation, but also the question of fines to be levied on those gentlemen who refused to take the knighthood to which they were entitled, the selection of new knights of the Bath, and 'the Mizes or Tallage in Wales'.[4] Liveries had to be prepared, and the sites of ceremonies made ready.

The church and city authorities were busy, too. At Westminster Abbey there were hangings to be put out, the altar to be suitably decked, and a stage to be built before it. In the city, the streets through which the royal procession would pass had to be swept and freshly gravelled, and parts of the route fenced.[5] The coronation pageants had also to be prepared. For all this, the tax payers of London were charged with a fifteenth and tenth.[6]

The coronation was intended to provide the lesser people of London with spectacle and entertainment, but it was also a means of distributing largesse to the upper ranks of society, and largesse on a considerable scale. On 4 February a proclamation had been issued requesting 'all the ... nobility, and other ... subjects claiming to do service' at the coronation to make their claims known to a court sitting for that purpose at Whitehall.[7] The court, chaired by the lord chancellor, Wriothesley, and consisting of the earls of Shrewsbury and Essex, Lord Lisle, Sir Richard Lister, the lord chief justice, and

---

[3] Strype, *Ecclesiastical Memorials*, iv, 310. For a full analysis of Henry VIII's funeral see J. Loach, 'The Function of Ceremonial in the Reign of Henry VIII', *Past and Present*, cxlii (1994), 56–66.

[4] PRO, SP10/1, no. 3.

[5] Bodleian Library, Oxford, Ashmole MS 817, fo. 1.

[6] Wriothesley, *Chronicle*, i, 182.

[7] PRO, SP10/1, no. 4; College of Arms MS I.7, fo. 30; Hughes and Larkin, 383 (no. 277).

Sir Edward Montague, chief justice of Common Pleas, worked hard. It had to judge the validity of the claims before it, often by the scrutiny of ancient documents, and to distinguish between rival claims.[8] Claims ranged from that of the earl of Arundel to act as chief butler for the day to a demand by Nicholas Leigh that he should be permitted to make for the king 'a Messe of Podage called Digeront'.[9] (Leigh's claim was allowed, although the court prudently decreed that the king's chief cook should be responsible for the actual preparation of the dish.)

Why were nobles and gentlemen so anxious to perform these tasks? Some, like Leigh, seem to have been moved by family pride and an antiquarian desire to see old customs maintained. Others, such as the bishop of Durham, who claimed a right, jointly with the bishop of Bath and Wells, to support the king at the ceremony, clearly wanted to have a role on so solemn an occasion. For others, the material benefits to be gained by such services may have been of major importance. Arundel, for instance, was rewarded by a present of all the wine left in the pipes, hogsheads and other vessels as soon as the wine in those vessels was 'drawn to the Bar', in addition to the best cup before the king at the feast, and all other pots and cups left in the wine cellar after dinner that were neither gold nor silver. Lisle, who was the panterer at the feast, was given the salt cellar laid before the king, and the carving knives and serving spoons. The barons of the Cinque Ports, who bore the king's canopy, were later given it, while the earl of Oxford, who offered the king water with which to wash his hands after dinner, was presented with the basins and towels. Since everything used at the coronation and the ensuing feast was of the best, these were substantial rewards.

Before the coronation, there was a procession from the Tower of London to Westminster. It left the Tower about one o'clock in the afternoon of 19 February.[10] The king was on horseback, and was dressed in a gown of cloth of gold and a cape furred with sable. Underneath, he wore a jerkin and cape of white velvet, embroidered with 'Venice silver' and garnished with rubies, diamonds, and

[8] PRO, SP10/1, nos 6, 7. See also BL, Stowe MS 579, fos 61–3.
[9] Leigh, who held a minor court post, was described as an esquire of the body at Henry VIII's funeral (PRO, LC2/2).
[10] There is a number of contemporary accounts of this procession. I have drawn in particular on College of Arms MS I. 7, fos 32–38v. See Plate 11, and below, 187–8 and note.

pearls arranged in lovers' knots.[11] His horse was trapped in crimson satin, embroidered with gold and pearls.

Before and after him went an elaborately ordered train. First, in twos, walked his messengers, followed by his gentlemen, the servants of the foreign ambassadors, and the trumpeters, 'clothed all in redde damaske'. After them came the chaplains 'with owte dignitie', the esquires of the body, the knights, the chaplains of dignity and, on horseback, the sons of various gentlemen and nobles. The barons followed, arranged after their degrees, then the bishops, the sons of earls, marquesses and dukes; they were followed by earls, marquesses and dukes. Next came the comptroller of the household, Sir John Gage, with the Venetian ambassador. The treasurer of the household accompanied an ambassador from one of the Protestant states, as did the king's almoner, Richard Cox, and Sir William Petre. Sir William Paget rode with Duke Philip of Bavaria, the lord admiral with a Scots ambassador, and the lord privy seal, Russell, with another. The lord great master of the household, Paulet, accompanied the French envoy, Antoine Escalin des Aimars, baron de la Garde, and the chancellor the French ambassadors. The imperial ambassador came next, with the archbishop of Canterbury; although he was in a position of great honour, close to the king, van der Delft did not enjoy himself, as, he reported, Cranmer 'acted the part of a dumb man all the way'.[12]

Then came the knight harbinger, Sir Percevall Hart, bearing the king's cloak and hat. He was followed by two gentlemen ushers, John Norris and William Rainsford, dressed in scarlet with caps of state on their heads and carrying scarlet velvet robes lined with ermine. They represented the estates of Normandy and Guyenne, over which English monarchs still claimed suzerainty, but the symbolism escaped van der Delft who described them merely as 'apparelled in antique fashion'. Garter king of arms, carrying the king's coat of arms, and the mayor of London, with a mace, rode next, followed by the sergeants at arms, with their maces. After them came the marquess of Dorset, as Constable of England, carrying one of the swords of state, with Lisle and Arundel, carrying the others, on either side of him. Somerset, who, van der Delft observed, 'kept always nearest to the person of the king', rode slightly before Edward and his canopy.

[11] Ibid., fo. 63v.
[12] *CSP, Spanish*, ix, p. 47.

Behind the king came his master of the horse, Sir Anthony Browne, leading a richly trapped steed. Nine henchmen rode next, bare-headed and wearing cassocks that were half of cloth of gold and half of cloth of silver; their horses were similarly arrayed. The master of the henchmen, Sir Francis Bryan, was followed by the horses of the gentlemen and grooms of the privy chamber, the guard, with their halberds, and the noblemen and gentlemen's servants, arranged according to the dignity of their masters. The central part of the procession, near the king, was flanked by both the henchmen, 'in their Riche cotes' and by the pensioners.

Along the first part of the route stood members of the craftsmen's guilds, and, on the other side of the road, priests and clerks in holy orders 'with their crosses & sensers and in their best ornamentes to sense the king'.[13] Houses on the route were hung with 'clothes of tapestry/ Arras, clothe of gold & clothe of Tyssue ... as Richely as might be Devysed', and with banners and streamers. At any point at which the royal party might pause there was music and singing, and on many sites tableaux and pageants.

Perhaps because they had only a few days in which to organize, many of the pageants the city authorities prepared for Edward were taken from an existing sequence, written by John Lydgate for another boy king, Henry VI. That 1432 pageant sequence had been published in 1542 in an adaptation of Robert Fabyan's. Anglo describes Edward's entry as 'perhaps the most tawdry on record', a judgement based largely on the decision to re-use the sequence prepared for Henry VI.[14] However, that sequence, written to greet Henry on his return from his coronation in France, had been particularly sumptuous and carefully prepared, and it is understandable that the city should wish to repeat a success. Whilst it is true that van der Delft, the imperial ambassador, who was feeling very peevish and refused to attend the coronation, recorded that there had been 'no very memorable show of triumph or magnificence',[15] the French ambassador, Odet de Selve, described how the young king of England 'feust mene en grand triomphe' when he entered, and how he was 'couronne et sacre a Wesmester avec le plus grand triumphe et solennite qu'il est possible'.[16] The plan was that Edward

[13] Bodleian Library, Ashmole MS 817, fo. 1.

[14] S. Anglo, *Spectacle, Pageantry and Early Tudor Policy* (Oxford, 2nd edn, 1997), 283–94.

[15] *CSP, Spanish*, ix, 47.

[16] G. Lefèvre-Pontalis, ed., *Correspondance politique de Odet de Selve ambassadeur de France en Angleterre (1546–1549)* (Paris, 1888), no. 121, p. 105.

should be greeted at Cheap conduit by four children representing Grace, Nature, Fortune and Charity, while the citizens were there refreshed from a wine fountain surmounted by a 'crowne imperyall of golde'. (One contemporary noted that on the day the local inhabitants 'with great diligence feched [the wine all] away' within six hours.) Further along Cheap, Sapience and the seven Liberal Sciences were to be found. Then came a display devised especially for Edward, in which a phoenix – the emblem of the Seymour family – made friendly with a crowned lion, and produced a young lion, who was himself then crowned by angels. At Cheap Cross the king was to be greeted by the city aldermen, who would present him with 1,000 marks in gold. At the little conduit at Cheap representations were planned of King Edward the Confessor, and of St George, on horseback, while Truth, Faith and Justice waited in the Fleet, with two hogsheads of wine.

Because of the pressure of time, Edward did not pause long at any of the pageants; even so, the journey took four hours.[17] However, the young king did stop for a tightrope walker outside St Paul's, who made him laugh.[18] By the time he reached Westminster he was obviously exhausted, and Somerset asked the foreign dignitaries to take leave of the King 'with as few words as possible'.[19]

Edward had to rise early the next day – his train had been warned to be ready at 7 a.m.[20] With his councillors and the gentlemen of the privy chamber, he went by river from Westminster Palace to Whitehall. There, in the chamber of the court of augmentations, he put on his parliament robes of crimson velvet. Another procession assembled, similar to that of the day before, although this time everyone was on foot, and the choir of Westminster Abbey, and the children and choir of the chapel royal were present. The nobles now wore their robes and caps of state, and the bishops their pontificals. Somerset carried the crown, with Suffolk on his right bearing the orb, and Dorset on his left with the sceptre. Edward's heavy train was carried by Lisle, assisted by the marquess of Northampton and Thomas Seymour, Edward's other uncle.

Edward VI was not the youngest boy to be crowned king of England, for Henry VI had been barely eight at his coronation in

---

[17] *CSP, Spanish*, ix, 47.
[18] R. Fabyan, *Fabyan's Cronycle* (London, 1559), 435.
[19] *CSP, Spanish*, ix, 47.
[20] Bodleian Library, Ashmole MS 817, fo. 5v.

1429.[21] Henry III was the same age as Edward when he was crowned, albeit in a somewhat makeshift ceremony, and Richard II was ten at his coronation. Few concessions had been made to the youth of these kings, although Henry VI was carried to the Abbey by his tutor, the earl of Warwick.[22] Edward had to walk to the Abbey, but some thought was given by the Privy Council to the problem of the 'tedious length' of the ceremony, which might 'weary and be hurtsome peradventure to the Kinges Majestie being yet of tendre age fully to endure and bide owte'.[23] The arrangements allowed Edward a rest from time to time,[24] and he was carried by four gentlemen ushers in a chair for the recognition ceremony.[25] However, the rites themselves were not significantly curtailed. The service followed the fourteenth-century form known as the 'Liber regalis', which was to remain in use until 1685.[26] The first part consisted of the presentation of the king to his people by the archbishop of Canterbury. Showing them Edward, 'whose consecration, enunction and coronation is appointed by all the nobles and peers of this land to be this day', Cranmer asked those present to show their consent 'as by your dewtyes of allegeance ye be bownde to do'.[27] The assembled nobles responded with shouts of 'yea, yea, yea, King Edwarde, King Edwarde, King Edwarde'. Having laid a pall and a piece of gold weighing one pound upon the high altar, the king lay prostrate before it on a velvet cushion while Cranmer prayed over him. He promised to keep the laws and customs of England, and to protect the Church and people.[28]

The second, and most solemn, part of the service was the blessing and anointing of the king. For this, Edward discarded his robes, and wore over his shirt a crimson satin and ermine coat down to 'the smalle of the legge', with ties at the front, back and shoulders that enabled his chest, shoulders and back to be anointed.[29] While the

---

[21] B.P. Wolffe, *Henry VI* (London, 1981), 48–9.

[22] Ibid.

[23] PRO, SP10/1, no. 9. See also *APC*, ii. 29.

[24] PRO, SP10/1, no. 9.

[25] Ibid.

[26] L.G. Wickham Legg, *English Coronation Records* (Westminster, 1901), xix. The 'Liber' itself is reproduced on 81–130. The council went over the arrangements with some care: see PRO, SP10/1, no. 9 and *APC*, ii. 29–33.

[27] *APC*, ii. 30.

[28] Wickham Legg, *English Coronation Records*, xxxi.

[29] Nichols, *Literary Remains*, i, xcv, ccc, cciv. There is some doubt about what he wore on his head at this point, one source describing a gold coif, and another a 'lytell cappe of estate' made of crimson satin.

king was changing, a general pardon was proclaimed. (This had been the subject of an earlier discussion between members of the council, who were not certain whether the pardon should come, as it were, from the dead Henry or from the new king. The advice of Somerset and Browne, which prevailed, was that the pardon should be linked to the coronation, since Henry, being in heaven, had no need of his people's gratitude, whereas Edward needed their 'preyse and thankes'.)[30] The anointing was done by Cranmer, the king being in part hidden by a pall held over him by Sir William Herbert and Sir Anthony Denny. Putting on then other, richer, garments of crimson satin, Edward offered his sword on the altar. Then the vestments and ornaments were blessed, and given to the king – St Edward's spurs were, however, taken off again almost immediately, so that they would not trip him up. Finally, Edward was crowned, the archbishop and the duke of Somerset together putting on his head, in turn, the crown of King Edward the Confessor,[31] the imperial crown,[32] and a third made specially for the occasion.[33] The

[30] PRO, SP10/1, no. 2.

[31] Because the crown was destroyed in 1649, there is no certainty about the appearance of this ancient, and honoured, relic. The best theory seems to be that it was, as it appears in Elizabeth's 'Armada' portrait, 'not an arched crown over a loose cap of estate', but rather had 'a smooth and apparently rigid hemispherical lining fitting close up to the arches, which cross it like the reinforcing bands of an early helmet', with small finials and pear-shaped pearls (M.R. Holmes, 'New Light on St Edward's Crown', Archaeologia, xcvii, 1959, 218). In other words, it resembled the early crowns of eastern Europe, such as that of St Stephen. Cf. also D. Hoak, 'The Iconography of the Crown Imperial', in D. Hoak, ed., Tudor Political Culture (Cambridge, 1995), 59.

[32] In Henry VIII's reign the state crown apparently consisted of five crosses, and five fleurs-de-lys, which had in them images, three of Christ, including one of him with the Virgin Mary, and one of St George. Sapphires, rubies, emeralds and pearls were set into this, as was the Black Prince's ruby (which was, at this time, set into a fleur, not cross, at the front of the crown – see Elizabeth's great seal: M.R. Holmes, 'The Crowns of England', Archaeologia, lxxxvi (1936), 82–4.)

[33] This crown was made by the king's goldsmith, Everard Everdayce, in the days before the coronation, using broken gold and two girdles taken for the purpose from the king's secret jewel house by the duke of Somerset (PRO, SP10/3, no.7). Numbers of rubies, diamonds and emeralds were used, as well as a large quantity of pearls, including ten larger ones set on stalks of gold, surmounted by pointed diamonds. The 'crown in the iron chest', described in 1649 as Edward's, contained 'one fair diamond' worth £200, as well as other diamonds, seventy pearls, rubies and one emerald. It also contained a sapphire worth £60, which may have been 'St Edward's' sapphire. It had a gold cross, enamelled in blue, on its arches (A.J. Collins, Jewels and Plate of Queen Elizabeth I (London, 1956) 12).

orb and the sceptre were presented to the young king,[34] who carried them with the assistance of the duke of Suffolk and the marquess of Dorset. He was enthroned, and a *Te deum* sung. The lords spiritual and temporal paid homage to their king in the accustomed form.

Although the council had noted that 'many poinctes' of the traditional ceremony were 'by the lawes of the realme att this present ... nat allowable',[35] little in the ceremony presaged the religious changes that were to come. The archbishop wore his mass vestments, the Latin litany was used and mass was celebrated in its accustomed form. Edward took the oaths on the sacrament, and used, it appears, the traditional words rather than a corrected form earlier devised by his father.[36] Like the later Plantagenets and his father and grandfather, Edward seems to have knelt to receive the unction.[37] (However, the oil used for the anointing was presumably not that which had been presented by the Virgin to Thomas Becket for the anointing of English kings.)[38] Cranmer and the duke of Somerset apparently invoked 'all Hallows' when they did homage, and the marquis of Dorset 'all saints'.[39] Only Cranmer's address gave a hint of what was to follow. Cranmer noted that the coronation oath prevented Edward from handing over power illegally to the pope and insisted that the rites of coronation did not in themselves confer royal authority.[40]

Unlike the slightly older Richard II, who had fallen asleep in the Abbey and was carried to the subsequent banquet by Sir Simon Burley, losing on the way one of the consecrated shoes that had been worn by King Alfred at his coronation in Rome,[41] Edward appears to have survived the coronation ceremony unscathed. He

---

[34] Edward was presented with a gold sceptre decorated with a dove, and a gold rod with a cross upon the top. The latter may have been the long-stemmed orb to be seen in a number of portraits of medieval monarchs. The gold 'globe' or orb was not a part of the coronation regalia, but a personal possession of the English monarchs.

[35] *CSP, Spanish*, ix. 247.

[36] Wickham Legg, *English Coronation Records*, 240–1.

[37] Ibid., xxxvi.

[38] Wolffe, *Henry VI*, 49.

[39] College of Arms MS I.7, fo. 41; Nichols, *Literary Remains*, ccxcvi.

[40] *Miscellaneous Writings and Letters of Thomas Cranmer*, ed. J.E. Cox (Parker Society, 1846), 126. For further discussion of this sermon in the context of the evolution of religious policy, see below, 48–9.

[41] L.C. Hector and B.F. Harvey, eds, *The Westminster Chronicle* (Oxford, 1982), pp. 414–16.

still had the banquet in Westminster Hall to sit through, however, with all its complicated rituals. Probably the king most enjoyed the entrance, accompanied by a trumpeter, of his champion, Sir Edward Dymoke, in splendid armour and on an elaborately trapped horse; Dymoke thrice threw down a gage and challenged to combat anyone who questioned Edward's right to the crown.[42] This episode is described in more detail than anything else in Edward's own account of the dinner, at which, the king rather glumly records, 'he sat with the crown on his head'.[43] There was, certainly, little else calculated to appeal to what must by then have been a very weary small boy. The entertainments of the following two days were probably more to his taste, with jousting and a tournament. On the evening of Shrove Tuesday there was a banquet at court, followed by an interlude and a masque of Orpheus; these entertainments involved the construction of a large and elaborate 'mount'.[44]

[42] The Dymokes were, as Sir Edward pointed out to the court dealing with coronation claims, hereditary champions. Dymoke's father served both Richard III and Henry VII in this capacity, and Sir Edward himself was to serve at the coronations of both Mary and Elizabeth (PRO, SP10/1, no. 7).

[43] Edward VI, *Chronicle*, 5. See also ibid., 53–4.

[44] A. Feuillerat, ed., *Documents Relating to the Revels at Court in the Time of King Edward VI and Queen Mary* (Louvain, 1914), 3–8; Lefèvre-Pontalis, *Correspondance politique de Odet de Selve*, 105. See also J. Leland, *De Rebus Britannicis Collectanea*, ed. T. Hearne, app., 161–2.

Chapter 5

SOMERSET'S PROTECTORATE

Edward was obviously too young to rule himself and the history of his reign must therefore be the history of those who ruled in his name. Somerset, the first of these, had established himself as protector immediately after the death of Henry VIII. What was he like, the new protector? Few sixteenth-century politicians have received more favourable treatment from twentieth-century historians than Somerset. From the publication in 1900 of A.F. Pollard's *England under Protector Somerset* he has been portrayed by most English and American scholars as an idealist, concerned primarily with reform of church and state: indeed, some have created a liberal dreamer who would not have felt out of place at early meetings of the Fabian Society. 'Ambitious he certainly was', wrote Pollard, 'yet his was an ambition animated by no mean or selfish motives, but by the desire to achieve aims that were essentially noble'; the protector, 'ardent and enthusiastic by nature', fixed his gaze on a distant goal 'and overlooked the obstacles that beset his feet'.[1] W.K. Jordan followed Pollard in his admiration: his verdict on Somerset is that he was 'a very great man whose magnanimity and high idealism were never to be forgotten as Englishmen spoke in quiet corners, in the fields and on the sea of the age of the "Good Duke"'.[2]

The real Somerset was, however, very different from the character whom historians have created in their own image.[3] He was, to begin

---

[1] A.F. Pollard, *England under Protector Somerset* (London, 1900), 317. The exception to this is, of course, M.L. Bush's magisterial study of *The Government Policy of Protector Somerset*, (London, 1975). Bush's suggestion that Somerset was preoccupied with Scotland has been widely accepted, but it has had surprisingly little impact on the general reputation of 'the good duke'.

[2] W.K. Jordan, *Edward VI: the Young King* (London, 1968), 523.

[3] It would be fair to note that a few historians have chipped away at Somerset's liberal reputation. C.S.L. Davies, 'Slavery and Protector Somerset: the Vagrancy Act of 1547', *Economic History Review*, 2nd series, xix (1966), 533–49, has teased out the implications of a particular piece of legislation, and M.L.

with, neither modest nor self-effacing. From the start of his protectorship, he conducted himself with great state; the imperial ambassador reported on 10 February 1547 that Somerset had two gilt
maces borne before him,[4] and he even took the royal jewels from
Catherine Parr and allowed his wife to wear them.[5] He was
extremely interested in money, a fact admitted even by Pollard, and
in his pursuit of material advantage he could be both ruthless and
cold-hearted.[6] Autocratic by temperament, he was to run Edward's
government as a private fiefdom, using his own men and rewarding
them from the king's coffers.

The picture presented by Somerset's admirers accords ill also
with the man of action that Somerset primarily was: knighted in the
field by the duke of Suffolk on the French expedition of 1523, he
had served in both Scotland and France in the last years of Henry's
reign; he had been appointed, briefly, warden of the Scottish
Marches, was responsible in 1544 for the sacking of Edinburgh
castle, and the next year for a spectacular defence of Boulogne
against the French. His actions as protector were to demonstrate his
interest in military matters; many of the earliest official letters of the
protectorship concern the south coast defences,[7] on which, between
March and August 1547, £6,000 was spent. (Another £4,800 was
paid out in the following year.)[8] And Somerset was preoccupied –
M.L. Bush would say, obsessed – throughout the protectorship with
the problem of Scotland, the strengthening of the fortifications of
the north being another of his early concerns.

Somerset was, then, as concerned about matters military as Henry
had been. Moreover – and in this Somerset was unlike his former

Bush (*Government Policy*) has more generally seen Somerset's social policy as
subordinate to military needs, though the thrust of his work is somewhat muf-
fled (see review by J. Hurstfield, *English Historical Review*, xliii, 1978, 613–15).

[4] *CSP, Spanish*, ix, 19.

[5] He may have gone further. One of the charges against him was that 'he hath
robbed and embesselled from the kinges majestie the tresure and Jewells left
by his majesties father' (BL, Add. MS 48126, fo. 2), and my own researches
into the coronation jewellery suggest that this charge may have some truth.

[6] See, for example, M.L. Bush, 'The Lisle–Seymour Land Disputes: a Study of
Power and Influence in the 1530s', *Historical Journal*, ix (1966), 255–64; H.
Miller, *Henry VIII and the English Nobility* (Oxford, 1986), 28–9 (Hertford sell-
ing the earldom of Bridgwater), 252–3.

[7] Edward Vaughan, captain at Portsmouth, wrote on 17 February 1547 of the
bad state of fortifications at Portsmouth (PRO, SP10/1, no. 77).

[8] H.M. Colvin, ed., *The History of the King's Works, Vol. IV 1485–1660 (Part II)*,
(London, 1982), 510–13.

master – his interests were, in the main, those of a soldier. Amongst the extant – and voluminous – accounts of Somerset's expenditure over the years there is little to suggest intellectual pursuits, although large sums were spent on jewellery and plate, and on building.[9] (He was also an inveterate gambler – winning, in 1542, 35 shillings 'the night he supped at Lambeth' with the archbishop of Canterbury.)[10] However, it would be unfair to deduce from the accounts alone that Somerset owned no books, for we know that, in fact, he owned two; both were entirely appropriate fare for a military man, one being a French translation of a racy tale, Boccaccio's *Decameron*,[11] and the other a manuscript volume of tide tables.[12] He also maintained a troupe of players.[13]

None the less, Somerset's admirers have often claimed that he had a considerable interest in education; after all, an Elizabethan source credits the protector with the view that

> if learning decay, which of wild men maketh civil, of blockish and rash persons wise and godly counsellors, and of evil men good and godly Christians; what shall we look for else but barbarism and tumult?[14]

One of the stated purposes of the dissolution of the chantries was to be the 'erecting of grammar schools to the education of youth in virtue and godliness, the further augmenting of the universities, and better provision of the poor and needy', but in the event most of the money went directly into the coffers of the crown; only those lands that were already used for the maintenance of schools appear to have been preserved.[15] One of those close to Somerset, John Hales,

[9] *HMC, Bath, Longleat Manuscripts, Vol. IV Seymour Papers 1532–1686* (London, 1968), *passim*.
[10] Ibid., 338.
[11] J.N. King, *English Reformation Literature. The Tudor Origins of the Protestant Tradition* (Princeton, 1982), 109.
[12] It was, poignantly, into these that he wrote some verses on the eve of his death.
[13] S.R. Westfall, *Patrons and Performance. Early Tudor Household Revels* (Oxford, 1990), 15, 143, 217.
[14] W. Harrison, in *The Description of England*, quoted and endorsed by Jordan in *Edward VI: the Young King*, 327. For sceptical discussion of this quotation, from a speech that 'reflects Harrison's obsessions, rather than Somerset's ideas', see G.T.R. Parry, 'Inventing "The Good Duke" of Somerset', *Journal of Ecclesiastical History*, xl (1989), 370–80.
[15] A. Kreider, *English Chantries: the Road to Dissolution* (Cambridge, Mass., 1979), 186–8.

had founded a school in Coventry at the end of Henry's reign, but in general Somerset and his circle are not distinguished for their interest in schools.

There is more evidence for an interest in university matters amongst those close to Somerset, and in 1548 the government ordered a visitation of Oxford and Cambridge.[16] One aim of the visitation was to remove all traces of popery from the universities, but it was also intended to produce a syllabus that was more practical, more 'relevant' to the needs of the day. A major proposal, which was much desired by the secretary to the council, Sir Thomas Smith, was to amalgamate, in Cambridge, the colleges of Clare and Trinity Hall, and in Oxford, parts of New College and All Souls, thus producing establishments committed to the study of civil law.[17] This suggestion offended not only the fellows of the institutions concerned, who took prompt, and effective, action to protect themselves, but also alienated those who felt, like Ridley, one of the commissioners for Cambridge, that it was 'a very sore thing, a great scandal ... to take a college founded for the study of God's word, and to apply it to the use of students in man's law'. To this, Somerset replied pragmatically, pointing out how great was the need for civilians to assist the government in its interpretation of treaties.[18]

There is, then, very little evidence to support the view that Somerset was particularly committed to the advancement of education. The same is true of things spiritual. W.K. Jordan declared that 'Somerset was an undoubted Protestant of moderate and Erastian persuasion',[19] but the evidence for any personal piety beyond the conventional is tenuous. Somerset had, of course, considerable religious patronage, and in Edward's reign he appointed a number of Protestants to positions within his household, including his physician, William Turner,[20] and Thomas Becon, his chap-

---

[16] C. Cross, 'Oxford and the Tudor State, 1509–1558', in J. McConica, ed., *The History of the University of Oxford, III*, (Oxford, 1986), 135–8.

[17] M. Dewar, *Sir Thomas Smith: A Tudor Intellectual in Office* (London, 1964), 40–2; Bush, *Government Policy*, 54–5.

[18] PRO, SP10/7, nos 16, 27, 30. Somerset made similar points in a letter to Gardiner: J.A. Muller, ed., *The Letters of Stephen Gardiner* (Cambridge, 1933), 493–5.

[19] Jordan, *Edward VI: The Young King*, 125.

[20] W.R.D. Jones, *William Turner: Tudor Naturalist, Physician and Divine* (London, 1988), 19–26. There is, however, *pace* Bush (*Government Policy*, 108), no reason to believe that Somerset 'summoned' him from exile.

lain.[21] He was also associated with Miles Coverdale, translator of the Bible, who had served as almoner to the duke's one-time sister-in-law, Catherine Parr. Because of the current political troubles John Hooper stayed with the protector briefly after his return from exile in 1549, and, according to one of the foreign *émigrés*, it was Somerset who was responsible for his later elevation to the see of Gloucester.[22] But in the circumstances of the late 1540s these associations are no more than one would expect of a man in Somerset's position; indeed, we might also observe that the duke was not, in general, conspicuous for his advancement of Protestant clients.[23]

Somerset's duchess can be much more positively linked with reformers. Anne Stanhope, whom Somerset married as his second wife some time before March 1535, was in 1546 involved with the radical Anne Askew, who was subsequently burnt for heresy; she was said to have sent a man in a blue coat with 10 shillings to help her.[24] It was more probably through the influence of Anne Stanhope than that of her husband that their six daughters received a scholarly education; Becon, dedicating a revised edition of his *Gouernans of Vertue* in 1550 to Lady Jane Seymour, praised her parents for bringing up both sons and daughters in 'good literature and in the knowledge of God's most holy laws'.[25] By 1549 the duchess was widely recognized as a woman of radical religious views, and the eminent academic and civil servant, Thomas Smith, found it necessary to justify himself to her in very defensive terms, saying that he was no religious neuter, but a man who had 'professed Christ' in 'the times of persecution'.[26]

But if Somerset left most matters intellectual and spiritual to his wife, why was he the recipient of no fewer than twenty-four book and manuscript dedications?[27] (His wife received the dedication of

---

[21] D.S. Bailey, *Thomas Becon and the Reformation of the Church in England* (Edinburgh, 1952), 54.

[22] H. Robinson, ed., *Original Letters relative to the English Reformation (Zurich Letters) 1537–1558* (Cambridge, 1847), ii, 68–9, 410.

[23] See, for example, Bush, *Government Policy*, 111 and Jones, *William Turner*, 21, 23.

[24] Foxe, v, 547.

[25] M. Dowling, *Humanism in the Age of Henry VIII* (London, 1986), 240–1. Jane, with her sisters, Margaret and Anne, was later to compose Latin verses on the death of Marguerite of Valois, for which they were lauded by Ronsard.

[26] BL, Harleian MS 6989, fo. 141.

[27] F. Williams, *An Index of Dedications and Commendatory Verse in English Books before 1642* (London, 1962); J.N. King, 'Protector Somerset, Patron of the English Renaissance', *Papers of the Bibliographical Society of America*, lxx (1976), 326–31, and *English Reformation Literature*, 107–8, 460–1.

eleven religious works between Edward's accession and October
1551.)[28] After all, even the king himself received only forty-nine,
and Warwick a mere seven.

Some of the dedications came from Somerset's clients. William
Turner dedicated to him *The Names of Herbes in Greke, Latin, Englishe*
... (1548)[29] and *A New Herball,* (1551)[30] and William Gray, one of
his household, gave him gifts of verse.[31] But a dedication did not
necessarily indicate that a relationship existed between the author
and the dedicatee; thus, William Gibson, a schoolmaster at
Sherborne, was probably unknown to Somerset until he sent him a
translation of one of Bullinger's works.

Only two of these works deserve specific attention. In April 1550
there appeared *An Epistle of Godly Consolacion ...*, a letter of Calvin's
written during the rebellions of the previous year.[32] The frontispiece claims that the work was 'translated out of frenshe' by the
duke, but the preface, which probably was indeed written by
Somerset, in no way supports this. The preface itself is of some
interest, for it rejoices in the coming forth of 'godly preachers' who
spoke out against the sin of rebellion, and in the fact that 'litle
England' was now successfully resisting foreign power. The second
work which sheds some light on Somerset himself is Miles
Coverdale's translation of Otto Werdmueller's *Spyrytuall and Moost
Precyouse Pearle* (1550), which appeared the following month.[33] This,
again, has a commendatory preface by Somerset, in which he says
that Werdmueller's book had given him consolation in his 'greate
trouble', and that he had asked 'hym of whom we had the copye' to
ensure its setting forth, in order that others might find in the book
the consolation in affliction that he had.[34]

Does all this justify a description of Somerset as 'a Protestant
patron and man of letters'? Book dedications are not, in truth, a
very helpful guide to the religious views of the dedicatee. William
Forrest dedicated to Somerset his 'Pleasaunt Poesy of Princelie

[28] Dakota L. Hamilton, 'The Household of Queen Katherine Parr', University
of Oxford D.Phil. thesis, 1992, 340–9, and note.

[29] *RSTC* 24359.

[30] *RSTC* 24365.

[31] On Gray, see E.W. Dormer, *Gray of Reading* (Reading, 1923).

[32] *RSTC* 4407.

[33] *RSTC* 25255.

[34] Jordan, *Edward VI: The Young King,* 126, implies that Somerset declared that
Werdmueller's book had consoled him after his fall: in fact, Somerset says that
it had been a comfort during the previous year's popular risings.

Practise' in 1548, for example, presumably because it dealt with matters agrarian, and he also dedicated to him his translation of the Psalms.[35] But Forrest was a conservative priest, who later became a chaplain to Queen Mary, and his best-known work is a history of the patient and badly treated 'Griseld', Catherine of Aragon; he made a strange bedfellow for Turner and Coverdale. Henry Parker, Lord Morley, who dedicated to Somerset a manuscript commentary on Ecclesiastes, was a member of the household of the Princess Mary, to whom he dedicated a number of other works; interestingly, Morley threw in his lot with Somerset's opponents very early in the coup of 1549.[36] Lord Stafford, another conservative, was responsible for the dedication to the protector of a translation of *De vera differentia*, a work by the Henrician bishop, Edward Fox, which would certainly have been disapproved of by the radicals.[37]

Any person in a position of power in the sixteenth century was likely to receive dedications from authors anxious to find patronage, for dedications were both a form of courtesy and a request for patronage. It is noteworthy that Somerset received no dedications before he became protector, and that his wife received none between his fall and the middle of Elizabeth's reign; it was their position rather than their beliefs that had brought them so many dedications.

Warwick's supreme authority did not produce the same result. Does this suggest that intellectuals and men of religion saw him in a different light from that in which they had regarded Somerset? The range of subjects amongst the books dedicated to Warwick is not unlike those addressed to the protector, some being religious – John Bale's *An Expostulation . . . agaynste the Blasphemyes of a Franticke Papyst . . .*, for example[38] – and there were also works on rhetoric and geography. A significant fact here is the total number of books being published: from the peaks of 1548 and 1550 when over 250 books were produced in a year, the average production slumped to about 150 in the early 1550s, not rising again to over 200 until

---

[35] Printed in part in *Early English Text Society*, extra series, xxxii (1878), lxxix–xcix.

[36] N. Pocock, *Troubles Connected with the Prayer Book of 1549* (Camden Society, new series, xxxvii, 1884), 94 (letter 52). This fact helps to support the theory (see below, 92) that the coup was initially thought to be a Catholic one.

[37] *RSTC* 11220 (London, 1548).

[38] *RSTC* 1294.

1555.[39] Although the change was in part due to the disastrous economic circumstances of the early 1550s, it is probably also true that the repeal, at the beginning of Edward's reign, of most of the various Henrician treason laws and of the Act of Six Articles,[40] together with a changed religious climate, produced in the late 1540s a particularly favourable environment for publishing,[41] and for this Somerset should be given credit.[42]

The changes in the treason and heresy laws that brought about this period of press freedom also permitted considerable religious discussion, and a number of people are known to have expressed openly opinions for which they would earlier have been burnt. No one was, in fact, burnt during the protectorate: a remarkable record for the sixteenth century. Somerset must take some credit for this; perhaps, as Jordan suggests, he did not believe that 'force was a proper or a useful instrument in religious policy'.[43] Certainly he was reported by Gardiner as having declared, pragmatically, that he 'wold not condemne other contries' that had different religious policies.[44] But the bulk of the praise for this toleration should go to Cranmer, who carried out some very delicate interrogations with tact and sympathy; even in the much more difficult conditions that prevailed after the 1549 risings, only two people were burnt.

Yet the liberal atmosphere of the early protectorate soon changed. From May 1548 preaching was strictly regulated, and in September of that year it was totally forbidden for the time being.[45] Moreover, in April 1549 a commission against heresy was issued, nominating twenty-five people, of whom two-thirds were clergy; a

[39] For a discussion of book production see J. Loach, 'The Marian Establishment and the Printing Press', *English Historical Review*, ci (1986), 136–7. The figures used here, however, are taken from 'A Quantitative Survey of British Book Production: Some Provisional Statistics', unpublished paper, Institute of Bibliography, University of Leeds, December 1990.

[40] Bush, *Government Policy*, 145; see 1 Edward VI, c. 12 for the repeal of certain statutes.

[41] J.N. King, 'Freedom of the Press, Protestant Propaganda, and Protector Somerset', *Huntington Library Quarterly*, xl (1976), 1–9.

[42] It should, however, be noted that in the Bill repealing the Henrician treason laws, it was not the government that was responsible for the bulk of the more moderate provisos: these were added by the House of Commons (Bush, *Government Policy*, 145).

[43] Jordan, *Edward VI: The Young King*, 126–7. For a most interesting discussion of Somerset's toleration, or lack of it, see Bush, *Government Policy*, 112–19.

[44] Muller, ed., *Letters of Stephen Gardiner*, 436.

[45] Hughes and Larkin, 432–3 (no. 313).

number of people were summoned before it, but the majority abjured.

What little direct evidence there is for Somerset's religious views in the late 1540s suggests a man of some piety but little specialized knowledge, whose inclinations were, perhaps as a result of his wife's influence, towards the radical rather than the conservative end of the spectrum.[46] He was thought to have abandoned mass in his own household by December 1547 – but the same was claimed of Warwick and of Catherine Parr.[47] (None the less, the use of English in the Chapel Royal in April 1547, and for parts of the mass for the opening of parliament in the following November cannot have occurred without the protector's specific sanction.) Somerset was not personally generous to the many distinguished Protestant scholars who flocked to England to escape the persecution of the Emperor Charles V – they depended on the charity of Cranmer and of the young king – but he did help the refugee Protestant community at Glastonbury; however, there his charitable instincts ran alongside a hope that the Walloon weavers might prove a sound investment. (In the event, neither side fulfilled its part of the contract.)[48]

Much of the religious change of this period – change that was sanctioned by the protector even if it was not initiated by him – should be seen primarily as an attempt to consolidate the royal supremacy and to extend lay control over the Church, rather than as an effort to move the Church in a specifically Protestant direction. Thus, the visitation of 1547 suspended the power of the bishops and other ordinaries, replacing it by that of thirty visitors, of whom twenty were laymen. Moreover, by an Act of 1547 'for the election of bishops' the old system, by then a formality, whereby the dean and chapter were issued with a *congé d'élire*, or licence to elect, was abolished, and replaced by letters-patent issuing directly from the monarch. Most important of all, the Prayer Book of 1549 was sanctioned merely by parliament, and not by the clerical gathering of convocation.

---

[46] For a much more positive account of Somerset's religious views, see King, 'Freedom of the Press', 1–9; idem, 'Protector Somerset, Patron of the English Renaissance'; and idem, *English Reformation Literature*, *passim*.

[47] *CSP, Spanish*, ix. 221.

[48] PRO, SP10/13, nos 70–9, 10/14, nos 4, 13–14; see also H.J. Cowell, 'The French Walloon Church at Glastonbury, 1550–1553', *Proceedings of the Huguenot Society*, xiii (1928), 483–515.

Other statutes of the period, such as the 1547 Act for the giving of chantries, colleges and religious guilds to the king, were clearly intended to provide the crown with much-needed funds. Although the preamble to the Act stated that the purpose of chantries involved 'phantasising vain opinions of purgatory and masses satisfactory, to be done for them which be departed', the Privy Council stated in a minute of the following year that the dissolution was intended primarily to relieve the king's 'charges and expences, which do dayly growe and encrease'.[49] Many bishops and their cathedrals were raided during the protectorate: Lincoln lost thirty manors, Bath and Wells twenty, Norwich twelve and Exeter nine.[50] (Indeed, Felicity Heal has characterized Somerset's attitude towards the Church as 'essentially acquisitive', noting that even when his main purpose was to secure additional funds for the crown, 'the choice of dioceses to be assailed seems to have been determined largely by his own personal concerns'.)[51] All clerics must have held their breath when the council ordered inventories of church plate to be made on a diocesan basis in December 1547, and then, in February 1549, asked for them to be done county by county: in the event, it was not until 1553 that the churches were finally stripped.[52] Thus, whilst the attack on the Church's wealth was not as fierce in the protectorate as it was subsequently to become, and Somerset seems to have been more sympathetic to the bishops than Warwick was to be, relations between church and state were throughout Edward's reign very much what might have been expected under a son of Henry VIII.

Yet, although in these respects there was continuity in attitudes towards the Church between Henry VIII in his later years and Somerset, under the leadership of Archbishop Cranmer there was a very marked change of direction in matters of faith and practice. This first became apparent over the question of images. Cranmer encouraged apparently spontaneous outbreaks of iconoclasm in London and Southampton in the first months of Edward's reign. He uttered phrases hostile to images in the course of his sermon at

[49] *APC*, ii. 184, cited by Kreider, *English Chantries*, 262 n. 48. Cf. E. Duffy, *The Stripping of the Altars: Traditional Religion in England, c. 1400–c. 1580* (New Haven and London, 1992), 454, for discussion of theological dimensions.

[50] F. Heal, *Of Prelates and Princes: A Study of the Economic and Social Position of the Tudor Episcopate* (Cambridge, 1980), 131.

[51] Ibid., 137.

[52] C.E. Challis, *The Tudor Coinage* (Manchester, 1978), 163–4. See below, 124.

Edward's coronation. In that address, he pointed out that the coronation oath the young king had sworn prevented him, as it had his predecessors, from handing over power illegally to the pope and his legates. Then he explained that although 'the solemn rites of coronation have their ends and utility', they in no way increased royal authority; the oil, he said, 'is but a ceremony; if it be wanting, that king is yet a perfect monarch notwithstanding, and God's anointed, as well as if he was anointed'. Comparing Edward with Josiah, an analogy that was to become a commonplace of the reign, Cranmer apparently told the king that his tasks were 'to see ... God truly worshipped, and idolatry destroyed, the tyranny of the bishop of Rome banished from your subjects, and images removed'.[53] This last phrase was startling, for the Henrician Church had set its face only against 'abused' images. But no contemporary observer remarked upon Cranmer's words, and no manuscript copy of the address is still extant, so some doubt must exist about whether these precise words were indeed used. The fact that Ridley undoubtedly did denounce images and holy water in a sermon preached at court only three days later, on Ash Wednesday, may perhaps lend some credence to the tale, since it suggests that Ridley believed the atmosphere to be conducive to radical reform, but the fact that Stephen Gardiner, bishop of Winchester, in a letter to Protector Somerset protesting about Ridley's sermon did not mention Cranmer's supposed words tends to undermine it.[54] Quite what Cranmer said remains uncertain.

But there is no doubt that the movement against images and the veneration of saints was well under way. The Injunctions of 31 July 1547 defined as superstitious the 'lighting of candles, kissing, kneeling, decking of images', permitted just two lights on the altar and, in an ambiguous phrase, allowed the removal of 'abused' images.[55] In some ways these were not dissimilar to the Injunctions issued in 1536 and 1538, but in practice the definition of 'abused' was widened. From the autumn of 1547 images and stained glass were being removed from churches in London and other radical areas.[56] Images before which candles were burnt were particular targets. Processions to shrines were now ruled out by the requirement that the Litany should be sung kneeling. The new Litany made no refer-

[53] T. Cranmer, *Writings and Letters*, (Parker Society, Cambridge, 1846), 126–7.
[54] Muller, ed., *Letters of Stephen Gardiner*, 255–63, 265–7.
[55] M. Aston, *England's Iconclasts I* (Oxford, 1988), 255.
[56] Ibid., 258–9, 255.

ence to saints. But the distinction between 'abused' and legitimate images was abandoned in February 1548. The council ordered Cranmer – had Cranmer persuaded them? – to see to the country-wide removal of all images. In the same year the traditional cere-monies for Candlemas, Ash Wednesday and Palm Sunday were forbidden, and Whit Sunday passed without the traditional releas-ing of doves from the roof of St Paul's.[57] Holy bread and holy water disappeared. The result was a very plain, educative, pattern of serv-ices. As an imaginary woman had been described as saying to her neighbour:

> Alas, gossip , what shall we do at church ... since all the godly sights we were wont to have are gone, since we cannot hear the like piping, singing, chanting and playing upon the organs that we could before? [58]

The dismantling of the chantries, colleges and guilds, while primar-ily driven by financial needs, significantly affected the provision of church services and music. In 1547 parliament enacted a statute with an apparently uncontentious title: an Act 'against all such as shall unreverently speak against the sacrament'.[59] Behind this title lay a clause allowing the laity to take both the bread and the wine at the eucharist – communion in both kinds. It was the first change in the order of service and on 8 March 1548 a royal proclamation put its provisions into effect. Into the Latin mass, after the celebrant had himself communicated, was inserted a section in English for the par-taking of communion by the laity. Although much of the text was drawn from medieval liturgies, the proclamation was an indication of the direction in which Cranmer and his supporters were going: communion in both kinds had been a highly visible feature of both Lutheran and Swiss Reformations.[60] So was the new freedom of clergy to take wives: a statute permitting clergy to marry was passed in the parliamentary session of 1548–9 against strong opposition from the conservative bishops in the Lords.[61] That measure had been petitioned for in the lower house of convocation two years earlier and many priests would take advantage of it, giving the

---

[57] Duffy, *Stripping of the Altars*, 459–60.
[58] The source for this quotation could not be traced.
[59] 1 Edward VI c.1 (*Statutes of the Realm*, iv. 2).
[60] MacCulloch, *Cranmer*, 384–6.
[61] 2 & 3 Edward VI, c.21.

Church a fundamentally different character: no longer would the clergy be set apart by their celibacy from the rest of society.

All those trends were confirmed and intensified by the Book of Common Prayer, prepared by a committee under Cranmer's leadership from September 1548, presented to parliament in December 1548, and given statutory authority in the Act of Uniformity early in 1549. At first sight it is surprising that the 1549 Prayer Book, with all its apparent doctrinal ambiguities, should have produced so much hostile reaction. Why should a book that Gardiner said he could use (although in the event he did not, and his willingness to accept it might have been tactical) cause so much trouble? The service laid down was to be conducted entirely in English, but that was not necessarily a Protestant measure (the bidding of the bedes and the sermon had always been vernacular parts of the mass); and much of the text was based on the liturgy of a Catholic reformer, Cardinal Quinones. After all, even though the Catholic doctrine of the sacrifice of the mass was absent, various parts of the 1549 Book could easily be taken to imply some corporeal presence – the words of adminstration, the fraction of the wafer, the epiclesis (the petition to God to send the Holy Spirit for the consecration of the bread and the wine in the eucharist), the commendatory prayers for the dead and the prayer of humble access. For these reasons, the Book was not well received amongst Protestants. Martin Bucer, the prominent reformer now in exile in England, thought it a concession to 'the infirmity of the present age' and believed that more instruction would be needed before a fullly reformed rite could be imposed.[62]

But the fact is that whatever the doctrines taught in the Book – and these may have been unclear even to many of the clergy – its message about ceremonies was unambiguous: they were to be drastically reduced. Only plain vestments were to be worn by the priest. Kneeling, the holding up of hands, and knocking the breast were left to the individual's choice, 'as every man's devotion serveth'. Elevation of the Host was forbidden. The wafers used for what was now described as 'the Holy Communion' were to be plain, and not, as in the past, decorated with religious images. In baptism, the exorcism of salt, the signing of the hand, the anointing of the breast and the giving of the candle were all abolished. In the marriage ceremony, the blessing of the ring was abandoned. And so on. The traditional cycle of feast and fast days, already 'nibbled at by successive

[62] See below, Ch. 9.

measures since 1536',[63] was reduced to the great festivals of Christmas, Easter and Whitsun, plus a very few saints' days. All but one of the feasts of the Virgin were abolished, for example, including the Feast of the Assumption. The result was a radical simplification. Irrespective of its doctrinal position, the 1549 Prayer Book thus involved, visually and orally, a great break with the past.

As under Henry VIII, Somerset's government remained preoccupied by problems of finance and defence. The foreign situation was, indeed, threatening. In 1545 the English had seized from the French the strategically important port of Boulogne, which, by a treaty of 1546, they were permitted to keep for eight years. However, some aspects of the treaty, in particular the future of another vital port, Calais, remained unresolved at Henry's death. With the death of Francis I on 31 March 1547, the resumption of formal war became almost inevitable, for the new French king, Henry II, was determined to avenge the loss of Boulogne.[64] Moreover, with his accession the influence of the Guise family grew, and so, too, did the likelihood of French intervention in the north, the dread of all English monarchs, for the dowager queen of Scotland was also a Guise.

The situation in Scotland was complicated by the fact that in 1543 Edward had been betrothed to Mary, the infant queen of Scotland, a union that promised to bring to an end centuries of conflict. However, in the event, neither the betrothal nor the treaty of which it was a part had secured stability in Scotland, and armed conflict remained endemic. Desultory negotiations took place throughout the summer of 1547, the English still, publicly at least, putting their faith in promises and agreements which, they said, would 'knit into one nacion' themselves and the Scots.[65] But all parties were meanwhile preparing for hostilities, and in the late summer Somerset led a vast army into Scotland, where, on 10 September, he won a notable victory at Pinkie.[66]

Despite this, and despite the subsequent failure of the Scots to capture even such exposed positions as Broughty castle, the English cause did not prosper, and in January 1548 the Scots began to dis-

---

[63] Duffy, *Stripping of the Altars*, 465.

[64] J. Delaborde, *Gaspard de Coligny* (3 vols, Paris, 1879), 53.

[65] PRO, SP10/2, no. 6: draft prayer for peace.

[66] For a very full account of the battle, see W. Seymour, *Ordeal by Ambition: An English Family in the Shadow of the Tudors* (London, 1972), ch. 12.

cuss a marriage between Mary and the dauphin. French involvement in Scottish affairs became more overt, and in June 1548 a substantial expeditionary force landed at Leith. The French besieged the English stronghold of Haddington, and pressed the marriage negotiations, which were finally completed on 7 July. Although the earl of Shrewsbury moved somewhat ponderously to the north and relieved Haddington, it was too late – Mary had been removed to France.

The government planned another offensive campaign for the summer of 1549, but the major rebellions of that year necessitated the withdrawal of troops to the south-west and Norfolk. The French, who had been much annoyed in the previous autumn by snide English remarks about the rebellion in Guyenne,[67] seized their opportunity, and on 8 August 1549 Henry II declared war on England and took personal command of the troops outside Boulogne. However, to his chagrin, the English resisted stoutly, and it was, in the end, by a treaty signed on 28 March 1550 that Boulogne was surrendered to the French.

What Edward felt about the loss of his infant bride or, later, that of Boulogne, we do not know, any more than we know whether he supported the immensely costly policy pursued by Somerset in Scotland.[68] What is clear is that the king enjoyed hearing about the exploits of his troops. For this we have the evidence of Edward's own *Chronicle*, which was probably begun as a school exercise to be presented to one of the king's tutors.[69] It opens with a brief account of Edward's birth and upbringing, and then proceeds to give a rather fuller description of his coronation. The first substantial entry tells the story of an encounter early in 1547 between the admiral of the Northern Sea, Sir Andrew Dudley, and a Scottish ship, the *Lion*.[70] This is shortly followed by a fairly detailed account of Somerset's Scottish campaign in the autumn of the same year. Almost all the

[67] G. Lefèvre-Pontalis, ed., *Correspondance politique de Odet de Selve, ambassadeur de France en Angleterre (1546–1549)* (Paris, 1888), 447.
[68] The strengthening of the Scottish fortresses between 1547 and 1550 cost £11,939, one third of the total costs of the establishment in the north. Garrisoning in Scotland, between September 1548 and April 1550, cost £72,000. (The total cost for the reign of all the troops in the north was £424,000.) In all, Edward's war in Scotland cost £604,000, almost twice as much as Henry's. (For this, and further details, see Colvin, *King's Works*, iv, 725–6.)
[69] Cf. Jordan's remarks in Edward VI, *Chronicle*, xvii.
[70] Ibid., 5–6.

longer descriptive passages over the next two years relate to matters military or to tournaments. This surely reveals something of the boy's own tastes and interests: treaties and negotiations are dutifully recorded, but Edward's account of the attack on Haddington, where the townsmen were 'in their shirts',[71] or a attempt on Boulogne by a galley loaded with stones and gravel,[72] has about it a zest and enthusiasm that other passages lack. Edward seems, too, to have had his heroes – Sir Andrew Dudley, the rash Sir Thomas Palmer, and the earl of Warwick, whose near-capture at Musselburgh was given more space than Somerset's efforts at the battle of Pinkie itself.[73]

From April 1550 the *Chronicle* becomes much more thorough, providing almost daily, though often brief, notes of events in the kingdom and, occasionally, overseas. The concern with military events and with tournaments persists; but the young king's interests widened to take in the visits of foreign envoys, epidemics, and economic affairs. By 1551 Edward was, as we saw earlier, analysing complex fiscal matters as well as monetary campaigns.[74] As a source for historians, the *Chronicle* is invaluable, providing a framework of events and, much more significantly, an insight into Edward's mind and growing maturity from 1550 until November 1552, when it comes to an end.

In the months after Pinkie, Somerset was in a position of great strength. Parliament, summoned for November, eased the government's financial difficulties by a statute permitting Edward to dissolve the chantries,[75] whilst the Bill repealing Henry VIII's treason legislation on the grounds that 'lighter garments' were more suitable now that 'tempest or winter' no longer threatened shows how confident the government felt in its own ability to govern.[76]

Somerset's personal position was strengthened by another bill of repeal, which abolished the curious statute of 1536 whereby future kings could suppress by letters-patent any statutes passed before they reached the age of twenty-four.[77] He was also named by letters-

[71] Ibid., 10.
[72] Ibid., 16.
[73] Ibid., 7–8.
[74] See above, 16.
[75] 1 Edward VI, c.14 (*Statutes of the Realm*, iv. 24).
[76] 1 Edward VI, c.12 (*Statutes of the Realm*, iv. 18).
[77] 1 Edward VI, c.11 (*Statutes of the Realm*, iv. 17).

patent of 3 November 1547 'our chief and principal councillor', authorized to sit upon the king's right hand in parliament. The same document changed the terms of his appointment as protector: originally authorized only until the king's eighteenth birthday, his power could now be terminated only at the king's pleasure. This document was signed on 24 December by all the peers who were present in parliament, by most members of the council, by thirteen bishops and by all the principal legal officers.[78]

Nevertheless, there were threats to Somerset's position. One threat came from very near at hand: Somerset's brother, Thomas, aggrieved since the time of Henry's death about his elder brother's pre-eminence, began to plot against him.[79] Thomas, who had married with unseemly haste Henry's widow, Catherine Parr, and then taken to flirting with the young Princess Elizabeth, who was living with her, was clearly a man of some charm, all of which he employed in his dealings with his young nephew. Through various chamber officials, he constantly sought access to the boy, flattering him and giving him presents and extra pocket money.[80]

From the establishment of the protectorship, Thomas Seymour had asserted – with some truth – that in minorities of the past it had been unknown, when the king had two uncles, for one to 'have all rule and the other none, but that if one were protector, the other should be governor'. His bid to secure control of the king's person seems to have been backed, albeit cautiously, by Edward himself who probably thought that Seymour would make a more enjoyable guardian than the aloof Somerset; 'my Unkell off Sumerset deylyth very hardly with me and kepyth me so strayt that I cane not have mony at my wylle,' he declared, 'but my Lord Admyrall both sendes me mony and gyves me mony'.[81] In return Seymour and Catherine tried to persuade Edward to write in favour of their marriage. After their marriage had, in fact, been solemnized, Edward did write a

---

[78] J.G. Nichols, 'The Second Patent Appointing Edward Duke of Somerset Protector', *Archaeologia*, xxx (1844), 463–9; Jordan, *Edward VI: the Young King*, 74–5.

[79] For a full account see G.W. Bernard, 'The Downfall of Sir Thomas Seymour', in G.W. Bernard, ed., *The Tudor Nobility* (Manchester, 1992), 212–40.

[80] BL, Harleian MS 249, fos 26–31v.

[81] Bernard, 'The Downfall of Sir Thomas Seymour', 220, citing BL Hatfield Microfilms, M485/39, vol. 150, fo. 112.

letter, dictated by Seymour, appearing to make out that the marriage was the result of a request to Catherine from himself. His own *Chronicle* entry shows that he was conscious of being on dangerous ground: 'the Lord Seymour of Sudeley married the Queen, whose name was Catherine, with which marriage the Lord Protector was much offended'.[82]

In the summer of 1547, when the protector was campaigning in Scotland, Seymour secured the support of some members of the king's privy chamber, passing messages and money to Edward through them. He urged Edward to take on the rule of the kingdom himself – to be 'rewler of his own thynges'. Asked by Seymour why he did not seek to bear rule as other kings did, Edward shrewdly replied that 'I needed not, for I was well enough'. When Seymour asked him to sign a letter to parliament asking its members to favour a suit from Seymour, Edward refused, on the advice of his tutor Cheke. The young king showed precocious discretion in saying that if Seymour's suit were good, the lords would allow it; if it were ill, then he would not write.[83]

Seymour's relations with the king are significant, for they show that Edward, even when he was aged only ten or eleven, was one of the principal keys to political power. Somerset was wise to keep his younger brother away from the king as far as he could. They also show that Edward was beginning to acquire a mind of his own, capable of recognizing the abundant dangers of the royal court.

Seymour's machinations did not stop with the young king. He also began to build up support amongst the peerage, to assemble quantities of men and weapons, and to fortify the castle of Holt. He promised Henry Grey, marquess of Dorset, that he would arrange a marriage between his daughter, Lady Jane, and the king.[84] Following the death of his wife, Catherine Parr, soon after giving birth in September 1548, Seymour was clearly interested in marrying Elizabeth.[85] There were suspicions that he was contemplating kidnapping the young king. John Fowler, one of the members of the king's privy chamber, testified how Seymour had once come to St James's Palace at 9 a.m. and voiced his surprise that there were so

[82] Edward VI, *Chronicle*, 6.

[83] Bernard, 'The Downfall of Sir Thomas Seymour', 219 and nn 60–64.

[84] PRO, SP10/6/7 (1–3); BL, Hatfield Microfilms, M485/39, vol. 150, fos 53–53v, 115, 84v (S. Haynes, *A Collection of State Papers . . . at Hatfield* (London, 1740), 83, 76, 98).

[85] Bernard, 'The Downfall of Sir Thomas Seymour', 216–17.

few people there: 'a man might stele away the king now for there cam more with me than is in all the howse besides'.[86] On 17 January 1549 he was arrested, interrogated, and then attainted by Act of parliament.[87] He was executed on 19 March. Edward commented laconically in his *Chronicle* that 'the Lord Sudeley, Admiral of England, was condemned to death and died the March ensuing'.[88] Elizabeth I later recalled Somerset telling her

> that if his brother had been suffered to speak with him, he had never suffered; but the persuasions were made to him so great, that he was brought in belief that he could not live safely if the Admiral lived; and that made him give his consent to his death.[89]

However, there is no contemporary evidence to suggest that the protector bemoaned his brother's death, and he certainly signed the death warrant. Yet, whilst it is an exaggeration to claim, as Jordan does, that Thomas Seymour's death 'did grave, perhaps irreparable damage to Somerset's reputation and position',[90] there is ample evidence that both protector and council felt uneasy in the early spring of 1549. Hugh Latimer preached a number of sermons denigrating Seymour as a man 'the furthest from the fear of God that ever I knew or heard of in England'; he tried hard to justify the government's actions, and, in particular, its decision to proceed by bill of attainder rather than by allowing Seymour a common law trial.[91]

The other threat to the security of Somerset's government and indeed of the realm lay in the agrarian disturbances of the spring and summer of 1549. These proved a greater danger and had more serious consequences for the protector than the fall of his brother.

[86] PRO, SP10/6/10 (6); cf. Bernard, 'The Downfall of Sir Thomas Seymour', 227–9.
[87] 2 and 3 Edward VI, c.18 (*Statutes of the Realm*, iv, 61–5).
[88] Edward VI, *Chronicle*, 10–11.
[89] Jordan, *Edward VI: the Young King*, 382.
[90] Ibid., 381–2.
[91] G.E. Corrie, ed., *The Sermons of Hugh Latimer* (Parker Society, 1844), 164. See also 238.

Chapter 6

ECONOMIC AND SOCIAL DIFFICULTIES

Edward reigned at a time of economic and social dislocation, accompanied by local protests and risings. Yet, for many groups the 1540s were a period of prosperity. Good harvests kept prices down; inflation, although growing, did not reach the staggering proportions sometimes suggested; and rents for the most part lagged behind prices. Indeed, not until the end of Elizabeth's reign was the short lease of twenty-one years widely adopted, so that most sixteenth-century tenants enjoyed long leases which had been fixed before prices began to rise markedly. Many tenants therefore occupied under-rented holdings, and some were even able to sub-let.

Why, then, were the 1540s a period of such rural violence? The 1540s was a time of marked population increase; Wrigley and Schofield suggest that a population of 2.774 million in 1541 had risen by 1551 to 3.011 million.[1] Inevitably, this led to pressure on land, especially in areas well placed to take advantage of the demand for food of a rising population, such as the counties around London, where there was a scramble to feed a city which grew from 60,000 in 1520 to 200,000 by 1603, and in East Anglia. There, a boom in the cloth trade, fuelled by a decline in the value of sterling which made English cloth appear very cheap to foreign buyers, together with the demand for meat of an increasing population, encouraged a rapid rise in the size of sheep flocks; one East Anglian family, the Townsends, for instance, who had a flock of 3,000 in 1544, had 4,200 in 1548. Theirs may have been quite a modest flock; it has been suggested that by the end of the 1540s several Norfolk farmers, like Sir Richard Southwell of Wood Rising, owned between 10,000 and 20,000 sheep.[2] Such large flocks rapidly exhausted grass supplies.

---

[1] E.A. Wrigley and R.S. Schofield, *The Population History of England, 1541–1871: A Reconstruction* (Cambridge, MA, 1981), 528.
[2] A. Simpson, *The Wealth of the Gentry, 1540–1660* (Cambridge, 1961) 183–4.

Another area subject to very intensive land use was the Weald of Sussex, Surrey and Kent. There, the iron industry consumed large quantities of wood and charcoal, and more timber was exported for other purposes.[3] During the Tudor and Stuart period enclosures for a variety of purposes withdrew land from common wastes in over a quarter of Sussex parishes: heaths replaced woodland, the decline in oak and other trees led to a reduction in swine-herding, and disputes between the keepers of forests and parks and those who commoned their beasts on the wastes increased.

Increased population led to increased land use. The tensions this caused had two consequences: increased rural violence, and, perhaps paradoxically, an increased recourse to the process of law. The number of cases heard in King's Bench went up,[4] whilst the newer courts of Star Chamber and Requests were kept busy with matters relating to land ownership and use. Recourse to the law was by no means confined to nobles and gentlemen: by 1560, 70 or 80 per cent of those using King's Bench and Common Pleas were from lower down the social scale.[5] Rural violence showed the same social spread. The riotous levelling of hedges, which was especially prevalent during the 1530s and 1540s,[6] often involved not only tenants and labourers, but also gentlemen and nobles. Enclosure riots have, indeed, been described as 'merely one species of violence employed by the gentry in pursuing quarrels with rival gentry or enforcing uniformity in agricultural usage upon their tenants'.[7]

None the less, the ubiquity during this period of one form of rural violence, the enclosure riot, is somewhat puzzling. Why did hedge-levelling acquire the status of a rural pastime?[8] Enclosure was much less of a problem than has sometimes been suggested: between 1455 and 1607 no more than 2 per cent of the land surface of England and Wales was newly enclosed. Even in areas such as the Midlands where there were relatively high levels of enclosing, less than 10 per

[3] R.B. Manning, *Hunters and Poachers: A Social and Cultural History of Unlawful Hunting in England 1485–1640* (Oxford, 1993), 113–14.

[4] E.W. Ives, 'The Common Lawyers in Pre-Reformation England', *Transactions of the Royal Historical Society*, 5th series, xviii (1968), 167.

[5] C.W. Brooks, *Pettyfoggers and Vipers of the Commonwealth: The 'Lower Branch' of the Legal Profession in Early Modern England* (Cambridge, 1986), 60–1, and appendix A.

[6] R.B. Manning, *Village Revolts: Social Protest and Popular Disturbances in England 1509–1640* (Oxford, 1988), 31.

[7] Ibid., 39.

[8] S.T. Bindoff, *Kett's Rebellion* (London, 1949), 9.

cent of the surface area was affected. Moreover, in the whole period from 1455 to 1607 it was *the second part of the fifteenth century* which saw the bulk of enclosing.[9] The real problems of *the mid-sixteenth century* were encroachment upon commons and waste and the extinction of tenants' rights over common land[10] – problems created as entrepreneurs and others jostled for access to limited resources.

So why was the enclosure riot so common? Forms of physical protest were still relatively primitive and undeveloped, and such anxieties seem to have found no outlet beyond the laying open of that which was closed: the hedge thus symbolized something that excluded and deterred. Interestingly, it was the outsider, the unintegrated newcomer, who was most frequently the victim of such attacks,[11] perhaps because he was less susceptible to other, more subtle, forms of pressure.

The crown, though naturally hostile to any action that threatened the peace, recognized that disputes over the ownership and use of land often involved matters touching on the good of the commonwealth as a whole. Self-sufficiency in food production and an adequate supply of healthy men for the defence of the realm were essentials on which all in government were agreed. A series of statutes from the early years of Henry VII's reign onwards had sought to prevent the decay of tillage, and from to time statute was reinforced by proclamation. On 1 June 1548 Edward's government took further action, with the announcement that, since 'of late by the enclosing of lands and arable grounds in divers and sundry places of this realm many have been driven to extreme poverty and compelled to leave the places where they were born', a 'view or enquiry' was to be held.[12] Commissioners were to be appointed, whose task it would be to travel round and empanel juries, in order to find out whether the relevant statutes from the reigns of Henry VII and Henry VIII were being observed. The enquiry thus followed the pattern of Wolsey's investigations of 1517–18, after which action had been taken against 264 persons.[13]

---

[09] J.R. Wordie, 'The Chronology of English Enclosure, 1500–1914', *Economic History Review*, 2nd series, xxxvi (1983), 483–505.

[10] Manning, *Village Revolts*, 36.

[11] Ibid., 52.

[12] Hughes and Larkin, 427–9 (no. 309).

[13] J.J. Scarisbrick, 'Cardinal Wolsey and the Common Weal', in E.W. Ives, R.J. Knecht and J.J. Scarisbrick, eds, *Wealth and Power in Tudor England: Essays Presented to S.T. Bindoff* (London, 1978), 45–67, esp. 52.

The concern of the government in June 1548 was explained in the proclamation as a response to the desire of the industrious poor for work, to a fear that too many sheep and 'beasts' were producing 'great rots and murrains', and to the comments of 'wise and discreet men'. However, defence considerations were also mentioned in the proclamation – the realm needed 'force of men', not 'flocks of sheep and droves of beasts' – and it seems probable that in the difficult circumstances of 1548 these were a major incentive to action.[14]

Interestingly, the proclamation was by no means solely preoccupied with the problems caused by sheep-farming, cattle being mentioned several times: where ten or two hundred people had once lived, it declared, now 'there is nothing kept but sheep or bullocks', and it stated that 'christian people by the greedy covetousness of some men [are] eaten up and devoured of brute beasts, and driven from their houses by sheep and bullocks'. The proclamation ends with the hope that the enquiry may result in a fall in the price of cattle, which it hopes will soon be 'in many men's hands as they be now in few'.

The proclamation states that the government has been 'advertised and put in remembrance' of these problems by the supplications and 'pitifull complaints' of the king's poor subjects,[15] and by the comments of 'other wise and discreet men'. Who were these wise men? Many preachers and moralists had taken up these complaints. They saw the problem as evidence of moral turpitude, arguing, as William Forrest did, that it was the greediness of rack-renting landlords that caused depopulation and unemployment. Such comments had obviously influenced the government.[16]

Somerset has been credited by some historians with the encouragement of a group of 'commonwealth' preachers and moralists who were anxious both to promote social reform and to advance the

[14] Hughes and Larkin, 427–9 (no. 309).

[15] These laments are often identified as *The Decay of England only by the Great Multitude of Sheep*, printed in *Four Supplications*, ed. J.M. Cowper (Early English Text Society, extra series, xiii, London, 1871) 93–102. For a contrary argument, see M.L. Bush, *The Government Policy of Protector Somerset* (London, 1975), 72–3. Hales's 'Defence' (BL, Lansdowne MS 238), printed in E. Lamond, ed., *A Discourse of the Common Weal of this Realm of England* (Cambridge, 1929), lxii–iii, also says that the commission was set up at the suit 'partlie of poore men' (p. liv).

[16] For a brief account, see W.R.D. Jones, *The Tudor Commonwealth 1529–1559* (1970), 67; Hughes and Larkin, 427–9 (no. 309).

cause of Protestantism; W.R.D. Jones, in his *Tudor Commonwealth,* *1529–1559,* writes of a 'Commonwealth Party which looked to Somerset for patronage and included in it John Hales and a number of divines such as Latimer and Lever'.[17] However, the evidence for the existence of such a group and for Somerset's active encourage- ment of it are alike tenuous. Although we can perhaps describe as 'commonwealth' the assumptions and rhetorical expressions fre- quently used in the middle of the sixteenth century by preachers and pamphleteers of a more radical persuasion, no commonwealth 'movement' or 'party' existed in this period in any organized or coherent form,[18] and Somerset's personal links with the men who most frequently expressed such ideas were limited. Of those he was known to have personally patronized, only Becon, who wrote in *The Jewel of Joy* that 'the cause of all this wretchedness and beggary in the commonwealth are [sic] the greedy gentlemen, which are sheep- mongers and graziers', and John Hales, clerk in the hanaper, can be described as having commonwealth tendencies. Yet Hales himself explicitly stated that he knew nothing of the setting up of the enclo- sure commission before he was named as a commissioner,[19] and there is no evidence to link Becon with the formulation of govern- ment policy. The majority of those usually described as belonging to the commonwealth movement were either court preachers, like Latimer, whose links were chiefly with Cranmer, or were without any government affiliations at all; thus, Robert Crowley, perhaps the most prolific of the Edwardian pamphleteers, was a stationer and bookseller before being ordained in 1551.[20]

It is true that commonwealth expressions did find their way into some government documents of the period; a proclamation of April 1549, for example, condemned the greediness of men who were 'blind and ignorant in brotherly love and charity, that ought to be between Christian man and Christian man, and the natural love and amity of one Englishman to another'.[21] But such phrases were no more than the rhetorical small change of the period; they had been

---

[17] Jones, *Tudor Commonwealth,* 32.
[18] G.R. Elton, 'Reform and the "Commonwealthmen" of Edward VI's Reign', in P. Clark, A.G.R. Smith and N. Tyacke, eds, *The English Commonwealth,* *1547–1640* (Leicester, 1979), 23–38.
[19] Hales, 'Defence', in Lamond, ed., *A Discourse,* liv.
[20] Crowley's only possible link, and a tenuous one, with Somerset, was through his patroness, Lady Fane, the wife of one of Somerset's clients.
[21] Hughes and Larkin, 451–3 (no. 327).

used by Wolsey in 1527, and continued to be employed until the Civil War.[22]

Certainly Somerset's fellow-councillors were, by the autumn of 1549, anxious to distance themselves from the commission of 1548 and that of 1549, but Hales may none the less have been correct in saying that councillors had originally been in favour of the 1548 enquiry. Only one councillor, the earl of Warwick, is known to have expressed reservations; Hales wrote to the earl on 12 August 1548 justifying the sending out of the commission 'in this troublesome tyme',[23] but later in the month he was able to reassure the protector that, after a meeting between them, the earl had agreed that it was necessary 'that the matter should go forward', and Warwick would now 'gladly further the same'.[24]

The first commission, to cover Oxfordshire, Berkshire, Warwickshire, Leicestershire, Bedfordshire, Buckinghamshire and Northamptonshire, was named on 1 June. It consisted of local gentlemen – Sir Francis Russell, son of Lord Russell, and later to succeed him as second earl of Bedford; Sir Fulke Greville of Alcester, Warwickshire; John Marsh, a London and Warwickshire merchant; William Pinnock of Hanley Castle, Worcestershire; and John Ames – and was chaired by Hales himself.[25] The council clearly intended to appoint a number of other commissions,[26] but it is not known whether or not men were so nominated.[27]

The commissioners were instructed to summon juries of twelve and enquire of them about the decay of tillage, the keeping of flocks of sheep of 2,000 or more, and about emparkment, the conversion of agricultural land into deer-parks.[28] The Midland commission speedily set to work; on 23 July Hales told Somerset that he had covered nearly the whole of his circuit, finding the people in gen-

[22] P.A. Slack, 'Dearth and Social Policy in Early Modern England', *Social History of Medicine*, v (1992), 5–9.

[23] BL, Lansdowne MS 238, fo. 321. Another set of articles against Somerset declared that 'a proclamation ... concerniung enclosures' went forth 'against the will of the whole council' (Foxe, v, 291).

[24] BL, Lansdowne MS 238, fo. 321v.

[25] Printed in J. Strype, *Ecclesiastical Memorials: Relating Chiefly to Religion and the Reformation* (London, 1816), vi. 330–2.

[26] Ibid.: 'the like shall be so directed to such others as shall be named'.

[27] In a letter of 24 July 1548 Hales begged Somerset to send out the other commissions, since in their absence 'we be thoughte men onely bent or set to do displeasure to some menn in these partes' (PRO, SP10/4, no. 33).

[28] *Calendar of Patent Rolls*, i. 419–20.

eral quiet.[29] But Hales, as his later career suggests, was a difficult man; an exile under Mary, he wrote at the beginning of Elizabeth's reign a contentious tract on the succession which earned him a stay in prison ended only by his death.[30] He was given to provocative statements about the duties and weaknesses of the rich, a habit which did not endear him to the local gentry and nobility.[31] Although Hales was careful to tell juries that neither they nor their neighbours should 'go about to take upon you to be executors of the statutes; to cut up men's hedges, and to put down their enclosures', he also declared that 'the people of this realm ... is greatly decayed through the greediness of a few men', and that God forbids 'the rich to oppress the poor'.[32] The 'greediness of the rich men', he declared, was one of the main reasons for the destruction of Sodom.[33] By 21 August Somerset was warning Hales that the people

> whether it be by any words by you to them vttered, wh[ich] they haue taken the more encouragement, or else by some other vpstires, are at this present in a marvelous trade of bouldness, some of them not lettinge to saye, that if other remedye be not presently had by the kinges maesties aucthoritie, for the redusinge of farmes a[nd] Copieholdes to the wonted state, that thei shall not fayle among themselves by a comen assent the reformacon thereof to be attempted.[34]

He ordered the commissioners to return through the towns they had already visited, telling the people that they should not take action themselves, since the king intended 'reformacion of thinges amysse', as soon as was expedient.[35]

Whether encouraged or not by the words of the commissioners, there were indeed a number of stirs in the summer of 1548. In June

[29] PRO, SP10/4, no. 33.

[30] For a brief account of his career, see S.T. Bindoff, ed., *The History of Parliament: the House of Commons, 1509–1558* (3 vols, London, 1982), ii, 276–7.

[31] Hales, 'Defence', lx–lxv. An apparently identical bill was passed in 1555. Hales also claimed (p. lix) that the landowners packed the juries empanelled by the commissioners.

[32] Strype, *Ecclesiastical Memorials*, vi, 333–48.

[33] Ibid., 333. In his 'Defence', Hales also talks of Sodom. He says of the nobility that 'they wrongfully reporte I shulde styrre and encourage with my wordes the comynaltie ayenst the nobilitie' ('Defence', lvi).

[34] BL, Lansdowne MS 238, fo. 316v.

[35] Ibid., fo. 319.

there had been a riot in Great Livermere, Suffolk,[36] and Bucking-hamshire was also uneasy, although Hales told Somerset dismissively that rumours of unrest had been exaggerated.[37] There was trouble in Northamptonshire, too, although that was apparently 'about the mass and the sacraments' rather than agrarian matters.[38]

However, in the autumn the country became quieter. Parliament sat from November 1548 to March 1549. In addition to some highly important legislation regulating the Church – clergymen were, in future to be allowed to marry,[39] the number of holy days was reduced,[40] and a new Prayer Book was authorized[41] – parliament also considered a number of bills dealing with agrarian matters. Hales himself introduced three bills: one, dealing with milk cattle,[42] was rejected by the Commons; a second, for maintaining tillage, failed in the Lords; and the third, against regrating – the cornering of markets – lapsed at the end of the session.[43] Hales subsequently compared the fate of his 'programme' bitterly to committing a lamb to a wolf.[44] However, another of his projects was more successful. A new form of taxation was introduced, involving a levy on sheep and cloth;[45] this has sometimes been interpreted as a device for limiting the size of flocks, but it seems more probable that it sprang from a concern in government circles about the decline in revenue from wool and woollens.[46] One private bill of the session is also of interest; this was a bill providing that all the Duke of Somerset's tenants should hold 'in the book or roll'.[47] Although the number of tenants affected by it was not great, and the improvement in their legal position only relative, the passing of the Act does suggest that

[36] B.L. Beer, *Rebellion and Riot: Popular Disorder in England during the Reign of Edward VI* (Kent, Ohio, 1982), 142, quoting PRO, Req. 2/17/73.
[37] BL, Lansdowne MS 238, fo. 320.
[38] PRO, SP46/5, fo. 218; 46/1, fo. 171.
[39] 2 and 3 Edward VI, c.21 (*Statutes of the Realm*, iv, 67).
[40] 2 and 3 Edward VI, c.19 (*Statutes of the Realm*, iv, 65–6).
[41] 2 and 3 Edward VI, c.1 (*Statutes of the Realm*, iv, 37–9). See 51–2, above.
[42] PRO, SP 10/5, no. 21.
[43] Ibid., nos 20, 22.
[44] Hales, 'Defence', lxii–lxiii; Bush, *Government Policy*, 49–51.
[45] 2 and 3 Edward VI, c. 36 (*Statutes of the Realm*, iv, 78–93).
[46] Bush, *Government Policy*, 52–3.
[47] 2 and 3 Edward VI, c.12 (*Statutes of the Realm*, iv, 54–5). See I.S. Leadam, 'The Security of Copyholders in Fifteenth and Sixteenth Century England', *English Historical Review*, viii (1893), 684–96; E. Kerridge, *Agrarian Problems in the Sixteenth Century and After* (London, 1969), 86–9; Bush, *Government Policy*, 55–6. In theory this act gave greater security of tenure.

Somerset took seriously the advice he gave to others about putting
their own houses in order.[48] Unusually, offenders against the
statutes against enclosure and conversion were included in the
Pardon Bill;[49] Hales later claimed responsibility for this, saying, 'I
sued to his grace for the generall pardon, whiche I opteigned'. But
he went on to claim that the rich had, none the less, soon
'retourned to ther olde vomyte'.[50]

Perhaps a belief in government circles that the rich had indeed
failed fully to reform also explains a proclamation issued on 11
April 1549, only a few weeks after the passing of the Pardon Bill.
This reports that although the commission had discovered that anti-
enclosure legislation was being widely ignored, the king had
decided to pardon offenders, believing that they were 'begin[ning]
to amend that that was past'; his mildness had not met a proper
response and so, the proclamation threatened, 'if gentleness will
not now provoke and cause that thing to be amended', then 'redress
and punishment' would speedily follow.[51]

With milder weather, unrest surfaced again. A contributory factor
seems to have been widespread misunderstanding of the government's position. After unrest the previous month,[52] a crowd at
Frome, Somerset, said to have consisted of some 200 people, chiefly
weavers, tinkers and other artificers, pulled down hedges and fences
in early May; those involved informing the magistrates who hastily
assembled that they had done nothing unlawful, as they knew of a
proclamation telling them 'so to do'.[53] Later that same month a
gathering near Salisbury pulled down Sir William Herbert's enclosure, saying that 'thay wylle obaye the kynges maieste and my lord
protector with alle the counselle, but ... thaye wyll not have ther
commonse and ther growendes to be inclosyd and soo taken from

[48] See, for example, PRO, SP10/8, nos 11–23, and a proclamation of 16 July
1549 (Hughes and Larkin, 75–6, no. 341).
[49] 2 & 3 Edward VI, c. 39 (*Statutes of the Realm*, iv, 95–8); read in the Lords on
8, 9, 13 March, and in the Commons on 13 and 14 (no second reading
recorded).
[50] Hales, 'Defence', lxi–lxii.
[51] Hughes and Larkin, 451–3 (no. 327); Bush, *Government Policy*, 46, 76;
and also R.W. Heinze, *The Proclamations of the Tudor Kings* (Cambridge,
1976), 217.
[52] F.E. Warneford, 'The Star Chamber Suits of John and Thomas Warneford',
Wiltshire Record Society, xlviii (1992), 91.
[53] *HMC Bath, Longleat, IV (Seymour)*, 109–10.

them'.[54] In Hereford, a man was reported as having said that 'by the king's proclamation all enclosures were to be broken up'.[55]

The government tacitly admitted its responsibility in a proclamation of 23 May which ordered an end to rioting, and condemned those who 'under pretense' of the earlier proclamation were destroying 'pales, hedges, and ditches at their will and pleasure'.[56] However, another proclamation, of 14 June, promised pardon to those who had 'plucked down men's hedges' and 'disparked their parks', provided they were sorry, since it recognized that the outrages had been committed 'of folly and of mistaking' the meaning of the earlier proclamation.[57]

On 8 July the council took the extraordinary step of establishing a fresh commission: moreover, whereas the 1548 commission had been intended, in Hales's words, 'onlye to enquyer, and not to here and determyn',[58] the new commissioners were told that if they discovered any commons or highways to have been enclosed or emparked 'contrary to right and without due recompense, that then the same shall be reformed by the said commissioners'.[59]

Where these second commissions were intended to operate and how many of them did so is unknown: a proclamation of 16 July declared that the king had 'directed his several commissions ... into every his counties',[60] but there is no clear evidence that this was so. Indeed, although on 29 June the council had told Lord Russell, by then in the west country, that he would 'shortly' be sent a commission 'for the inquery of decayes and unlawfull inclosures',[61]

[54] *HMC Rutland*, I, 36. Edward's *Chronicle* claims that Herbert 'did put them down, overrun, and slay them' (W.K. Jordan, ed., *The Chronicle and Political Papers of King Edward VI*, 1966, p. 12), and Wriothesley's *Chronicle* also says that Herbert 'slewe and putt to death diuers of the rebells' (ii, 13). In addition the commons 'broke downe certaine parkes' of Lord Stourton (Wriothesley, *Chronicle*, ii, 13).

[55] *HMC, Thirteenth Report*, app. iv (London, 1892), 317–18.

[56] Hughes and Larkin, 461–2 (no. 333).

[57] Ibid., i, no. 334, 462–4.

[58] Hales, 'Defence', lxi.

[59] PRO, SP10/8, no. 10. Reproduced in Hughes and Larkin, 471–2 (no. 338). See also E. Kerridge, 'The Returns of the Inquisitions of Depopulation', *English Historical Review*, lxx (1955), 212–28.

[60] Hughes and Larkin, 475–6 (no. 341).

[61] N. Pocock, ed., *Troubles Connected with the Prayer Book of 1549* (Camden Society, new series, xxxvii, 1884), 17–18.

there is no reason to believe that his commission ever arrived. On 16 July it was also stated in a proclamation that the king had 'by special ... letters missive' instructed the commissioners 'to redress and amend their own proper faults'. However, the proclamation went on, the commissions were only partly in operation, some being delayed by 'the folly of the people seeking their own redress unlawfully'.[62] There is in the Public Record Office a number of letters about the importance of the commission, and the need for those appointed to begin by reforming themselves; these are signed by Somerset; some are dated July 1549 and others left undated.[63]

But even if all the planned commissions did not operate, some did. On 13 July Somerset wrote 'with spede' to William Cecil; the letter implies that some activity has taken place, for it says that despite words to the contrary in the commission, it was important that commissioners should sit together, rather than dividing up.[64] Other letters dealing with the manner in which the commissioners should meet, remain unaddressed, and in some cases undated.[65]

It seems probable that the commissioners in Kent – Edward Wotton, James Hales, the attorney general, George Harper and John Norton – had begun work, for a letter of 18 July explains that in order to suppress unrest the commissioners have had to give out letters of assurance, and also to pay towards the cost of the demonstrators' journey home,[66] the money coming from the Canterbury Mint.[67] Hales's remarks in his 'Defence' make it clear that his own Midland commission also operated.[68] Indeed, the seventeeth-cen-

---

[62] Hughes and Larkin, 475–6 (no. 341).

[63] PRO, SP10/8, nos 11–23.

[64] Ibid., no. 25. The commission, as printed, does not say anything about the commissioners dividing up.

[65] Ibid., nos 26–9.

[66] *HMC Salisbury*, i, 54. The editor ascribes the letter to 1548, but the mention of other proclamations seems to fix it firmly in 1549; the commissioners ask, for instance, for the proclamation for tale-bearers to be sent to them, by which they presumably mean the proclamation of 8 July (Hughes and Larkin, 469–70, no. 337). See also *APC*, ii. 199.

[67] *HMC Salisbury*, i, 52–4; PRO, SP10/8, nos 50, 56; T. Wright, 'On the Municipal Archives of the City of Canterbury', *Archaeologia*, xxxi (1846), 211. A year later, in June 1550, the imperial ambassador reported that there had been trouble in both Sittingbourne and Maidstone, and that 'two rebellious peasants who werre taken prisoners last year were pardoned and set free' (*CSP, Spanish*, x, 116).

[68] He claims that 'the last yeare ... the lyke tales wer spredde ageynst me', thus making it clear that the instructions and the charge to the jury that he enclosed referred to the 1549 commission, not that of 1548 (Hales, 'Defence', lvi).

tury antiquarian, Dugdale, recorded notes of evidence laid before the Warwickshire commissioners, Sir Richard Catesby, his step-brother, Thomas Lucy, Sir Fulke Greville, Roger Wigston and Hales.[69] Moreover, on 10 July Sir Thomas Darcy and Sir John Gates, both from Essex, wrote to Cecil saying that they had passed on 'the contentes of the comyssion to vs and others directed'. Puzzlingly, they then ask for the sort of powers actively to redress offences which they had in fact been given by the second commission: they requested authority to enable them to summon those who had severed land from houses and those who kept excessive numbers of sheep, and to enable them to make presentments against thcm, because, they declared, the people might otherwise think 'we do but only delay time with them'.[70] Perhaps Darcy and Gates were simply confused.

By this time confusion was, in fact, widespread. Four days after the establishment of the commission, on 12 July, a proclamation pardoned those who had been involved in 'sundry unlawful and riotous assemblies', provided that they were repentant.[71] However, on 16 July those who gathered unlawfully to pull down enclosures were threatened with severe punishment; this proclamation reminded people of the instructions issued to the enclosure commissioners, and stated that the only impediment to their speedy implementation was 'assemblies, riots, conventions, stirres and uproars'.[72] On 22 July yet another proclamation accused bailiffs, constables and other officials of being sometimes 'the very ringleaders and procurers' of the unrest.[73]

The issuing of the second enclosure commission, to the general implications of which we shall return, was the more astonishing because the minor agrarian disturbances of 1548 and early 1549 had by this time turned into something infinitely more substantial: rebellion.

---

[69] I.S. Leadam, *The Domesday of Inclosures, 1517–1518* (1897), ii, 656–66. Dugdale says that in 1653 these documents were in the possession of John Hales of Coventry; their present whereabouts are unknown.

[70] PRO, SP10/8, no. 24.

[71] Hughes and Larkin, 474 (no. 340).

[72] Ibid., 475–6 (no. 341). Hughes and Larkin print 'stittes' which we have amended to 'stirres'.

[73] Ibid., 476–7 (no. 342).

Chapter 7

THE REBELLIONS OF 1549

THE WESTERN RISING

In Cornwall, there was a gathering around Bodmin on 6 June, according to the later indictment of the rebels, involving some thousand men – commons and clergy as well as the mayor and two local gentlemen, Humphrey Arundell and John Winslade.[1] Only the previous year there had been trouble in that county: William Body, an unsavoury minor official who had been involved in the removal of images, had been murdered at Helston.[2] It had been claimed by those involved in Body's death that 'they would have all such laws as was made by the late King Henry VIII, and none other until the king's majesty that now is' had reached the age of twenty-four and that if anyone tried to defend Body 'or follow such new fashions as he did, they would punish him likewise'.[3] Ten of the rioters had been convicted and sentenced to death, although, in the event, only seven, including a priest from Keverne named Martin Geoffrey, were executed.[4] Possibly unrest remained endemic in the area. However that may be, the renewed Cornish rioting at Bodmin in June 1549 very likely helped provoke disturbances at the Devon vil-

[1] H.M. Speight, 'Local Government and the South-Western Rebellion of 1549', *Southern History*, xviii (1996), 1–23 esp. 6 citing PRO, KB8/17, m.9.
[2] Wriothesley, *Chronicle*, ii, 4. See also E. Duffy, *The Stripping of the Altars: Traditional Religion in England, c.1400–c.1580* (New Haven and London, 1992), 456–8.
[3] R. Whiting, *The Blind Devotion of the People: Popular Religion and the English Reformation* (Cambridge, 1989), 76, 118; F. Rose-Troup, *The Western Rebellion of 1549* (London, 1913), 108, (n.2).
[4] H.M. Speight, 'Local Government and Politics in Devon and Cornwall, 1509–49, with Special Reference to the South-western Rebellion of 1549', University of Sussex D.Phil. thesis, 1991, 184.

lage of Sampford Courtenay, just off the Launceston–Crediton road.[5]

On Whit Sunday, 9 June, the Edwardian Prayer Book, sanctioned by parliament in the preceding winter, had come into use. The villagers at Sampford allowed their priest, William Harper, to conduct services in accordance with the new order, but when he attempted to use the Prayer Book again on the Monday, his congregation instead forced him to put on his 'olde popishe attyre' and celebrate mass in Latin, rather than follow the new English procedures set out in the Prayer Book. The unrest spread to Crediton, and then to Clyst St Mary. By late June all north Devon was disturbed. Meanwhile the Cornish had successfully laid siege to St Michael's Mount, where a group of gentry families had taken refuge, and Trematon castle, and moved on to take Plymouth (but not the castle). They then joined up with the Devon rebels and on 2 July a siege of Exeter began.[6]

By 12 July Somerset was in despair. Not only was the south-west in revolt, there were also risings in Oxfordshire and Buckinghamshire. Writing to Lord Russell, whom the council had dispatched to deal with the siege of Exeter, Somerset declared: 'We had determined to send down to you the Lord Grey, with a band of horsemen' and some soldiers,

but that uppon occasion of a sturr here in Bucks and Oxfordshire by instigation of sundery preists (kepe it to your self), for these matyers of religion, we have been forced to kepe him a while …[7]

For a week or so the situation in Oxfordshire was shaky, until Grey defeated the rebels at the battle of Enslow Hill. He then rode, with 250 cavalry and 350 infantry, to reinforce Russell. This brought the crown's forces in the south-west to more than 3,000 men, of whom nearly half were foreign professional mercenaries. That proved to be sufficient to turn the tide. On 6 August, Lord Russell was able to lift the siege of Exeter, which had lasted for thirty-five days; he then crushed the insurgents in pitched battle at Sampford Courtenay.

What provoked the rising in the south-west? There is little direct evidence about motivation, beyond the lists of rebels' grievances,

[5] On the whole history of the Cornish rising, see Speight, 'Local Government and Politics in Devon and Cornwall', 189–199.

[6] Speight, 'South-Western Rebellion', 1–23.

[7] Pocock, *Troubles Connected with the Prayer Book of 1549*, (Cambridge, 1884), 26.

which have, as always, to be treated with some caution since we do not know who composed them or in what circumstances. Moreover, there is a number of versions of the rebels' articles, and it is not possible to say which is the final and 'definitive' text. First, probably, came the eight articles to which the government replied in *A Message Sent by the Kynges Maiestie to Certain of his People, Assembled in Devonshire*, published on 8 July.[8] Somerset drafted a reply a few days later to what appears to have been a list of nine articles.[9] On 27 July a public 'letter' supposedly written from Russell's camp near Ottery St Mary mentions fifteen articles.[10]

The striking thing about all versions is their concentration on religious issues. As well as complaining about changes they supposed to be taking place in the Church's practices relating to baptism and confirmation, the rebels asked for the sacrament to be administered to the laity in one kind only, and reserved. They demanded the restoration of holy bread and holy water, images and 'all other auncient olde ceremonyes'. They wanted the doctrine of transubstantiation reasserted, and the Act of Six Articles of 1539, which had been repealed in 1547, to be restored; the articles to which Somerset replied also asked for the return of the Act creating the offence of treason by words. In addition the rebels demanded that 'all the general Councils and holy decrees of our forefathers [be] observed, kept and performed', and asked for the restoration of 'the mass in Latin as before'. Significantly, all versions of the articles show a marked contempt for the new Prayer Book, described as a 'Christmas game' or a 'Christmas play'.

Only a very few articles dealt with grievances other than religious ones. In the fifteen articles there are some clauses that relate to purely local matters – the rebels apparently asked for the release from detention of two local clergymen of conservative tendencies, John Moreman and Richard Crispin, and for the recall and pardon of Cardinal Pole, whose family came from the south-west. The rebels claimed that Cornishmen could not understand the English of the new Prayer Book, which provoked the authors of the 'official' responses, Cranmer and Philip Nichols, to various sarcastic com-

---

[8] *RSTC* 7506.

[9] Rose-Troup, *Western Rebellion*, appendix G. These articles are more 'Cornish' than other versions, and seem to have argued that a service in English was incomprehensible to the Cornishmen, who understood no English.

[10] Ibid., appendix K. These are the articles to which Cranmer replied.

ments about the ability of Cornishmen to understand Latin. The rebels also suggested that half the former monastic and chantry land now in lay hands should be handed back to the Church to establish two abbeys in every county, where 'devout persons' should pray 'for the King and the commonwealth'. There is, finally, a rather puzzling demand that the number of servants kept by gentlemen should be restricted, a demand that prompted Nichols in his reply to comment that such a measure would surely increase vagabondage and unemployment.

There are one or two clauses dealing with economic grievances. In his reply to the nine articles, Somerset noted that 'you require to have the relief granted unto us by parliament ... to be remitted'; the newly introduced tax on sheep and cloth, described by one historian as 'a device for extracting revenue from subjects whose poverty safeguarded them' from the longer-established subsidy,[11] clearly caused unhappiness in the south-west, and the correspondence between Russell and Somerset indicates that a special remission of the tax for that area was considered.[12] Unhappiness about the fiscal impact of the tax may have been heightened by the need for all sheep to be registered, a process which had probably begun in the south-west.[13] Given the weakness of mid-sixteenth-century communication systems it is not surprising that these assessments caused public anxiety. Rumours abounded; in a letter of 29 June to Lord Russell the Privy Council mentioned a story circulating in the south-west that 'after the payment for shepe thay should paie for theyr geese and piggs and such like'.[14] Somerset mentioned as another grievance the dearth 'of vittaies and other thinges', asking ironically, 'is this the way think you to make plenty?'[15]

However, none of this adds up to the kind of overall economic and social explanation of the rising which Joyce Youings, for example, has postulated.[16] In Devon, the cloth industry may have

[11] M.L. Bush, 'Tax Reform and Rebellion in Early Tudor England', *History*, lxxvi (1991), 391.

[12] Pocock, *Troubles*, letters 33, 35, 39.

[13] The date of commencement of the assessing of flocks for the sheep tax was 1 May, and Joyce Youings has shown that in at least three parishes near to Exeter, the numbering of sheep did take place. The assessment of cloth was intended to start on 25 June (J. Youings, 'The South-Western Rebellion of 1549', *Southern History*, i, 1979, 99–122, esp. p. 106).

[14] Pocock, *Troubles*, 16.

[15] PRO, SP10/8, (no. 5).

[16] Youings, 'South-Western Rebellion'.

been in difficulties, for the Privy Council urged Russell on 24 June
to see that clothiers, dyers, weavers and fullers were occupied,[17] and
at the end of August the council complained that the clothiers'
'malignity at the relyefs pulling a waye of theyr workmen, ye and
pryvie insencing and encouragment' had been the 'kindling' which
had allowed a 'spark of rebellion' to come to a great flame.[18] But sixteenth-century governments always, in a crisis, worried about unemployment in the cloth industry, and we should not attach too much
significance to the council's comments. In Cornwall tin-mining had
slumped, and it is tempting to imagine that the miners who tried to
breach the walls of Exeter were men driven to despair by unemployment; however, the fate of the tin-miners and their industry is
nowhere mentioned in contemporary explanations of the rising.
Although economic problems of this sort may indeed have created
an environment in which men were ready to take violent action, the
evidence does not permit us to argue that such problems 'caused'
the rebellion.

   Popular discontents are in themselves readily explicable. What
needs to be asked is why they were not contained. There was at this
time no dominant regional magnate in the south-west, no one who
could have emulated the actions of the earl of Shrewsbury who led
the resistance against the rebels in the north in 1536. The leading
nobleman, the marquess of Exeter, had fallen for treason in 1538,
and John Russell, Lord Russell, who had then been endowed with
lands in Devon, especially from the former priory at Tavistock, had
not yet built up a strong local following, mainly because he was too
active at court and on the Privy Council to spend any significant
time in the south-west. He visited the region just twice between
1539 and 1549, never maintaining a permanent household there,
and even alienating some of his lands, unlike Charles Brandon,
duke of Suffolk's much more successful development of his influence in Lincolnshire.[19] The absence of a magnate who could arbi-
trate gentry quarrels has been seen as allowing local rivalries
between gentry families to grow in the 1540s: Speight identifies
tensions between Sir Thomas Denys, Sir Hugh Pollard and Sir
Richard Edgcumbe on the one hand and Sir Peter Carew, a con-

[17] Pocock, *Troubles*, 10.
[18] Ibid., 67. Speight notes that many of the rebels came from the cloth-pro-
ducing areas of east Devon, around Crediton ('Local Government and Politics
in Devon and Cornwall', 213).
[19] Speight, 'South-Western Rebellion', 3.

frontationally minded newcomer, and the Powderham Courtenays on the other.[20] In Cornwall, too, there was no dominant figure who could inspire loyalty. Sir John Arundell of Lanherne had the potential, given his estates and his family's connections, but he pursued a resolutely apolitical career and he seems to have held aloof in 1549, saying he was too ill when the rebellion began, and excusing himself for having masses said, and processions held on Corpus Christi day, which he had done, he claimed, 'to appease the people', not out of sympathy. He may have been away on his estates in Dorset when trouble occurred.[21] There was thus a vacuum of power at the top of regional society in the south-west: there was no one powerful enough to set an example and to co-ordinate the enforcement of law and order, and no alternative arrangements had yet evolved on the lines of those English counties without a resident and dominant peer in which a group of larger gentry in effect supervised the county. What allowed discontent to turn into open revolt in the south-west was the failure of the local gentry to halt the rebellion.

Divisions within the gentry were worsened by differences over religion. In Devon Sir Peter and Sir Gawen Carew, who had close associations with Protector Somerset and were committed to religious reform, tried aggressively to resist the rebels. But they were not strong enough to succeed. Sir Peter had not been resident in Devon; Sir Gawen was more of a courtier. Nor did they show the political skills such a situation required. They were suspected of having barns set ablaze at Crediton. Other leading gentry, notably Sir Thomas Denys and Sir Hugh Pollard, preferred to temporize and to conciliate the rebels, not out of sympathy but out of a more realistic appreciation of their options, in much the same way that magnates elsewhere listened to grievances and urged the commons to disband. At one point Denys thought he had persuaded the rebels to go home, though on condition that religious innovation would cease, a concession which he had no authority to make but which may reveal the perceived causes of revolt. That led to a quarrel between Denys and Pollard on the one hand and the Carews on the other. Not surprisingly, Russell himself suggested that the 'lack of

---

[20] Ibid.
[21] Speight, 'Local Government and Politics in Devon and Cornwall', 193, 225–8.

good order amongst such as ought to rule the commons' was an important factor in the rebellion.[22]

So we are left with religion as, at the least, the main driving force of the risings in Oxfordshire, Buckinghamshire and the south-west. Why was this? According to the government, it was because the 'popish-inclined' clergy had misled their simple parishioners. Somerset and the council constantly asserted that the risings were the work of priests. On 29 June, for example, councillors told Russell that the rebels were moved 'by the provocation only of certen popyshe presrs' who wanted to subject the people once more to the pope 'by whome they leved as in a kyngdom, And all other the kyngs loving subjects in a thraldome',[23] and Somerset on 11 June declared that

> in the most parties of the Realme sundry lewde persons have attempted tassemble themselfes, and first seking redresse of enclosures, have in some places by seditious priests and other yvel peple set forth to seke restitucion of tholde bluddy lawes.[24]

The government view was taken up by the pamphleteers. Nichols's reply to the rebels claims that 'rank Papists' had stirred the 'simple people' first 'under the colour and name of the commonwealth'; they made it 'a querele of religion for their sacrament of the altar'.[25]

Not surprisingly, several priests were later condemned to death for their part in the rising, and some at least were actually executed. In Exeter, Robert Welsh was hanged in his mass vestments, with his beads and 'a holy water bucket' around his neck. According to Foxe, eight priests were condemned in Cornwall, while in Oxfordshire, Henry Matthews of Deddington was ordered to be hanged, as were Henry Joyes, who was to be strung up from the steeple of his church at Chipping Norton, Richard Thompson of Dun's Tew and John Wade of Bloxham.[26] It seems improbable that all these sentences

[22] Ibid., 90–1, 201–11; Speight, 'South-Western Rebellion', 3–4, 11–14; HMC, Report on the Records of the City of Exeter (London, 1916), 21.

[23] Pocock, Troubles, 16.

[24] PRO, SP10/7, (no. 31).

[25] Pocock, Troubles, 1, 146, 151. The author was probably not Nicholas Udall but Philip Nichols, a Devon gentleman: see G. Scheurweghs, 'On an Answer to the Articles of the Rebels of Cornwall and Devonshire', British Museum Quarterly, viii (1934), 24–5.

[26] According to Wriothesley, James Webbe, vicar of Burford, was hanged, drawn and quartered at Aylesbury in August (Wriothesley, Chronicle, ii, 21).

were carried out: indeed, Frances Rose-Troup found no evidence for the rapid change-over of parochial clergy in the south-west that one would have expected had the executions taken place. In the sixteenth century the bark of governments was not infrequently worse than its bite. It is certainly suggestive that William Harper of Sampford Courtenay, who does not seem to have been a reluctant participant in the events of Whit Monday 1549, was still in his parish at the end of Mary's reign.[27]

Of course, even if the government was correct in attributing a considerable share of the blame for the risings in the south-west and Oxfordshire and Buckinghamshire to the instigation of priests, it is still not clear why priests in those particular areas should be more opposed to the new Prayer Book than were their colleagues elsewhere, or if a large number of priests everywhere were opposed to the Book, why parishioners in these central and south-western areas were so susceptible to clerical objections.

Robert Whiting has produced some evidence about the greater than normal involvement of priests in education in the south-west at this time, which may be pertinent.[28] The bishop of Exeter, Veysey, was non-resident, and not especially diligent, but his deprivation in 1551 indicates that his religious views were conservative, and this would have had some impact on the other clergy in his diocese. The see was a poor one, which had suffered further deprivations from greedy courtiers in the 1540s;[29] clerical stipends were generally low, but so too, surprisingly, was the level of non-residence. Julian Cornwall noted that in the great survey of 1522 nearly every parish in the south-west 'enjoyed the ministrations of a resident priest, often two or more'.[30] (This contrasts with Rutland, where nearly a quarter of townships did not.) In general it would appear that we are dealing with an area in which the hold of the clergy over their parishioners was stronger than the norm.

And, as has been argued above, the overall effect of the religious changes of the first two years of Edward's reign was very great. Traditional ceremonies – holy bread, holy water, singing, kneeling, feasts – had yielded to a very plain pattern of services designed to educate. However much the government may have seen the Prayer

[27] Rose-Troup, *Western Rebellion*, 427–9.
[28] Whiting, *Blind Devotion of the People*, 232–3.
[29] W. G. Hoskins, *The Age of Plunder* (London, 1976), 142.
[30] J. Cornwall, *Revolt of the Peasantry* (London, 1977), 50–1.

Book of 1549 as a compromise or as a gentle introduction to reform, however many passages some conservative bishops found which they could tolerate, the Prayer Book confirmed and deepened a striking visual and oral break with the past. Unsurprisingly, it was much disliked in areas where attachment to traditional religion was strong, such as the south-west and the Thames Valley – and indeed Yorkshire, where a minor rising also took place.

KETT'S REBELLION

The other major rising of 1549 had no such strong religious component, although it began, in early July, with a riot at Wymondham amongst those assembled for a play to mark the anniversary of the translation of Thomas Becket.[31] By 12 July it had become a full-blown rising, with rebels encamped on Mousehold Heath, just outside Norwich. The unrest soon spread to other places in Norfolk, with camps at Castle Rising, King's Lynn and Downham Market, and into Suffolk, where there were camps at Bury St Edmunds, Melton and Ipswich.[32] There was also trouble in adjoining counties: in Cambridgeshire, Essex and Lincolnshire, as well as in Kent, at Canterbury and Boxley.[33] An attempt on 31 July by William Parr, marquess of Northampton, to put down the revolt was ignominiously unsuccessful, and the camp at Mousehold flourished until it was brutally suppressed by Warwick in late August, when according to Alexander Neville, Matthew Parker's secretary, some 3,500 rebels were slain in battle. Some of the other camps also survived until that date, although Sir Anthony Wingfield and John Gosnold apparently dispersed the Melton rebels by offering them pardons in late July and the end of August, and Northampton may have succeeded in neutralizing the Bury camp on his way to Norwich.[34]

What was the cause of this rising? Although it began with the

---

[31] This account is taken from Sotherton's narrative, BL, Harleian MS 1576, fos 251–9, edited by B.L. Beer, ' "The Commoyson in Norfolk, 1549": a Narrative of Popular Rebellion in Sixteenth-century England', *Journal of Medieval and Renaissance Studies*, vi (1976), 80–99, and by S. Yaxley, Sotherton, *Commoyson* (Stibbard, 1987).

[32] D. MacCulloch, 'Kett's Rebellion in Context', *Past and Present*, lxxxiv (1979), 36–59.

[33] P. Clark, *English Provincial Society from the Reformation to the Revolution: Religion, Politics and Society in Kent, 1500–1640* (Hassocks, 1977), 78.

[34] D. MacCulloch, *Suffolk and the Tudors* (Oxford, 1986), 77.

throwing down of hedges, first of all of Robert Kett's 'close' at Wymondham, and later of that of his arch-enemy, the lawyer turned squire, John Flowerdew, there is little evidence that enclosure was a problem in the area. Indeed, the only mention of enclosure in the rebels' articles, although somewhat ambiguous, suggests that it was entirely acceptable when undertaken for the laudable purpose of saffron-farming. The main thrust of the rebels' grievances appears to have been twofold: anxiety about the overuse of land, and in particular the overuse of common land – entirely comprehensible in the light of economic conditions – and a belief that corruption and the pursuit of self-interest had seriously undermined the ability of the gentry to administer the area. The articles also complain about potential or real increases in prices and rents; they ask, for example, that copyhold lands should be charged at the death of a tenant or at the time of sale with 'an easy fine such as a capon'.

The articles and actions of the rebels breathe a spirit of resentment against the gentry. As the duke of Somerset told Philip Hoby, ambassador to the court of Charles V, in a letter of 24 August:

> And in deed all hathe conceved a wonderfull hate against gentilmen, and taketh them all as their ennemyes ... In Norfolke gentilmen, and all seruing men for their sakes, are as evell-handeled as may be.[35]

The articles certainly seek to restrict considerably the economic activities of the gentry: no lord of the manor, they claim, should be able to use common land, which should be enjoyed by more humble freeholders and copyholders; landlords should take over the cost of collecting various traditional rents; private leet jurisdictions (which often were very profitable) were to be abolished; and those worth over £40 per annum (the level of gentility) were to maintain sheep and bullocks only for the provisioning of their households.

Moreover, the rebels took some gentlemen prisoner; interestingly, several of these were lawyers, including Thomas Gawdy, Richard Catlyn, who had also served as a chantry commissioner, and the Appleyards.[36] The sheriff of the two counties, Sir Nicholas l'Estrange, was forced to leave his brother and his son as pledges of

[35] BL, Harleian MS 523, fos. 52v–53.
[36] F. Blomefield, *An Essay towards a Topographical History of the County of Norfolk* (Norwich, 1745), ii, 161.

his good faith, as was Sir William Woodhouse. According to Sotherton's account of the rising, Richard Wharton was also seized.

Sotherton records that the gentlemen were badly treated by their captors:

the gentyllmen they tooke, they browte to the tree of reformacion, to bee seene of the people to demande what they would doe with them, where some cryde 'hang him', and some 'kill him'.[37]

However, Sotherton was anxious to present the rebels in a bad light, and there is no evidence that any gentleman was hanged; even the evidence for actual physical mistreatment is scanty, consisting of stories of gentlemen being tumbled into ditches, and poor Mr Wharton running the gauntlet.

Perhaps in order to show up the misgovernment which they believed was characteristic of the existing county ruling class, the rebels organized their own affairs with particular efficiency. They named councils to run many of the camps; that at Mousehold consisted of two representatives from each of twenty-two Norfolk hundreds and one representative from Suffolk. At Downham Market another seven Norfolk hundreds were represented. From Mousehold the rebels issued quasi-official writs for food requisition, some of them written in Latin: they may have used for this purpose one of their captives, Thomas Godsalve, a lawyer and Somerset's clerk of the signet.[38]

The ease with which the rebels established themselves in Norfolk and Suffolk does give some credence to their argument that the counties were not well governed. There is much evidence that many of the gentlemen, whose task it should have been to act at the first stir, were absent in London. Indeed, as late as 15 August it was necessary for the government to issue a proclamation ordering all gentlemen from Essex, Suffolk and Norfolk to 'depart from the court and the city of London' and await further instructions from Warwick and other government officials.[39]

Some historians, notably Diarmaid MacCulloch, have suggested that Norfolk was particularly vulnerable at this time because of the recent fall of the potential leader of county society, the duke of

[37] Sotherton, *Commoyson*, ed. Yaxley, 12.
[38] Cornwall, *Revolt of the Peasantry*, 146.
[39] Hughes and Larkin, 481–2 (no. 348).

Norfolk; his fall, it is claimed, left the forces of repression leader-less.[40] MacCulloch goes further, describing Kett's rebellion as 'a cel-ebration of the passing of the Howard family'; the third duke of Norfolk was, he argues, 'an unusually oppressive landlord who had made the most of his family's conservatism in estate management and had exploited the remaining serfs on his estates at a time when most East Anglian manors had freed their bondmen'.[41] It is an inter-esting theory. However, it should be noted that much of the Howard land-holding was not in Norfolk, but in Surrey – and Surrey was largely undisturbed by risings in 1549.

In any case, the rural component of the East Anglian rising – and, indeed, of that in the south-west – has been much exagger-ated. In not one, but two, senses it is erroneous to describe the events of 1549 as 'peasants' revolts'. First, few of the rebels who can be identified – and these are only a small part of the whole – were peasants in the true sense of being physically involved in the cultivation of the land they occupied or owned. Robert Kett, the leader of the Norfolk rising, was a tanner, owning land worth at least 40 marks (£26 3s 4d) a year; in the 1545 assessment he was estimated to possess goods worth £160.[42] His brother, William, who was also later executed, was a butcher and a mercer. The other leaders of the Norfolk rising came from the same level of society, just below gentry status – thus, Robert Brand of the Ipswich camp had 'held second-rank offices in the borough of Ipswich in the 1540s', and was to leave a house, lands and a weir together with several hundred pounds in cash in his will made in 1558, while his brother-in-law, John Harbottle, already in 1549 owned two manors and by the time of his death in 1578 had risen to the status of 'esquire'.[43]

The other striking thing about the Norfolk rising is its urban con-tent. When Barrett Beer analysed the social origins of the rebels whose names were known he found that in Norfolk, 'artisans con-stitute the largest occupational category' of those indicted.[44] He

[40] MacCulloch, *Suffolk and the Tudors*, esp. 75–7.

[41] D. MacCulloch, 'Bondmen under the Tudors', in C. Cross, D. Loades and J.J. Scarisbrick, eds, *Law and Government under the Tudors* (Cambridge, 1988), 91–109.

[42] Cornwall, *Revolt of the Peasantry*, 139.

[43] MacCulloch, *Suffolk and the Tudors*, 303–4.

[44] B.N. Beer, *Rebellion and Riot: Popular Disorder during the Reign of Edward VI* (Kent, OH, 1982) 189, 192.

counted thirteen husbandmen and one yeoman amongst those
indicted, exactly half the number of artisans – tanners, tailors, mer-
cers and eight butchers.

The urban component of the south-western revolt was also considerable. There, artisans formed a larger contingent 'than the combined total of yeomen, husbandmen and labourers'. Some may, like
the shoemaker, Maunder, have been itinerant and unemployed, but
others, such as the smith, John Hammon, and the fish-driver,
Ashridge, were probably more substantial figures. John Hooker, an
eye-witness, tells us about 'Captain Underhill', a tailor of Sampford
Courtenay, whose family, according to Julian Cornwall's survey of
their tax assessment, were probably well-to-do yeoman farmers,
whilst the 'labourer', William Seager, turns out to have been
assessed in 1544 at £8, which makes him one of the richest men in
his parish.[45] There were eight gentlemen amongst those indicted,
although none of them were gentlemen of any great weight – they
were of 'parish' rather than 'county' status. Humphrey Arundell of
Cornwall, for example, was a mere 'military adventurer',[46] and the
more established members of his family did not flock to his cause.
Fourteen clergymen were indicted, as were ten urban officials.

These urban officials were by no means insignificant: they
included the mayors of Bodmin and Torrington, both of whom
were subsequently hanged. In Norwich the situation was not dissimilar, although there the urban oligarchs were more persuasive in
their plea that they had connived at rebellion only in order to control the savagery of the rebels.

Given this, it is very surprising that obviously urban grievances
play no part in the rebels' demands. Perhaps this was because there
was no strong tradition of the articulation of such grievances, or perhaps they were subsumed into what we too readily describe as 'rural'
complaints.

One of the most interesting of these 'disguised' complaints is, of
course, enclosure. Enclosure of common land was almost certainly
a greater problem for the urban labourer who wanted to keep a pig
or a cow than it was for his rural colleague. It is with this in mind
that we should note the presentments made in Cambridge (most
likely during the disturbances of 1549) one of which alleges that a
certain Mr Hind had 'unlawfully' brought into Cambridge Field 'a

[45] Cornwall, *Revolt of the Peasantry*, 66.
[46] Youings, 'South-Western Rebellion', 117–18.

flock of shepe to the number of vi or vii^{ci}, to the undoing of the fer-
mors and great hyndraunce of all the inhabitauntes of
Cambrydge'.[47] Equally, in the aftermath of the disturbances in
Norwich, John Somerd was reported to have said, 'that if the towen
close were not put down within thies iiij dayes, he wold be one of the
viiij that would put it downe, dykes and all, him self'.[48]

THE LESSONS OF THE REBELLIONS OF 1549

What do these events tell us about England in 1549? They suggest
that there was strong resistance to religious change in many parts of
the kingdom. They also suggest that there existed a large amount of
anti-gentry feeling; even Humphrey Arundell and the Winslades,
who were themselves gentlemen, seem to have succumbed to the
prevailing atmosphere and urged the commons to kill all gentlemen.[49] Both in East Anglia and in the south-west[50] there was tension
between the ruling élite and the men of substance immediately outside that charmed circle: men like Kett and John Harbottle, or, in
the south-west, John Winslade, a wealthy landlord with an income
from land of about £108, who yet was never appointed to any local
government office.[51] Russell, indeed, saw this as a contributory
cause of the revolt.[52] Such tension helps to explain another feature
of the risings: the fact that the forces of repression were not, at the
county level, very well organized. But, above all, the risings tell us
that all was not well with central government.

The events of 1549 raise a number of important questions about
central government in England. First, was the government in any
way responsible for the risings? Secondly, did it handle the crisis
properly? Thirdly, how united was the government in its approach
to the country's problems?

As far as the western rising and the other protests against the new

[47] R.H. Tawney and E. Power, eds, *Tudor Economic Documents* (3 vols, London,
1924), i, 45.
[48] Ibid., i., 52.
[49] Speight, 'Local Government and Politics in Devon and Cornwall', 197;
Speight, 'South-Western Rebellion', 9, both citing PRO, KB8/17, m.9.
[50] Speight, 'Local Government and Politics in Devon and Cornwall', 190, and
passim.
[51] MacCulloch, 'Kett's Rebellion in Context', p. 46; Speight, 'Local
Government and Politics in Devon and Cornwall', 191–2.
[52] *HMC, Exeter* (1916), 21.

Prayer Book are concerned, there can be no doubt that the protector and council had sanctioned, and even encouraged, religious change; in the debates before the first formal reading of the new Book in parliament only three laymen had taken part, but these three – Somerset, Warwick and the secretary to the council, Sir Thomas Smith – were all part of the government and all hostile to the conservative position.[53] Possibly the council thought that the new Prayer Book, with its theological ambiguities and doctrinal conservatism, was unlikely to incite popular resistance; possibly events in London and the home counties, where the radicals were in the ascendant, had misled the government into a belief that the country as a whole was more in favour of change than it actually was.

The Prayer Book was, then, a misjudgement; and it was a misjudgement for which Cranmer was largely responsible – the principles enshrined in the Book, like the language it uses, are his – but other members of the government, and indeed parliament, had concurred in its implementation. Thus, whilst the risings of 1549, and the part played in them by the clergy, weakened still further the position of conservative bishops such as Gardiner and Edmund Bonner, bishop of London, who were soon ousted from their sees, they also, in the long run, discredited Cranmer's moderate and piecemeal approach to reform, leaving him vulnerable to more extreme reformers. But the events of 1549 also left the protector exposed to attack both by those who felt that no change should take place in the Church during a minority and by those who felt that nothing less than full-scale Protestantism would serve.

What of the handling of the risings? Somerset ignored Paget's advice that he should cause 'justice to be ministered in solemn fashion'. Instead, on 8 July he had taken the extraordinary step of establishing a fresh commission: moreover, whereas the 1548 commission had been intended merely to enquire, the new commissioners had been told that if they discovered any illegal enclosures or emparkments, they should reform matters.[54] Undoubtedly the issue of this second enclosure commission hampered the ability of the authorities to handle the unrest effectively. But did the com-

[53] A. Gasquet and E. Bishop, *Edward VI and the Book of Common Prayer*, rev. edn (London, 1928), 127–37, drawing upon BL, Royal MS 17B, xxxix.
[54] PRO, SP10/8, no. 10, printed by R. Grafton. Cf. Hughes and Larkin, 471–2 (no. 338). See also E. Kerridge, 'The Returns of the Inquisitions of Depopulation', *English Historical Review*, lxx (1955), 212–28. Cf. above, 67, note 58.

missions, as Edward himself suggested, provoke those risings? In his *Chronicle* the young king suggested that the agrarian risings of 1549 began 'because certain commissions were sent down to pluck down enclosures'.[55] Was he correct? Hales, of course, thought not. He pointed out in the 'Defence' which he wrote in the autumn of 1549 that there had been risings in Hertfordshire, at Northall and Cheshunt, 'before this commyssyon was sent forthe',[56] and he noted that the first rising of the year had been in Somerset,[57] followed by others in counties where no commissions had operated (Gloucestershire, Wiltshire, Hampshire, Sussex, Surrey, Worcestershire, Essex and Hertfordshire).[58] All this, he added, happened before the parts in which he and his commission were operating were 'therwith infected'.[59] Hales pointed out that there had been calm in many of the places covered by the commission, despite the justifiable grievances felt by many of the people.

Certainly there had been disturbances in Wiltshire and Somerset before the issuing of the second commission.[60] Equally, Warwickshire, with both a history of recent enclosures and an operative commission,[61] saw no trouble. On the other hand, there were disturbances in Kent and Essex, where the commissions were in operation.[62] A great number of the commons of Kent had given the commissioners certain articles for Protector Somerset's consideration, but we do not know exactly what they contained.[63] According

---

[55] Edward VI, *Chronicle*, 12–13.

[56] Hales, 'Defence', (BL. Lansdowne, MS 238), printed in E. Lamond, ed., *A Discourse of the Common Weal of the Realm of England* (Cambridge, 1929), p. lviii. Which commission did Hales mean? The list in Edward VI, *Chronicle*, 12, is pretty similar, but also has Kent, Suffolk, Warwickshire, part of Leicestershire, and Rutland.

[57] Presumably he meant the Frome riot, although there was also trouble at Odiham (*HMC, Bath, Longleat, IV: Seymour Papers* (London, 1968), 109–11).

[58] The park of the military engineer, Sir Richard Lee, near St Albans, was attacked in early July (BL Add. MS 48018, fo. 390v, now printed by E.H. Shagan, 'Protector Somerset and the 1549 Rebellions: New Sources and New Perspectives', *English Historical Review*, cxiv, 1999, 61).

[59] Hales, 'Defence', lviii.

[60] *HMC, Manuscritps of the Duke of Rutland* (London, 1888), i, 36.

[61] I.S. Leadam, ed., *The Domesday of Inclosures 1517–1518* (2 vols, London, 1897), ii, 656–66.

[62] Clark, *English Provincial Society*, 78.

[63] *HMC, Salisbury*, i, 54. No details of the grievances from Essex survive, but we know from a reply to the Essex men which mentions the information given to Darcy and Gates that 'sondrie textes of Scripture' decorated the Essex com-

to a letter written by the imperial ambassadors on 19 July, risings in Kent and Essex had subsided when the pricing proclamation appeared:[64] the date of this proclamation is 2 July, nearly a week before the issue of the second enclosure commission,[65] which suggests that the commission was not the cause of the trouble. However, Kent and Essex rose again, according to the ambassadors, 'because a few of the prisoners were kept in the Tower'.[66] This may have been correct; or the issuing of the commission may have been the spark for the second rising. The Kentish men were not finally dispersed until August.

Overall, then, there is no clear evidence of a causal link between the commission and agrarian unrest. What is very apparent in 1549, however, is that some of those involved in the risings thought that there was sympathy for them amongst the country's rulers. The Frome rioters declared that they were acting legally, and so did many others.[67] The proclamation of 22 July which, as we have seen, accused bailiffs, constables and other officials of being sometimes 'the very ringleaders and procurers' of the unrest,[68] suggests that some risings had about them a spurious air of official action. More significantly still, there existed in 1549 a widespread belief that the government was sympathetic to the plight of the lower orders, and this belief encouraged violence. By the following September a gentleman was reporting that a rebel was to be found 'in every towne and typplyng house my lordes graces name in hys mouthe, sayng that hys grace hathe allowed all hys doynges for good, and in every towne and vyllage receyvyng bylls of complaynte of dyuers of hys sourte'.[69] If the risings were in any way encouraged by a belief that there was sympathy for such actions in government circles, the fault was Somerset's – or, at least, it was laid at his door. He had said some unwise things: Hales himself recorded, admiringly, in August 1548 that the protector had declared that despite 'the devil, private profit, self-love, money and suchlike the devils instruments', the

---

plaints (BL, Add. MS 48018, fo. 391, now printed in Shagan, 'Protector Somerset and the 1549 Rebellions', 62–3).

[64] *CSP, Spanish*, ix. 405; cf. *HMC, Salisbury*, i, 54 for dispersal in Kent.

[65] Hughes and Larkin, 464–9 (no. 336).

[66] *CSP, Spanish*, ix, 405.

[67] *HMC, Bath, IV Seymour Papers*, 109–10.

[68] Hughes and Larkin, 476–7 (no. 342).

[69] B.L. Beer and R.J. Nash, 'Hugh Latimer and the Lusty Knave of Kent: the Commonwealth Movement of 1549', *Bulletin of the Institute of Historical Research*, lii (1979), 175–8, esp. 176–7.

commission of that year should go forward, and the tone of his letters to Somerset in the summer of 1548 exhibits a confident belief
that the protector shared his aims and beliefs. The usually well-
informed imperial ambassadors reported on 13 July 1549 that the
protector had told his colleagues on the council that

> the peasants' demands were fair and just; for the poor people who
> had no land to graze their cattle ought to retain the commons
> and the lands that had always been public property, and the noble
> and the rich ought not to seize and add them to their parks and
> possessions.[70]

Only a month later Paget wrote complaining about the protector's
liking for the prayers of the poor.[71] Thus, his colleagues' subsequent
complaint that Somerset had often declared that 'the people had
good cause to reform ... things themselves' is substantiated by
earlier evidence.

Although Somerset was never the leader of a party committed to
social reform, he was more sympathetic to the plight of the lower
orders than some of his colleagues thought wise. There is no reason
to assume that the initial establishment of the enclosure commission was the work of Somerset alone – only one councillor, the
earl of Warwick, is known to have expressed reservations in the
summer of 1548, and even he subsequently agreed to it[72] – but
the risings of 1549 alarmed a number of Somerset's colleagues, and
made them doubt the wisdom of his policy. On 7 July 1549 Paget
wrote from Brussels advising the protector that if the whole council
urged something, he should give way. 'I know in this matter of the
Commons,' he said, referring to the outbreak of the Western rising,
and Somerset's unwillingness to take tough measures,

> every man of the council have misliked your proceedings ...
> would to God, that, at the first stir you had followed the matter
> hotly, and caused justice have been minstered in solemn fashion
> to the terror of others ...[73]

---

[70] *CSP, Spanish*, ix. 395. According to the articles drawn up on his fall,
Somerset had declared 'that the covetousness of the gentlemen gave occasion
to the common people to rise' (Foxe, v, 291).

[71] J. Strype, ed., *Ecclesiastical Memorials* (Oxford, 1822), II, ii, 430.

[72] BL, Lansdowne MS 238, fos 321–321v.

[73] Strype, *Ecclesiastical Memorials*, II, ii, 431–3.

But Somerset ignored Paget's advice. Unlike Hales, most of the governing groups in the counties did not care for his approach to these issues, and they were soon to have their revenge.

Chapter 8

THE FALL OF THE PROTECTOR

Somerset's handling of the crisis of 1549 had been neither fast nor effective, in part at least because of the coincidence of popular rising and foreign threats. But most of the difficulty lay in the protector's personality. Somerset's reaction to the crisis had not been well judged. His temper had soured; he shouted at his colleagues and contemptuously ignored their advice. Never generous to his commanders in the field,[1] he now blamed them publicly for their shortages of men and armaments.[2] He also issued a series of – occasionally contradictory – proclamations that seemed to justify the rebels' actions. His fellow councillors began to plot against him and, finally, in early October they overthrew him.[3]

On 5 October the young king publicly summoned 'all his loving subjects' to repair to Hampton Court 'with harnes and weapon', to defend him and the protector.[4] On the same day a letter was sent in Edward's name to his uncle, Sir Harry Seymour, the protector's younger brother, informing him about 'a certen conspiracy' and ordering him to levy men and bring them to court.[5] Somerset himself sent his son, Edward, to Lord Russell and Sir William Herbert – who had recently put down the south-western rising and who, cru-

---

[1] For his treatment of the earl of Shrewsbury, see G.W. Bernard, *The Power of the Early Tudor Nobility: A Study of the Fourth and Fifth Earls of Shrewsbury* (Brighton, 1985), 126–8.

[2] See, for example, N. Pocock, *Troubles Connected with the Prayer Book of 1549* (Cambridge, Camden Society, new series, xxxvii (1884), 44–5 (letter 22), 68–72 (letter 36).

[3] For the argument that the plot to overthrow the protector began early in the summer of 1549, see J. Berkman, 'Van der Delft's Message: a Reappraisal of the Attack on Protector Somerset', *Bulletin of the Institute of Historical Research*, liii (1980), 247–52.

[4] PRO, SP10/9, no. 1; Pocock, *Troubles*, 76 (letter 40).

[5] PRO, SP10/9, no. 3; Pocock, *Troubles*, 77–8 (letter 41). Sir Henry, it seems, did nothing, and was rewarded accordingly by Warwick: S. T. Bindoff, *The House of Commons, 1509–58* (3 vols, London, 1982), iii, 290–1.

cially, were returning to London with their troops – begging them
to come to his aid.[6]

What had alarmed the protector was an assembly of his council
colleagues in the capital. As they later said – disingenuously – 'as
soone as he harde that certaine of the Lordes of the Counsail had
met and consulted together', he had begun to levy troops.[7] The protector had correctly diagnosed what was going on. The councillors
in the capital, later known as 'the London lords', startled the citizens by going around armed, and 'their servants likewise weaponed,
attending upon them in new liveries'.[8] A number of men responded
to Somerset's appeal, and he brought the king out to them 'into the
base court and to the gate', according to a letter sent by the London
lords to the ambassadors, where he 'had the king pray them to be
good to him and his uncle'.[9] However, on the evening of 6 October
he and the king moved to the fortified castle of Windsor, a journey
which seems to have given Edward a bad cold.[10] The following day
the king wrote to the bailiffs and constables of Uxbridge, Hillingdon
and Colham Green asking that they should assemble 'the whole
force of our subjects', who would find weapons and armour at
Windsor.[11] 'Watch and ward', the king tells us, was kept every
night.[12]

For some days claim and counter-claim were exchanged. The
councillors in London drafted aggrieved statements, rejecting the
protector's 'falsehoods', and expounding their own position.
Handbills urging the people to rise and save the duke were also circulated; if these were indeed produced by Somerset or his supporters, which is not certain, they were counterproductive, alienating
and offending the propertied and socially conservative. The king
sent a letter on 8 October to the London lords, asking that the quarrel should be ended, and enclosing a promise by Somerset to agree
to a process of arbitration.[13] The lords responded with a reminder
that the protector's power came from them, and had not been

[6] Pocock, *Troubles*, 78–9 (letters 42, 43).
[7] Ibid., 98 (letter 53).
[8] R. Grafton, *Chronicles* (2 vols, 1809 edn), ii, 522, cited in S. Brigden,
London and the Reformation (Oxford, 1989), 497.
[9] PRO, SP10/9, no. 41.
[10] Ibid., no. 42.
[11] Ibid., no. 15.
[12] Edward VI, *Chronicle*, 17.
[13] PRO, SP10/9 (no. 24).

granted by Henry VIII's will.[14] They also wrote to the king's advisers still at Windsor, who included Cranmer, Paget and Sir Thomas Smith, complaining about their willingness to allow the king 'to remain guarded by the duke's men, sequestered from his old sworn servants'.[15] To this the advisers replied that the king was 'well and merry', although he wished to leave Windsor, where he felt he was a prisoner.[16]

The protector was becoming increasingly isolated; on 9 October the city authorities threw in their lot with the London lords, and Somerset's last hope, Russell and Herbert, still commanding troops deployed in the repression of the south-western rebellion, soon did the same. On 11 October Wingfield, the king's vice-chamberlain, arrived at Windsor and moved the duke from his room next to the king's, putting him in the lieutenant's tower, under guard.[17] The next day the London lords set off for Windsor. Somerset surrendered without bloodshed, and he and the king came back to London on 14 October. Somerset was interrogated in the Tower by his former colleagues, and 'confessed' on 24 October to a list of twenty-nine articles laid against him.[18] The main thrust of these articles concerned, as Edward wrote in his *Chronicle*, the duke's

ambition, vainglory, entering into rash wars in mine youth, negligent looking on Newhaven [Ambleteuse, near Boulogne], enriching of himself of my treasure, following his own opinion, and doing all by his own authority, etc.[19]

Many commentators, including some contemporaries and near-contemporaries, have seen this coup as the work of one man – John Dudley, earl of Warwick. Observing the subsequent rise of Somerset's old rival, they interpreted all the events of the protectorate in that light, suggesting that Warwick was plotting to seize power from the moment of Henry VIII's death.[20] It is impossible totally to disprove such conspiracy theories, but two points argue

[14] Ibid., (no. 35).
[15] Ibid., (no. 38).
[16] Ibid., (no. 42).
[17] Ibid.
[18] These formed the basis of a statute 'for the fine and ransom' of the duke, passed by parliament the following January (3 and 4 Edward VI, c. 31).
[19] Edward VI, *Chronicle*, 18.
[20] See, for example, BL, Add. MS 48126, fos 6–7, and Add. MS 48023, fo. 350.

against such an interpretation: first, Warwick did not become pre-eminent until some months after Somerset's fall, and secondly, for a time, it seemed as if his fortune was very closely linked with that of the discredited protector.

Initially, the most likely outcome of Somerset's fall appeared to be the predominance of a 'Catholic' party led by the earls of Arundel and Southampton, perhaps with the Princess Mary as regent.[21] Many at the time interpreted the events of October 1549 as a Catholic backlash – in Oxford the conservatives were so cock-a-hoop that Peter Martyr found it prudent to withdraw, whilst in London Gardiner, still in prison, confidently believed that his release was imminent.[22] As early in the coup as 8 October the London lords had found it necessary to reassure the mayor and aldermen of London assembled in the Guildhall that the seditious rumours circulating to the effect that they would 'reduce mattiers of religion to the state they were in afore' were untrue.[23] A proclamation of 30 October sought to quash rumours that 'the good laws made for religion should be now altered and abolished, and the old Romish service, mass and ceremonies eftsoons renewed and revived',[24] but unsuc-cessfully, since another proclamation, on Christmas Day, noted that

> divers unquiet and evil disposed persons, since the apprehension of the Duke of Somerset, have noised and bruited abroad that they should have again their old Latin service, their conjured bread and water, with such like vain and superstitious ceremonies . . .[25]

In his New Year's gift to the disgraced duke, Somerset's servant, William Grey, declared that 'the papistes' were 'never more lustyer then they are nowe'.[26]

Perhaps all this was a simple misunderstanding; perhaps, as an Elizabethan account suggests, Warwick deliberately fostered the

[21] D. Hoak, *The King's Council in the Reign of Edward VI* (Cambridge, 1976), 241.

[22] It was also rumoured that the duke of Norfolk and Edward Courtenay were to be released (BL Add. MS 11043, fo. 53, ed. H. James, 'The Aftermath of the 1549 Coup and the Earl of Warwick's Intentions', *Bulletin of the Institute of Historical Research*, lxii, 1989, 91–7).

[23] *APC*, ii. 336.

[24] Hughes and Larkin, 484 (no. 352).

[25] Ibid., 485–6 (no. 353).

[26] Cambridge University Library, D.IX.31, fo. 13. I owe this reference to Dr Philippa Tudor.

impression of a Catholic coup by plotting with all Somerset's ene-
mies, 'as well those that was for religion as other wayes'.[27] But if
Warwick was at first willing to make common cause with the conservatives, he was then forced by events to throw in his lot with the radicals. One account suggests that Southampton, anxious to be
revenged for his earlier dismissal,[28] decided that he could eliminate
the duke and Warwick at the same time: they were 'traytors bothe;
and bothe is worthie to dye', he declared after his examination of
Somerset.[29] Arundel concurred, but the ever-cautious Paulet, now
the earl of Wiltshire, hastened away and informed Warwick of what
was going on; knowing that his fate was bound up with Somerset's,
Warwick softened his attitude towards the duke, and, with
Cranmer's assistance, petitioned the king on his behalf. In mid-
January there was a confrontation between Warwick and his ene-
mies in the council, after which Arundel and Southampton were
banished from court.[30] On 2 February 1550 they were turned off the
council. (Southampton subsequently died of grief.) Four days later
Somerset was released from the Tower, under house arrest and on
a recognizance of £10,000.[31] On 18 February he received a free
pardon from the king, and on 10 April he was restored to the council. These events surely suggest that, as in the last months of Henry
VIII's life, Somerset and Warwick had for the moment made
common cause.

[27] BL, Add. MS 48126, fo. 8v.
[28] See above, 25–6.
[29] BL, Add. MS 48126, fo. 15v.
[30] Bodleian Library, Ashmole MS 861, fo. 340; S. Brigden, ed., 'The Letters of
Richard Scudamore to Sir Philip Hoby, September 1549–March 1555'
(Camden Society, fourth series, xxix, 1990), 107–11; James, 'The 1549 Coup',
94.
[31] APC, ii. 384.

Chapter 9

NORTHUMBERLAND'S RULE

THE NEW REGIME

Somerset's fall was followed by a major reorganization of Edward's domestic life. Sir Michael Stanhope was dismissed, and his position as 'chief gentleman' abolished. To replace him, four additional or 'principal' gentleman were appointed to the chamber on 15 October; these were Sir Andrew Dudley, Sir Edward Rogers, Sir Thomas Darcy and Sir Thomas Wroth.[1] However, Rogers was to be replaced in January 1550 by Sir John Gates, a close adherent of John Dudley, earl of Warwick, later duke of Northumberland: Gates's appointment to the chamber, and his subsequent elevation in April 1551 as vice-chamberlain of the household,[2] are clear indications of Warwick's increasing power – Gates was, indeed, to play an important part in the attempted coup of July 1553, and to die with his patron on the scaffold. Darcy was also replaced in April 1551, but for a different reason – he was elevated from his position as vice-chamberlain of the household to that of chamberlain,[3] and his position as one of the four chief gentlemen was taken by Henry Sidney,[4] a son-in-law of Warwick's, and formerly the holder of a new appointment, that of chief cup-bearer: the four gentlemen were assisted by another new officer, a chief carver, who was Warwick's son, Robert Dudley.[5] In April 1550 it was decided, to improve still further the king's safety, that

[1] Edward VI, *Chronicle*, 18; Hoak, *The King's Council*, 98.
[2] S.T. Bindoff, *The House of Commons, 1509–58*, ii, 198–9.
[3] Edward VI, *Chronicle*, 57.
[4] Ibid., 75.
[5] R.C. Braddock, 'The Royal Household, 1540–1560: a Study of Officeholding in Tudor England', Northwestern University Ph.D. Thesis, 1971, 80.

three of the outer Privy Chamber gentlemen should always be here, and two lie in the palat [pallet] and fill the room of one of the four knights; that the esquires should be diligent in their office, and five grooms should be always present, of which one to watch in the bed-chamber.[6]

The events of October 1549, and in particular Somerset's attempt to protect himself by controlling physically the person of the young king, made the Privy Council very anxious about access to Edward. It therefore decided in October 1549 to appoint six 'attendant lords', who would attend the king two at a time.[7] These lords were, of course, leaders of the opposition to Somerset: the marquess of Northampton, the earls of Arundel and Warwick, Lords Wentworth, St John and Russell. However, after Warwick became lord president of the council, Arundel, whose relationship with him had always been shaky, was banished from court, according to the king for 'certain crimes of suspicion against him, as plucking down of bolts and locks at Westminster, giving of my stuff away, etc'.[8] His place as an attendant lord was probably taken by Clinton.[9] (Arundel's position as chamberlain was filled by Wentworth.) At much the same time, Sir Anthony Wingfield, who had arrested Somerset at Windsor, was elevated to the position of comptroller of the household in the place of Somerset's adherent, Paget.[10]

The two bodies responsible for the king's security were also affected by political events. The older body, the Yeomen of the Guard, was increased in numbers from 100 to 400. The younger, the Company of Gentlemen Pensioners, sometimes known as 'the spears', founded in 1539 as an élite corps of mounted guardsmen, had dwindled in number to thirty-eight by 1549. Several of this small band were too elderly to fight and were paid off with annuities, their places assigned to sixty demobilized 'men-of-arms' from the Boulogne garrison after its return to France, early in 1550.[11]

[6] Edward VI, *Chronicle*, 26.

[7] *APC*, ii. 344–5.

[8] Edward VI, *Chronicle*, 19. The imperial ambassador reported that Arundel was accused of having distributed 'certain garments and furs no longer required by the king for his use', and having appropriated certain pieces of plate (*CSP, Spanish*, x, 14).

[9] D. Hoak, *The King's Council in the Reign of Edward VI* (Cambridge, 1976), 60–2.

[10] Edward VI, *Chronicle*, 19–20.

[11] *APC*, iii. 29–30; Hoak, *King's Council*, 93.

Whether this, as Dale Hoak suggests,[12] should be linked with the
readmission of Somerset to the council in the previous month, or
whether it is primarily to be seen in the context of financial
rearrangements, is unclear. These guards were strengthened still
further in February 1551 by the appointment of 850 cavalry, or
'gendarmes', not to be confused with the pensioners or 'men-of-
arms'. However, these gendarmes were disbanded as an economy
measure in the autumn of 1552; their main purpose seems to have
been the maintenance of law and order in general, rather than the
specific protection of the king's person.[13]

All contemporary commentators remarked on how much more
hold Warwick had over Edward than Somerset had ever had. A
French observer noted, for instance, that the duke

> auoit donné de soy telle opinion a ce jeune Roy qu'il le recevoit
> comme s'il eust esté subiect a luy. Tellement que les choses qu'il
> cognois soit estre désirées du duc de Northumberland il les com-
> mandoit comme de soy mesme pour gratiffier le duc.

The French were convinced that it was through his control of the
privy chamber staff that Warwick was able to control the king.[14]

> Quand il y auoit chose d'importance qu'il vouloit estre faites ou
> dicte par le Roy, sans qu'on sceust qu'elle procedait de son sua-
> sion, venoit la nuict secretment en la chambre du dict seigneur
> apres que tout estoit couché et nestoit veu de personne. Le lende-
> main ce Jeune Prince venoit en son Conseil et comme de soy
> mesme proposoit des choses dont chacun s'esbahissoitt pensant
> quelles procedassent se son esprit et invention.[15]

[12] Hoak, *King's Council in the Reign of Edward VI*, 94.
[13] Ibid., 199–200; idem, 'The King's Privy Chamber', in D. Guth and J.
McKenna, eds, *Tudor Rule and Revolution* (Cambridge, 1982) 92.
[14] BN, Fonds français 15888, fo. 216. ('The Duke had given the young king
such an opinion of himself that he [Edward] treated him [the duke] as if he
were his subject. So much so that in order to please him he ordered as if they
were his own ideas those things which he knew the duke wanted.')
[15] Ibid., fo. 217. ('Whenever there was something of importance that he
wanted done or spoken by the king without anyone knowing that it came from
him [Warwick], he would come secretly at night into the prince's chamber
after everyone was abed, unnoticed by anyone. The next morning this young
prince would come to his council and, as if they came from himself, advocate
certain matters – at which everyone marvelled, thinking they were his own
ideas.')

Northumberland 'auoit de sorte gaignee le coeur du roy'.

> Il estoit comme Mr absolu des tous. Le duc tellement se con-
> duisoit que les choses qu'il vouloit estre faictes par le Roy par
> mediateurs et instrumens a sa devotion les sensoit conduire telle-
> ment que en parlant au Roy sembloit que le Roy de soy mesme les
> voulust.[16]

This French account is confirmed by a letter from Jehan Scheyfve,
the imperial ambassador, reporting early in 1551 that when he
demanded a final answer from the council on the question of allowing Mary her private mass, he was told that they would have to
'confer with the king'. But four days later he wrote that Paget had
told him privately that the council had conferred together without
consulting Edward. When dining at court a year later Scheyfve
related how he had watched Edward carefully, finding him very
quick mentally, but subject to Dudley. He 'kept his eye turned
toward the duke' and eventually withdrew 'because of signs the
Duke of Northumberland had made to him'.[17]

Over the four years from 1549 to his death in 1553, Edward was,
however, gradually growing in maturity and becoming anxious to
play a larger role in public affairs. Northumberland had to recognize that he would shortly be of age and able to wield full authority.
He must therefore be educated in matters of government without
being allowed to slip out of Northumberland's control. Part of his
political education was undertaken by the clerk to the Privy Council,
William Thomas, who committed himself to providing Edward with
'discourses' each week on selected topics of government.[18] The pro-
cesses of education and maturing are reflected in Edward's own
writings and from them W.K. Jordan has concluded that Edward
showed 'precocious maturity'.[19] Jordan sees Edward as 'having a sen-
sitive and stubborn interest in administrative reforms'; as being

[16] Ibid., fo. 224. (Northumberland 'had won the king's heart'; 'he was the
chief. The duke so directed himself that the matters he wanted done by the
king by mediators and others devoted to him who behaved so that it appeared
as if the king himself wanted them.')

[17] Hoak, *King's Council in the Reign of Edward VI*, 315 nn. 87–8; *CSP Spanish*, x,
234–7, 437–8.

[18] E.R. Adair, 'William Thomas: a Forgotten Clerk of the Privy Council', in
R.W. Seton-Watson, ed., *Tudor Studies* (London, 1924), 139–44.

[19] Edward VI, *Chronicle*, xviii.

'deeply and intelligently concerned with social and economic problems' as well as 'devoutly protestant in his personal faith'. Admitting that Edward 'had something of the clerk – the bureaucrat – in his nature' and that there was in him 'a certain coldness and an almost frightening hardness of character and temper', Jordan nevertheless believes that 'potentially he may have been, after his great sister, the ablest of his incredibly gifted family'. Further, in Jordan's opinion, 'Edward had very nearly completed his tuition and was already beginning to rule before his untimely death occurred'.[20]

How far are these claims borne out by the evidence of Edward's writings? Certainly, from March 1550 his *Chronicle* becomes much fuller and begins to engage with complicated problems. For instance, in September 1551, perhaps helped by one of Thomas's discourses, he provides an admirable analysis of the state of the coinage and the proposals for restoring its value.[21] Several memoranda in his handwriting survive among the manuscripts of the British Library. They include a 'discourse on the reform of abuses in church and state'; arguments for establishing a mart for the export of cloth in England; a short memorandum on ways and means; rules for the dispatch of council business; and rather mysterious notes on the English occupation of France in the reign of Henry VI.[22] Some are draft agenda papers for the council.[23] There is a very thorough set of rules for the conduct of council business in January 1553 and another for the regulation of the commissioners for requests;[24] and there is a list of statutes proposed for parliament, with a draft bill for the restraint of apparel.[25]

The question of course is to know what to make of these. They are, mostly, in Edward's hand. But is he really the author? All the documents depend on a detailed knowledge of affairs which could only have been supplied by men closely involved in the business to hand. For instance, the reasons for establishing a mart in England are concerned with highly technical matters in the conduct of trade; and the piece on 'ways and means' contains figures which must have been derived from financial officers. Of the position papers only

---

[20] Ibid., xviii; W.K. Jordan, *Edward VI: the Threshold of Power* (London, 1970), 532–4.

[21] Edward VI, *Chronicle*, 80.

[22] Ibid., 157–90; Nichols, *Literary Remains*, ii, 475–86, 504–38, 550–1, 555–60.

[23] Ibid., ii, 489–90, 491, 543–9.

[24] Edward VI, *Chronicle*, 181–4; Nichols, *Literary Remains*, ii, 502–3, 552–5.

[25] Ibid., ii, 491–8.

one, the 'discourse on the reform of abuses', seems likely to give any insight into Edward's own views. Written in 1551, it looks as if it was inspired by Martin Bucer's *De regno Christi*, presented to the king by its author as a New Year's gift at the start of the same year.[26] The parts dealing with secular matters are, however, independent of Bucer and discuss the ills of the land through an extended and conventional metaphor of the human body. The language is vigorous and the argument flows well. Jordan, the most recent editor of the document, claimed that Edward was influenced by the 'thought and aspirations of the commonwealth party'; and at first sight that might seem to be so, for initially the king urges a check on the rich, insisting that merchants only be allowed land up to the value of £100, that no man have more than two farms or more than 2,000 sheep. But, having criticized merchants, husbandmen, artificers, serving men and most other groups in society for their greed and idleness, he turns to the condition of nobles and gentlemen, complaining that they have 'alone not increased the gain of living'. They have not increased their rents, while their expenses are all greater. If this continue it 'will bring that state into utter ruin'; this is hardly the language of Latimer, who scourged the landowners for oppressing the poor. The remedies proposed are good education, the strict execution of the laws and 'engendering friendship in all parts of the commonwealth'. The paper could not have been written without a good deal of help, possibly from William Thomas, and the remedies suggested are vague; but it is nevertheless a remarkable effort for a fourteen-year-old boy.[27]

The rules for council business, drawn up by Edward and Secretary Petre in 1553, laid down a procedure for the king to be informed by one of the secretaries each Sunday evening of forthcoming business, for him to assign particular matters to particular days, and for the secretaries to report to him each Friday evening what has been done in the past four days. The rules are detailed and precise, but apart from the parts relating to the king, they are largely based on earlier procedural articles devised by Paget.[28] Even so, they do show that Edward was becoming interested in the business of government and determined to play his part. So do the agenda papers for the council drawn up in the king's hand. The specific items must have

[26] BL, Royal MS 8B.VII.
[27] Edward VI, *Chronicle*, xiv–xv, 159–67.
[28] Ibid., 181–3; Hoak, *King's Council in the Reign of Edward VI*, 91–3, 118–19.

been produced by others, but their careful ordering reflects a care
and an interest in detail on the part of the king remarkable in someone of his age. However, it would be unwise to conclude from them
that Edward was beginning to shape the conduct of government
business. This seems unlikely: the drawing up of agendas is a skilled
matter and could not have been achieved by a sixteen-year-old boy;
more probably Edward copied out the agendas, or parts of them,
presented by the secretaries.[29]

In August 1551 Edward noted in his *Chronicle* that it was
'appointed that I should come to, and sit at, Council, when great
matters were in debating, or when I would'.[30] Jehan Scheyfve
reported a little later that 'the king is usually present at Council
meetings now, especially when state business is being transacted'.[31]
Yet there is no record that he attended the Privy Council itself or
that the agendas that he drew up were followed in practice. The
conclusion reached by the principal historian of the council, Dale
Hoak, is that Edward was attending a special committee 'for the
state', rather than sessions of the working council. Matters might be
debated in this committee, but decisions were taken elsewhere. It is
significant that no minutes survive of the 'council of state'.[32]

What may appear at first to reflect Edward's direct personal intervention in business, on inspection becomes more problematic. For
instance, in Grafton's *Chronicle*, we learn how after hearing Ridley
preach on the hardships of the London poor, Edward sent for the
lord mayor and instructed him to do something for their relief,
making over the royal palace of Bridewell to house them.[33] The difficulty with accepting this later account at face value is that the
system of London hospitals was a long time in the making, from
c.1544 to 1557. The City of London had been in touch with the
council (not least, earlier, with Somerset) and had a succession of
committees planning schemes. The future of Bridewell was in the
air before Ridley's sermon. It is unlikely that Edward's gift, if it was
really made in this way, was as spontaneous a royal gesture as it
appears.[34]

---

[29] Hoak, *King's Council in the Reign of Edward VI*, 122.
[30] Edward VI, *Chronicle*, 76.
[31] Hoak, *King's Council in the Reign of Edward VI*, 120.
[32] Ibid., 121.
[33] R. Grafton, *Chronicle or History of England* (2 vols, London, 1809), ii, 529–31.
[34] P. Slack, 'Social Policy and the Constraints of Government, 1547–58', in J.
Loach and R. Tittler, eds, *The Mid-Tudor Polity c.1540–1560* (London and

Close examination of the evidence does not suggest that Edward was beginning to control the government in these years. He was being given a sound education in political affairs, was learning to order and present information, and was becoming very well informed, as his increasing interest in detail and in broader problems shows. He combined this interest in the procedural aspects of government with a passionate concern for the courtly side of the kingly role. He could also intervene on matters of religion, notably confronting his sister Mary over services in her household. But it is impossible to predict from such occasional actions or from his writings whether or not he would have made an effective monarch. And government in the later years of Edward's reign was very much Northumberland's government.

But even with his followers in positions of influence around the king, Northumberland was never secure. Whereas Somerset had ruled in a period of comparative prosperity and good harvests, the latter part of Edward's reign was marked by bad harvests, dearth and disease. Popular discontent, and the council's anxiety about a repetition of the troubles of 1549, were marked characteristics of these years. The government was desperately short of money, money that was needed for the proper maintenance of law and order. The reaction of religious conservatives to the 1549 Prayer Book, coupled with the increasing influence in London and the south of foreign Protestant *émigrés*, led to considerable religious tension. Finally, political life was less stable than before: whereas Somerset, as the king's uncle, had a traditional and widely recognized claim to authority over his young nephew, Warwick did not, and his authority was not infrequently threatened. Somerset, despite Warwick's generosity in the aftermath of the coup of autumn 1549, came to plot against his successor. In June 1550 Somerset's daughter Anne was married to Warwick's son John, but as a contemporary chronicler noted about 'the mariage betwene the two duckes at Shene', 'Northumberland suspecteth he should haue ben betraied there and therfore cam not thither'.[35] Soon there were rumours of plots. Gradually Warwick and Somerset began to quarrel: largely, it seems, this was Somerset's fault. In June Warwick warned Somerset that he was not 'in that credit and best opinion with the kings majesty as he believeth ... and

Basingstoke, 1980), 110–11; *pace* D. Loades, *John Dudley, Duke of Northumberland 1504–1553* (Oxford, 1996), 194.
[35] BL, Add. MS. 48023, fo. 350.

by some fondly persuaded'.[36] By mid-February 1551 rumours that Somerset and Warwick 'shulde not be in full and perfecte amytie' were current.[37] In that month the council questioned the earl of Rutland (who had earlier been interrogated on his involvement in Thomas Seymour's plots) about a conversation he was alleged to have conducted with Somerset's steward, Richard Whalley.[38] Whalley was examined 'for perswading divers nobles of the realme to make the duke of Somerset protectour at the next parleament'.[39] Early in March Somerset and Warwick 'fell into dispute in open council', although the matter was soon calmed down. When a gentleman from Somerset's household claimed that Somerset was better qualified to govern than Warwick, Warwick had him imprisoned.[40] In April Somerset seems to have reached an understanding with two noblemen, the earls of Shrewsbury and Derby, who had been growing uneasy at the drift of religious policy in a more Protestant direction, though within a few weeks Warwick appears to have neutralized their discontents.[41] Just what Somerset was seeking to achieve remains obscure, but he was clearly hoping to harm Warwick in some way. Sir Thomas Palmer, one of Warwick's close associates and thus by no means a wholly credible witness, claimed that Somerset had planned to invite Warwick, the marquess of Northampton and others to a banquet at which they would be killed, allowing Somerset to recover power.[42] In October Somerset was duly arrested, and in December he was tried by his peers. Acquitted of the charge of treason, he was none the less convicted of felony (for bringing together men for the purpose of a riot) and was executed in January 1552.[43] Writing of the execution in his *Chronicle*, Edward merely reported that 'the Duke of Somerset had his head cut off upon Tower Hill between eight and nine o'clock in the morning', a startlingly arid comment on the death of his uncle and mentor. The

[36] PRO, SP10/10, no. 9.
[37] BL, Cotton MS, Titus B. ii, fo. 29; J. Strype, *Ecclesiastical Memorials* (Oxford, 1822), ii, 279–80.
[38] *APC*, iii. 217.
[39] Nichols, *Literary Remains*, ii, 303.
[40] *CSP, Spanish*, x, 262.
[41] G.W. Bernard, *The Power of the Early Tudor Nobility: the Fourth and Fifth Earls of Shrewsbury* (Brighton, 1985), 65–70.
[42] PRO, SP10/13, no. 65.
[43] *APC*, iii. 389–91; Wriothesley, *Chronicle*, ii, 62–5; J. Bellamy, *The Tudor Law of Treason* (London, 1979), 244–5; Hoak, *King's Council*, 73–80.

king fails to record any effort to save Somerset or grief at his death.[44] While relations between the two had never been close, and it had been possible for the protector's younger brother Thomas to play upon the king's sense of grievance about his pocket money, the lack of emotion displayed by Edward at this time has led most historians to charge him with coldness and hypocrisy.

How far can we give credence to an account found in an unpublished text in the Harleian MS and in John Hayward's *Life and Raigne of King Edward the Sixth*,[45] that contradicts traditional assumptions about Edward's supposed lack of 'personal warmth' and 'boyish affection'?[46] This account documents a depth of feeling going beyond the skeletal entries in the king's diary and attributes Edward's outward composure at the time of his uncle's death to a sense of royal decorum preventing 'maiestie openly to declare himselfe'. Although it agrees outwardly with the chronicles that interpret courtly revels and entertainment as part of Warwick's plot against Somerset,[47] it alone describes a confused youth who blames himself for failing to save his uncle.

Upon the death of the Duke albeit the King gave noe token of any ill distempored passion, as takeinge it not agreeable to maiestie openly to declare himselfe, and albeit the Lords had laboured with much variety of sports, to dispell any dampy thoughts, which the remembraunce of his Unckle might rayse, yet upon speech of him hee would often sigh and lett fall teares, Sometymes holdinge opinion that his Unckle had done nothinge, or if hee had it was very small and proceeded rather from his wife than from him-

---

[44] Edward VI, *Chronicle*, 107. Edward's longer description of the trial in his letter to Barnaby Fitzpatrick, 20 December 1551, is similarly factual (Nichols, *Literary Remains*, i, 71).

[45] BL, Harleian MS 2194, fos 19–20; B.L. Beer, ed., *The Life and Raigne of King Edward the Sixth by John Hayward* (Kent, OH, 1993), 147. The paragraphs that follow (down to '*The Vanitee of this Worlde*', 104) are largely by Professor John N. King of the Ohio State University and are drawn from an unpublished paper 'The Trial and Execution of Edward Seymour, Protector of the Realm under Edward VI: an Unpublished Account', by John N. King with the collaboration of Jennifer Loach.

[46] Edward VI, *Chronicle*, xxiii.

[47] Thomas Lanquet, *An Epitome of Chronicles* (2nd edn, 1559), sig. 4E3 r–v. The expansion by Robert Crowley covers the reigns of Edward VI and Mary, and the accession of Elizabeth. Richard Grafton's *Chronicle* (1809 edn), ii, 523–7, incorporated Crowley's accusation against Warwick and passed it on to later historians.

selfe, and where then said hee was the good nature of a Nephew? where was the clemency of a Prince? Ah how infortunate have I beene to those of my bloud, my mother I slewe at my birth, and since have made away two of her brothers, and happily to make away for others against my selfe, was it ever knowne before that a Kings Unckle, A lord Protectour one whose fortunes had much advanced the Honour of the realme, did lose his head for felony; for a felony neither cleere in Law, and in fact weakely proved. Alas so how falsely have I beene abused? how weakely carried? howe little was I master of myne owne Judgement, that both his death and the envy there of must bee layd upon mee.[48]

The king's acceptance of moral responsibility presented here accords well with the pietistic temper of the Reformation court, which took seriously the medieval themes of mutability and *de contemptu mundi*. This account reveals Edward dramatizing his own consciousness according to conventional attitudes of English 'mirror' tragedies, notably those concerning the evanescence of human life and the fickleness of fortune. Before Somerset's fall, the king had dedicated his own handwritten translation of a collection of scriptural commonplaces to his uncle with the admonition that the Bible is the sole source of constancy in the face of 'la vanite du monde, la mutabilite du temps, et le changement de toutes choses mondaines'.[49] As exercises in language study, neither this collection nor another holograph manuscript entitled 'A lencontre les abus du monde'[50] displays any originality of thought. They do define, however, prevailing pietistic ideals that were inculcated at court during the royal minority. Another example is the courtier William Thomas's *de contemptu mundi* treatise entitled *The Vanitee of this Worlde* (1549).

All this is very suggestive, even moving. But can this account of Edward's reaction to Somerset's execution be taken at face value? Is the Harleian MS an independent source, on which Hayward drew, as Barrett Beer, the most recent editor of *The Life and Raigne*, suggests?[51] Or is it simply copied from Hayward's text? Hayward, Diarmaid MacCulloch has suggested, was prone to inventing

---

[48] Beer, ed., *Life and Raigne of Edward the Sixth*, 147; BL, Harleian MS 2194 fos 20r–20v.

[49] BL, Add. MS 9000, fos 1r–1v.

[50] BL, Add. MS 5464.

[51] Beer, ed., *Life and Raigne of Edward the Sixth*, 16.

speeches or adapting them from Tacitus. It is possible, then, that what we have here is what the early seventeenth-century historian believed Edward ought to have felt, rather than compelling evidence that he did feel such emotions. And yet the possibility remains that Hayward or the author of the Harleian MS was drawing on credible memories.

It is clear from Edward's *Chronicle*, full of rumours about 'a stir' here and a riot there – in June 1550, for instance, the watches were increased in London 'because of the great frays', a search was undertaken in Sussex for 'all vagabonds, gypsies, conspirators, prophets, ill players and such-like', there were rumours of a conspiracy in Essex[52] – that king and council alike felt considerable anxiety during this period about the risk of another popular rising. The problem was attacked in a variety of ways. In the parliamentary session of November 1549 to February 1550 a bill was introduced to deal with the difficult legal status of riot. Introduced in the Lords as a measure against 'the rioting of the common people', this became, after a great deal of attention in both houses, a statute that made it high treason for twelve or more to assemble together to kill or imprison a member of the council, and for forty or more to break down enclosures. It also became a felony for twelve or more persons to destroy parks, or to seek to lower rents and prices.[53] Another Act, for the control of poaching, sought to prevent the 'owtragyous disorders' produced by illegal hunting.[54] The government also sought to improve its control of the localities – control which had proved in 1549 to be very weak – by a variety of means. It introduced lord-lieutenants into the counties to direct those involved in the suppression of unrest, it established loyal men in areas of particular concern such as the Welsh Marches and the north, and it issued licences to councillors and others allowing them to 'retain' large numbers of armed men. It also, when finances permitted, employed some foreign mercenaries.

The government was clearly anxious about security. But it did also take more positive measures. Another Act passed, reaffirming the statute of Merton, concerned some of the agrarian conditions that had produced unrest.[55] It has sometimes been claimed that this

[52] Edward VI, *Chronicle*, 37.
[53] 3 & 4 Edward VI, c.5 (*Statutes of the Realm*, iv. 104–8).
[54] 3 & 4 Edward VI, c.17 (*Statutes of the Realm*, iv. 117–18).
[55] 3 & 4 Edward VI, c.3 (*Statutes of the Realm*, iv. 102–3).

measure gave landlords *carte blanche* in relation to their tenants,[56] but this is not the case, for the Act did not involve the repeal of existing statutes about the maintenance of tillage, and one of its clauses, permitting settlement on waste, was obviously intended to alleviate the lot of the peasant. The Act should be seen in the context of a subsequent proclamation of May 1551 dealing with enclosure and engrossing,[57] and of Edward's comment that the object of the proclamation was 'to give warning to all those that keep many farms, multitudes of sheep above the number limited in the law ... regrators, forestallers, men that sell dear ...'.[58]

Perhaps most important of all, the Privy Council in these years tried very hard to galvanize local authorities into activity, and sought to maintain good relations with the most important of local authorities, that of the capital.[59] The government was concerned about the social impact of high prices and in September 1550 a proclamation reinforcing statutes against the export of grain pushed forward the activities of central government by requiring justices of the peace to make grain surveys.[60] (Edward carefully recorded the provisions of this measure in his Chronicle.)[61] The next month a further proclamation allowed for the compulsory purchase of grain stocks.[62] The proclamation was accompanied by circular letters to local authorities,[63] and in York and Shrewsbury at least the searches were carried out.[64] (However, the pricing requirements of the proclamation produced a storm of opposition from the counties, and were withdrawn on 6 December.)[65]

---

[56] Jordan, *Edward VI: the Threshold of Power*, 40.

[57] Hughes and Larkin, 520–2 (no. 373).

[58] Edward VI, *Chronicle*, 62. In 1552 another Act for the increase of tillage ordered that land that had been cultivated for four years since 1509 should be kept under the plough. Interestingly, this Act very much echoed earlier moves by sanctioning the establishment of commissions to discover what land was being ploughed up; there is, however, no evidence that the commissions ever operated (5 & 6 Edward VI, c.5 [*Statutes of the Realm*, iv. 134–5]). Also in that session, two Acts were passed to deal with regrating (5 & 6 Edward VI, c.14, c.15 [*Statutes of the Realm*, iv. 148–51]).

[59] 5 & 6 Edward VI, c.2.

[60] Hughes and Larkin, 499–503 (no. 365).

[61] Edward VI, *Chronicle*, 46–7.

[62] Hughes and Larkin, 504–9 (no. 366).

[63] PRO, SP10/10, nos 42, 41, 40, 43.

[64] Slack, 'Social policy,' 105–6; R.W. Heinze, *The Proclamations of the Tudor Kings* (Cambridge, 1976), 259–61.

[65] PRO, SP10/11, (no. 15).

Although these measures obviously originated in an anxiety to prevent a repetition of 1549, they were not essentially different from, or more repressive than, the policies promulgated under 'the good duke'. Thus, the harsh and vicious Poor Law of 1547, which had permitted the enslavement of the poor, was replaced by a respectable and traditional statute that looked back to the statute of 1531, and parish responsibility.[66]

FOREIGN POLICY: WAR AND PEACE

The government had planned another offensive campaign against the French for the summer of 1549, but the major rebellions of that year necessitated the withdrawal of troops to the south-west and Norfolk. The French seized their opportunity, and on 8 August 1549 Henry II declared war on England, and took personal command of the troops outside Boulogne. However, to his chagrin, the English resisted stoutly. They were, therefore, able to secure slightly better terms than might have been predicted in the peace treaty agreed in late March 1550. By this, the English agreed not to intervene further in Scotland unless, as Edward put it, 'new occasion be given',[67] Boulogne was surrendered to the French in return for a 'ransom', and six hostages were exchanged, the English ones including most of Edward's schoolfriends.[68]

After the surrender of Boulogne, Anglo-French relations were cordial. In April 1551 Henry II was elected a knight of the Garter, and Edward was elected to the French order of St Michael.[69] Shortly before the arrival of the French mission, Northampton and a substantial English train had departed for France, where they were to invest Henry II with the Garter and to carry out further negotiations.[70] When Northampton raised again the question of Edward's marriage to Mary, queen of Scots, he was told, according

---

[66] 3 & 4 Edward VI, c.16 (*Statutes of the Realm*, iv. 151–2); 22 Henry VIII c.12. C.S.L. Davies, 'Slavery and Protector Somerset: the Vagrancy Act of 1547', *Economic History Review*, 2nd series, xix (1966), 533–49. In 1552 another attempt was made to create an effective statutory Poor Law, this time using parish collections.

[67] Edward VI, *Chronicle*, 21.

[68] Ibid., 22. The duke of Suffolk, the earl of Hertford, Lord Talbot, Lord Fitzwarren, Lord Maltravers, Lord Strange. See also above, 9, 12.

[69] See below, 143.

[70] Edward VI, *Chronicle*, 63.

to Edward, that 'they had taken too much pain and spent too many lives for her, also a conclusion was made for her marriage to the Dauphin'.[71] Since this was the reply he expected, Northampton was able to regroup rapidly, and asked instead about the prospect of an alliance for Edward with Henry II's eldest daughter, Elizabeth, whose portrait had been sent to the English court in the previous December.[72] After lengthy haggling over the dowry, agreement was reached on 19 July.[73] The next January, Edward sent her 'a fair diamond', from Catherine Parr's collection, as a gift.[74]

Now that any prospect of a marriage between Mary and Edward had been abandoned, Mary of Guise felt able to leave Scotland for a protracted visit to her homeland and to her young daughter. The English government granted her a safe-conduct, and in October 1551 the dowager queen landed in England.[75] Her visit allowed Edward to put on an impressive display, which he described in detail in his *Chronicle*. The queen was given an escort of 120 gentlemen when she visited the king at Hampton Court, and dined with him in great state, two services of plate, one gold and the other silver, being put out on display;[76] in the previous June four parcels of plate 'of the best sorte and guilte that can be found' had been ordered, worth, in all, £3,700.[77] In matters of foreign policy, therefore, the second part of the reign had its successes.

FINANCIAL DIFFICULTIES

But the government, despite the peace, was in acute financial difficulty. One reason for this was the ending of the policy of debasement, a policy which had substantially cushioned the crown since the mid-1540s.

Coins contain a mixture of precious metal and base metal;

[71] Ibid., 68.

[72] *CSP, Foreign 1547–1553*, 109; E. Auerbach, *Tudor Artists* (London, 1954), 74.

[73] Edward VI, *Chronicle*, 69, 74. See also *APC*, iii. 453.

[74] Edward VI, *Chronicle*, 107.

[75] The initial plan had been that Mary of Guise should travel through England on her outward journey, but in the event she came, driven by bad weather, on her return from France.

[76] Edward VI, *Chronicle*, 89–94.

[77] *APC*, iii. 288. For similar displays of plate at an earlier period, see P. Glanville, 'Cardinal Wolsey and the Goldsmiths', in S. Gunn and P. Lindley, eds, *Cardinal Wolsey* (Cambridge, 1991), 131–48.

debasement is the process of reducing the precious metal content of coins while retaining the face value. To do this the crown, which alone had the right to mint coin, had to secure plate for the Mint, either by confiscations from the Church or by persuading private individuals to bring in plate or coins – they got back, of course, a number of coins. The crown charged 'seigneurage', and also, more directly, gained by the increased quantity of coin it received for its own input of precious metal.

The process of debasement had begun in 1542, with two 'experimental' years, which produced for the crown £6,000 profit, and then had become much more bold. In the last years of Henry's reign, the ratio of silver to base metal in the coins was reduced from 11.1 oz. per 12 oz, to 4 oz. by 1546. By this means, from 1542 to 1547 the crown made £450,000 profit, or £75,000 per annum. (This sum later rose to £150,000 per annum.)

Those bringing coin and plate to the Mint profited enormously. A later, Elizabethan, calculation suggests that by December 1549 Warwick, Arundel, Southampton and Sir William Herbert had received over £36,000 each by this means. In December of that year Paget and Dorset were to receive much the same, perhaps as a reward for their part in the political settlement.

Between 1542 and 1551 it is probable that the 'circulating medium', that is, the amount of money in the economy, doubled. There were two results of this. First, such a tremendous increase in rate of production required the opening of new mints at Canterbury, York and Southwark and, in 1546, at Bristol. (The choice of Bristol, only the third city of the kingdom, rather than Norwich, the second, is interesting. Is the explanation perhaps, as Challis suggests, linked to the patronage of Sir William Sharington, groom of the privy chamber, and subsequently under-treasurer of the Bristol Mint?)

Secondly, such a substantial increase in the circulating medium seems likely to have had inflationary effects; twice as much money was pursuing roughly the same amount of goods. At first the increase could be absorbed, because there had probably previously been a shortage of silver coin, but by the late 1540s there may have been some pernicious consequences.

By 1549 there was certainly confusion amongst consumers, who could now see and feel the difference in their coins. Latimer, in a sermon of March 1549, commented:

> We have now a pretty little shilling ... the last day, I had put it away almost for a groat... this pretty little shilling...

while John Heywood wrote in the same year that

> These testons looke redde: how like you the same?
> Tis a tooken of grace: they blushe for shame.[78]

The effects were not, however, felt equally by all. A London chronicler noted in 1550 that

> Moste poore men were muche greeued, for theyr whole sub-
> staunce lay in that kind of money, where as the richer sorte, part-
> ley by friendship vnderstanding the thing beforehande, dyd put
> that kynd of money away.[79]

In Norwich, a woman reported that she had heard the baker speak
of 'extortioners and breybours of the country and said that if it
would please the king ... he would be hangman to a hundred of
them'.[80]

By late 1550, when the silver content of coins had sunk to about
a quarter of its pre-1542 standard, and there had been a spectacular drop in the value of sterling on the foreign exchanges, it was
obvious that the process of debasement had to stop. But the government made one last raid on the nation's pockets. In April 1551
Warwick decided to gain £160,000 by a final reduction in the weight
of the coins to 3 oz., a procedure described by the young king as a
means whereby 'the debt of the realm might be paid, the country
defended from any sudden attempt, and the coin amended'.[81] In
the end, the council settled for £120,000 profit.

Debasement was then halted. A proclamation of 8 May announced
that from the following 31 August the rate at which shilling coins
passed was to be reduced to 9d. Those who could 'get out' of coinage
did so as quickly as possible, leaving the little men to discover that
their own coinage was already being rejected or accepted for less
than its face value. The *London Chronicle* declares that

> by reason of wh. proclaymacion ensewed great dearth of all thyn-
> ges, for the people coueytinge to rayse the losse of theyr money

[78] R. H. Tawney and E. Power, eds, *Tudor Economic Documents* (3 vols, London,
1924), ii, 179.
[79] Ibid., ii, 187.
[80] Ibid., ii, 189.
[81] Edward VI, *Chronicle*, 58.

1. The Chapel Royal at Hampton Court, the setting for Prince Edward's christening. The interior had been altered by Henry VIII and was to be altered again in subsequent centuries.

2. A contemporary drawing of Edward's christening, artist unknown, showing the porch and the eight-sided platform, with the marchioness of Exeter carrying the baby prince. College of Arms MS M6, fo. 82v.

3. *Edward VI as a Child*. The earliest painting of Edward and the only one by Hans Holbein. It is probably the one recorded as given by the artist to Henry VIII as a New Year's gift in 1539, when the prince was aged 14 months. National Gallery of Art, Washington, Andrew W. Mellon Collection.

PARVVLE PATRISSA, PATRIÆ VIRTVTIS ET HÆRES
ESTO, NIHIL MAIVS MAXIMVS ORBIS HABET.
GNATVM VIX POSSVNT COELVM ET NATVRA DEDISSE,
HVIVS QVEM PATRIS, VICTVS HONORET HONOS.
ÆQVATO TANTVM, TANTI TV FACTA PARENTIS,
VOTA HOMINVM, VIX QVO PROGREDIANTVR, HABENT
VINCITO, VICISTI, QVOT REGES PRISCVS ADORAT
ORBIS, NEC TE QVI VINCERE POSSIT, ERIT.

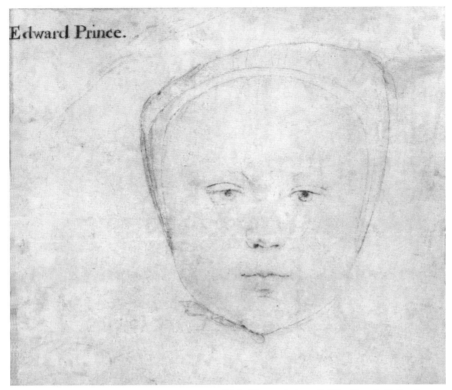

Edward Prince.

4. The drawing by Hans Holbein upon which Plate 3 is based. The Royal Collection.

5. The anamorphosis by William Scrots, 1546. National Portrait Gallery, London.

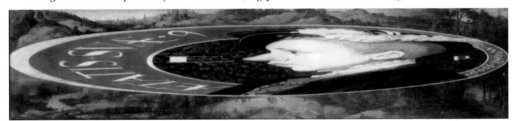

6. The prototype, painted in 1546 by an unknown artist, for later portraits of Edward as king. The Royal Collection.

7. Portrait of Edward by William Scrots sent to the French
Court in 1552. The Louvre.

8. *The Family of Henry VIII*, artist unknown, *c*.1545. Henry VIII, Jane Seymour (then already deceased), Prince Edward, and the two princesses, Mary and Elizabeth, in Whitehall Palace. The Royal Collection.

9. *An Allegory of the Tudor Succession*, attributed to Lucas de Heere, *c*.1572. Edward, kneeling at the side of his father, is dwarfed by the figure of Elizabeth, hand-in-hand with Peace. Mary is shown on the left with Philip and accompanied by Mars. The National Museum of Wales, on loan to Sudeley Castle, Glos.

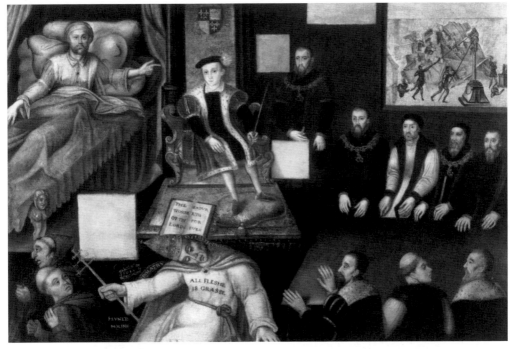

10. *Edward VI and the Pope*, artist unknown. The message is clearly the destruction of popery and of idols, but the date has been disputed. National Portrait Gallery, London.

11. The procession of Edward from the Tower to Westminster, 19 February 1547, before his coronation. Society of Antiquaries of London.

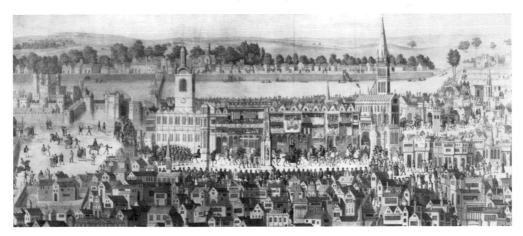

12. Edward VI at the opening (or possibly the closing) of Parliament, by Sir Gilbert Dethick, 1553. The Royal Collection.

13. Edward listening to the preaching of Hugh Latimer at court, 1549. J. Foxe, *Actes and Monuments*, 1563.

The newe Testament of our Sauiour Iesu Christe. Faythfully tranflated out of the Greke.

Wyth the Notes and expoficions of the harke places therein.

Mathew.xiy f.
Vnio,quem præcepit emi seruator Iesus,
Hic situs est, debet non aliunde peti.

The pearle, which Christ cōmaunded to be bought Is here to be founde, not elles to be sought.

14. Edward as a protestant king. From the frontispiece to Tyndale's *New Testament*, 1552. Engraving taken from the Scrots portrait (Plate 7).

15. The gold coronation medal, 1547. Typical of the coins and medals of the reign; the king is shown wearing his crown and carrying the orb and the sword of state. British Museum.

16. Princess Mary, aged 28, in 1544 by Master John. National Portrait Gallery, London.

17. Princess Elizabeth, painted in
1542–7 by an unknown artist.
The Royal Collection.

18. Queen Jane Seymour, mother
of Edward VI, by Hans Holbein,
1536. Mauritshaus, the Hague.

19. Queen Catherine Parr, Henry VIII's last queen, probably by William Scrots, date unknown. She married Thomas, Lord Seymour of Sudeley, after Henry's death. National Portrait Gallery, London.

20. Edward Seymour, duke of
Somerset, lord protector,
1547–9, by an unknown artist.
He was uncle to Edward VI.
Collection of the Marquess of
Bath, Longleat.

21. Thomas, Lord Seymour of
Sudeley, younger brother of
the duke of Somerset, husband
of Catherine Parr, artist and
date unknown. National
Portrait Gallery, London.

22. Thomas Cranmer, archbishop of Canterbury, painted after the death of
Henry VIII by an unknown artist. This portrait differs markedly from the earlier
and better known work by Gerlach Flicke. Cranmer's beard is a sign of his
rejection of the Old Church and his commitment to Protestantism. Lambeth
Palace Library.

23. *The Chronicle* of Edward VI for the period 5–14 June 1550. The British Library, Cotton MS Nero C.x, fo. 22v.

24. Edward's 'devise for the succession', 1553. The crucial alteration is in the fourth line where 'L Janes heires masles' is changed to 'L Jane and her heires masles'. Inner Temple, Petyt MS 538, vol. 47, fo. 317.

vppon soche kynd of wares or victualles as they occupyed, dyd dayly inhaunse and encrease the prises both of wares and victualles, most miserably oppressynge the poore.[82]

A tanner in Norwich became involved in a dispute in a pub when the landlord refused to accept shillings at even half their value, declaring that he had heard a rumour that they were to be reduced to the value of a groat (that is, 4d).[83]

On 8 July the council did what it should have done earlier, and announced an immediate implementation of its 25 per cent reduction. But anxiety remained about a further calling down, as a proclamation on 24 July makes clear, and on 16 August the council did in fact further reduce the value of the shilling to 6d. In October 1551 new shilling coins were issued, with a much higher silver content (although one still lower than that of the 1542 coinage).

By bringing debasement to an end and introducing a new and improved currency, Warwick did something to improve the immediate state of the economy. But the whole question of the long-term impact of debasement is a complicated one on which historians disagree. It is not clear that debasement was entirely a bad thing, for, by leading to a fall in the value of the pound on the foreign exchanges, it probably stimulated demand: above all, at least for a time, demand overseas for English broadcloth.[84] Moreover, if debasement was responsible for the increase in prices which occurred in this period, it is surprising that some prices rose so much more sharply than others, and that they did not fall very much after debasement ended. None the less, it seems probable that during the years 1548 to 1551 manipulation of the coinage did have a deleterious effect, if only by producing uncertainty. Even in those years it is difficult, however, to distinguish the inflationary impact of debasement from that of war expenditure.

But the end of debasement caused a major crisis in government

---

[82] C.L. Kingsford, *Two London Chronicles* (Camden Society, 3rd series, xviii, 1910), 23.

[83] Tawney and Power, *Tudor Economic Documents*, ii, 189.

[84] F.J. Fisher, 'Commercial Trends and Policy in Sixteenth-century England', *Economic History Review*, x (1940), 95–117, esp. 103–4. However, J.D. Gould, in *The Great Debasement* (Oxford, 1970), 114–60, argues that the growth of London exports was simply reflected a shift from the remainder of the country, rather than an overall increase, and that in any case the real drop in the value of sterling occurred too late to explain the increase that there was.

finance. Between 1547 and 1551 the crown had received about three-quarters of a million pounds from debasement – a large sum if it is remembered that sale of crown lands in the whole period from 1539 to 1554 produced only £1.2 million. How would the government deal with the shortfall once further debasement was eschewed? Clearly, it was necessary both to increase income from other sources and to reduce expenditure. The Privy Council therefore set up various commissions to recover moneys owed to the crown and to gather information about crown revenues. On 30 December 1551, for example, a six-member commission was established to call in royal debts.[85] In March 1552 a sub-committee was added to the commission, to gather information about royal income. These groups reported in December 1552: they suggested various improvements in the handling of royal revenues, such as the proposal implemented in a statute of 1553 that revenue officers should give sureties before taking up their positions.[86] They also suggested that enquiries should be instituted into the way in which the goods of the monasteries and of attainted persons had been administered in the past, and this was done. Most important, the report considered the question of how crown finances should be administered in the future, proposing that one all-inclusive department should be created to take over all the tasks currently carried out by the numerous revenue courts established by Thomas Cromwell in the 1530s. This, it was argued, would produce economies in staff and salaries, a saving of perhaps £11,050 a year.

These various enquiries of 1552 revealed how great was waste and corruption within government. The salaries of augmentations officials, for example, had risen from £4,748 in 1536 when the court was established, to £7,084 in 1551.[87] Henry Brinkelow, satirist and social critic, commented in The *Complaint of Roderick Mors*, that 'it is a common saying amongst the people, Christ, for thy bitter passion, save me from the Court of Augmentations.'[88] The most famous example of the corruption revealed by these enquiries is the case of

[85] Edward VI, *Chronicle*, 102; J. Alsop, 'The Revenue Commission of 1552', *Historical Journal*, xxii (1979), 511–33, esp. 512.

[86] 7 Edward VI, c.1 (*Statutes of the Realm*, iv. 161–4).

[87] W.C. Richardson, ed., *The Report of the Royal Commission of 1552* (Morganstown, West Virginia, 1974), 30; W.C. Richardson, *History of the Court of Augmentations* (Baton Rouge, Louisiana, 1961), 334, n.17.

[88] J. Meadows Cooper, ed., *Henry Brinklow's 'Complaynt of Roderyck Mors'* (Early English Text Society, extra series, xxii, 1874), 24.

John Beaumont, receiver-general of the court of wards from 1545 to late December 1550, who turned out to have robbed the crown in that time of £11,823.[89]

However, some of the charges of corruption brought at this time may have been politically motivated, such as attacks on known associates of the duke of Somerset: in May 1552, for instance, Lord Paget, Somerset's greatest ally, was charged with corruption as chancellor of the duchy of Lancaster, whilst Sir John Williams, treasurer of augmentations, and Sir John Thynne, both also followers of the dead duke, were prosecuted.

The reports also resulted in a proposal finally to finish off the last of the Cromwellian revenue courts, with a recommendation that either all departments should be subsumed back into the exchequer, or that a new court be established, called the court of king's revenue, to deal with augmentations and duchy of Lancaster moneys. In the event it was Mary who implemented the report, taking all courts except that of wards and Lancaster into the exchequer.

Almost everything done by the governments of these years can be explained as a result of their desperate need to cut costs or to save money: Northumberland, for example, accepted the somewhat ignominious surrender of Boulogne to the French under the treaty of May 1550, and subsequently courted Henry II with the hope of securing a marriage alliance between Edward and a French princess. He did this not because he was intellectually committed to peace – he was, after all, a soldier and, according to many contemporaries, a good one – but because he had no resources with which to fight a war.

Overall, Warwick – Northumberland – seems to merit many of the plaudits offered to him by Dale Hoak.[90] He was energetic and efficient (except when he allowed a proclamation to be issued that merely gave notice of the crown's intentions about the coinage). Among his closest associates was William Cecil, originally one of Somerset's private secretaries, who, after being imprisoned at the time of Somerset's fall, wisely sought employment with the rising star on his release. In September 1550 Cecil became one of the secretaries of state: as such he prepared the agendas of council meet-

<hr />

[89] Edward VI, *Chronicle*, 109, 128–9; J. Hurstfield, 'Corruption and Reform under Edward VI and Mary: the Example of Wardship', *English Historical Review*, lxviii (1953), 25–7.

[90] D. Hoak, 'Rehabilitating the Duke of Northumberland', in J. Loach and R. Tittler, *Mid-Tudor Polity* (London, 1980), 74–93.

ings, often on Northumberland's instructions, and wrote many of
the council letters. When Northumberland was away from court,
which he often was because of illness or service elsewhere, Cecil
wrote to him daily about what was going on. It is from their correspondence that we learn of Northumberland's concern for the
minutiae of council business. On 28 December 1552, for instance,
we find Northumberland explaining to the council how the government should present to the parliament that was about to begin the
crown's need for money. Parliament should be told that the debt
was all the fault of Henry VIII and 'the wilful government of
Somerset'.[91] On 14 January 1553 he explains that there is no reason
why they should 'make an oration to the commons of his majesties
liberality and bountyfulness' and he enquires who should be elected
as speaker, and who should preach the sermon at the opening of
the session.[92] On 19 January Northumberland consulted Cecil
about whether certain peers' sons might be summoned to the upper
house.[93] Numerous drafts of legislation survive. We know little about
the parliaments held at this time, but the care taken by
Northumberland is obviously very different from the situation
under Somerset, when we find Paget telling the protector to get on
with drafting the subsidy bill 'for the time goeth awaye and yt had
bene meter to have bene nowe in levienge of yt then about to aske
yt'.[94] Northumberland held less power than Somerset, and he recognized the need to consult his fellow councillors. But he was also
ambitious, greedy and corrupt. In this, as in much else, he closely
resembled Somerset. Although their methods of government were
very different, their policies and priorities were similar. Somerset
governed against a relatively optimistic background, whereas
Northumberland was constantly concerned about the possibility of
a repetition of the rising of 1549, not least because of the three bad
harvests in a row between 1549 and 1551. That context of economic
gloom and heightened anxiety among the propertied classes in
general about the risk of further popular risings explains why government responses and policies, in Northumberland's period of
power, such as the restoration in early 1551 of much of the
Henrician treason legislation,[95] look more reactionary or repressive

[91] PRO, SP10/15, no. 73.
[92] PRO, SP10/18, no. 6.
[93] Ibid., no.8.
[94] B.L. Beer and S.N. Jack, eds, 'The Letters of William, Lord Paget of
Beaudesert, 1547–1563' (Camden Society, 4th series, xiii, 1974), 21.
[95] 5 & 6 Edward VI, c.11.

than those of Somerset's protectorate; but essentially Somerset and Northumberland approached the problems confronting them in much the same way. This is true even in social matters, in which a marked contrast has been perceived in the past; closer examination reveals both that Somerset's policy was largely traditional, and that no major change of policy occurred on his fall. In many respects this was also true of religious policy under Northumberland.

Chapter 10

RELIGIOUS POLICY UNDER
NORTHUMBERLAND

We have seen how, in the first years of the reign, the movement against images and the veneration of saints, the dissolution of chantries and religious guilds, the relaxation of the heresy laws, the ending of clerical celibacy, and the introduction of a new Prayer Book amounted, not least visually and orally, to a great break with tradition, sufficient to provoke armed rebellion. Religious policy in the years after Somerset's fall is often presented as an acceleration of change in the direction of full-blooded Protestantism; but it may be more accurate to see it as no more than a series of further developments of what had already been decided upon, in response to critical reactions to the first Prayer Book.[1] In that light the renewed attempts at the codification of doctrine, notably in the second Prayer Book of 1552 and in the Forty-Two Articles, have been given disproportionate weight. They were, of course, of obvious significance theologically. But such developments did not have the novel impact on most people that the changes in the first half of the reign had had. And in significant respects the years of Northumberland's ascendancy revealed serious and growing divisions within Protestantism. Theologians quarrelled over doctrine and liturgy. The country's lay rulers and, not least, several bishops sympathetic to Protestant ideas, proved more concerned with maintaining order than with building Jersualem through any fundamental structural reform of the Church.

Theological developments were much influenced by the growing number of foreign Protestants in England. Archbishop Cranmer,

---

[1] Cf. P. Williams, *The Later Tudors: England 1547–1603* (Oxford, 1995), 75–6; and remarks of D. MacCulloch, *Thomas Cranmer: A Life* (New Haven and London, 1996), 365–6: 'there was an essential continuity of purpose in a graduated series of religious changes over seven years'. See MacCulloch, *Cranmer*, chs 9–12 for the most recent account of them.

very conscious of the lack of strong enthusiasm amongst the English clergy for the changes that he personally desired, had early in the reign written to a number of important continental reformers, such as the Polish nobleman, John à Lasco, and the Germans, Martin Bucer and Philip Melanchthon. He offered to pay their travelling expenses to England, and to accommodate them in his own house-hold.[2] Although Melanchthon stayed in Wittenberg,[3] other conti-nental reformers poured into England. Peter Martyr and Bernardino Ochino arrived in November 1547, Francis Dryander came the following February, and John à Lasco that summer. In 1549 Martin Bucer and Paul Fagius arrived.

These were the great men, but a large number of humbler refugees also flocked in. In the first year of Edward's reign it became clear that England, alone in Europe, offered 'a very safe haven' to such foreign Protestants.[4] They were driven, in part at least, by the persecutions that began in the empire after Charles V's victory over the Schmalkaldic League at the battle of Muhlberg in April 1547 and the subsequent imprisonment of Lutherans such as John Frederick of Saxony and Philip of Hesse. The Interim of Augsburg, which effectively forbade Lutheranism throughout the empire, was promulgated by the Imperial Diet in July 1548. Preachers and theologians fled: Martin Bucer deplored the fact that they escaped 'like water poured out'.[5] Protestants also fled from persecution in the Low Countries, and, in smaller numbers, from France and Italy. By 1550 it was deemed necessary to organ-ize these foreign Protestant communities in London into what were called the 'stranger churches'. Edward noted in June 1550 that the Germans should have the church at Austin Friars,[6] whilst the French Protestants were gathered into a church in Threadneedle Street, and there was also a small Italian church. In all, these church communities may have numbered between three and four thousand souls.[7]

Cranmer welcomed them all; as the Ferrarese Jew, Emmanuel

[2] H. Robinson, ed., *Original Letters Relative to the English Reformation* (Parker Society, 1846–7), i, 337.
[3] Ibid., 16–22.
[4] Ibid., 20–1.
[5] Ibid., ii, 531.
[6] Edward VI, *Chronicle*, 37.
[7] A. Pettegree, *Foreign Protestant Communities in Sixteenth-Century London* (Oxford, 1986), 77–8.

Tremellius, later wrote, 'his palace was a hotel open to all learned men and godly people. Host, Maecenas and father in one, he knew how to welcome strangers and could speak their language.'[8] He had, of course, close ties with the continent, having spent some months in Germany, where he married Andreas Osiander's niece; indeed, he wrote so regularly to his friends there that he kept a messenger for the transport thither of his letters.

The archbishop's purpose was in part practical, in part charitable, but he also nourished an idealistic scheme for an international Protestant conference, a godly alternative to the council of Trent. In July 1548 he told à Lasco that if 'learned and godly men...might meet together, comparing their respective opinions' on the chief subjects of ecclesiastical doctrine, it might be possible for them to 'set forth among all nations, an illustrious testimony...that all posterity may have a pattern to emulate'.[9] Later, he asked Calvin to help him remove dissension amongst the Protestants, who held so wide a variety of opinions over the sacrament,[10] and he urged Melanchthon to emulate the example of the apostles, who met together to resolve their disputes.[11] The king, he believed, was sympathetic, and willing to 'put his kingdom at their disposal'.

But protestantism in England under Northumberland was characterized more by divisions than by such inclusiveness, and foreign theologians were involved in such debates.

The first disputes arose over the introduction of a reformed ordinal shortly after Somerset's fall. Provision for the ordination of clergy and the consecration of bishops had been omitted from the Prayer Book of 1549, perhaps because Cranmer was not confident of carrying all the bishops with him. Parliament had in late 1549 passed an Act sanctioning the drawing up of a new ordinal,[12] which was speedily ready, based on the Canterbury Pontifical and Martin Bucer's *De ordinatione legitima*. All mention of sacrifice disappeared from the service, which meant that some of the more conservative bishops, such as Heath of Worcester, felt unable to accept it. However, enough of the medieval past was retained to make the ordinal equally unacceptable to radicals such as John Hooper, who in his Lenten sermons before the king denounced it. Hooper, who

[8] J. Strype, ed., *Memorials of Thomas Cranmer* (Oxford, 1840), ii, chs xiii, xxii.
[9] Robinson, ed., *Original Letters*, i, 16–18.
[10] Ibid., 24.
[11] Ibid., 25–6.
[12] 3 & 4 Edward VI, c.12 (*Statutes of the Realm*, iv. 161–4).

had spent many years in Germany and had lived in Zurich between 1547 and 1549, was nominated as bishop of Gloucester in the early summer of 1550. This provoked an immediate crisis over the ordinal, for he realized that the ceremony of consecration would require him to swear an oath that he described as 'shameful and impious', since it involved swearing by saints, and to wear vestments – the surplice and the cope – that he found hateful.[13] He therefore refused the bishopric.

Uproar ensued, involving the Privy Council, most of the existing bishops, the foreign Protestants, and the king himself. According to a letter written to Bullinger, Edward agreed that Hooper need not take the oath invoking the names of saints; asking 'are these offices ordained in the name of the saints, or of God?', he erased 'with his own hand' the offending phrase.[14] But on those 'anti-Christian habits and vestments', as Hooper described them, there was no agreement. Hooper apparently 'obtained a letter from the king to the archbishop of Canterbury, that he might be consecrated without superstition', but this did not appease Ridley, the bishop of London, on whom the task of consecration had fallen, for he 'refused to use any other form of consecration than that which had been prescribed by parliament'.[15] Ridley was a convinced Protestant, issuing injunctions as bishop of London that forbade kissing the communion table, washing fingers, using the paten to bless, moving the altar book, breathing on bread or chalice, using sacring bells, exhibiting the sacrament, placing candles on the table, as well as any ceremonies not included in the Book of Common Prayer. Such measures show a commitment to further reformation. Ridley was to die at the stake for his faith five years later. But, for all his Protestant zeal, he seems at this time to have been fearful lest religious discipline should break down and Anabaptism and other more radical ideas become widespread. His diocese included a number of such dissident groups, as well as the stranger churches. Desperately anxious to maintain control, Ridley appealed to the council, arguing that to allow such contraventions of the law as Hooper desired would be 'the very root and wellspring of much stubborn obstinacy, sedition and disobedience of

[13] Robinson, ed., *Original Letters*, i, 87.
[14] Ibid., ii, 416.
[15] Ibid., 567. Strype dates this letter 5 August (Strype, ed., *Memorials of Cranmer*, i, 302).

the younger sort against their elders'.[16] The council, constantly worried about popular disorder in the aftermath of the 1549 risings, supported him. Hooper then appealed to Warwick himself, only to be reminded that 'the king must be obeyed in matters of indifference': however, for Hooper, the vestments were not 'a thing indifferent'.[17] For months deadlock ensued: Hooper was imprisoned for a time,[18] whilst support for him waned, save from the German Church and John à Lasco. Finally, in February 1551, Hooper capitulated: he was consecrated in the form prescribed, without the contentious phrase about saints that the king had struck out, but, crucially, wearing the hated vestments.

The whole episode had deeply divided the foreign Protestant community. Hooper appealed to the foreign theologians, but not all of them agreed with him; Bucer and Peter Martyr both urged him to submit.[19] However, John à Lasco and Martin Micron, the pastors of the German stranger church, as well as others, supported him ardently.[20] For a time, their support of Hooper threatened the very existence of the stranger churches: Micron told Bullinger in October 1550 that 'by canvassing and persuasion the bishops have procured from the king's council that we are not to enjoy the free use of the sacraments, but must be fettered by the English ceremonies, which are intolerable to all godly persons'.[21]

Although in the end Hooper submitted, and although in the end Ridley and the stranger churches hammered out a working relationship, the vestments controversy had very wide-ranging repercussions. From now on many of the council must have regarded Hooper and his sympathizers as zealous hotheads who put the scruples of the individual conscience before the laws of the land. The consequences of the injury done by the episode to 'the Christian commonwealth' were also great. Although Cranmer seems to have continued to believe in his 'counter-Tridentine' conference, asking Calvin and Bullinger for their assistance in

[16] A. Townsend, *The Writings of John Bradford* (Parker Society, 1848–53), ii, 390–408. See also C. Hopf, 'Bishop Hooper's Notes to the King's Council', *Journal of Theological Studies*, xliv (1943), 194–9.

[17] Robinson, ed., *Original Letters*, ii, 571.

[18] *APC*, iii. 191.

[19] Robinson, ed., *Original Letters*, ii, 486–8; C. Hopf, *Martin Bucer and the English Reformation* (Oxford, 1946), 131–70; G.C. Gorham, *Gleanings of a Few Scattered Ears* (1857), 187–206.

[20] Robinson, ed., *Original Letters*, ii, 559–60, 466–7.

[21] Ibid., 573.

1552,[22] the bitter dissensions that the vestments controversy had aroused showed how improbable it was that agreement could be reached amongst the warring Protestant factions.[23]

The religious climate after 1549 did become more repressive. Several bishops had voted against the introduction of the 1549 Prayer Book. One of them, Thirlby, declared that he had only subscribed to a draft as a basis for discussion, and declared that he wanted 'the verity of the body and blood ... spoken plainly in the sacrament'. The subsequent rebellions in summer 1549 raised acutely the question of these clerics' loyalty, and many of them were to be harried, removed, even imprisoned, and then replaced by radicals in subsequent years. Edmund Bonner of London was deposed in favour of Nicholas Ridley, promoted from Rochester in June 1550: Ridley was soon plucking down altars in the capital. At the same date John Ponet went to Rochester, and then, in April 1551, to Winchester, to succeed the ousted Stephen Gardiner.[24] Constant efforts had been made to persuade Gardiner to accept the new Prayer Book in full, but after much prevarication, in the course of which he declared his willingness to accept it in part, he was finally deprived in February 1551.[25] Day of Chichester, despite preaching a sermon against transubstantiation in April 1550,[26] was deposed in October 1551, and succeeded by Scory of Rochester.[27] Similar fates overtook Heath of Worcester and Tunstall of Durham. In August 1551 Miles Coverdale went to Exeter to replace the conservative Veysey, and Hooper was promoted to Gloucester in July 1551 and then to Worcester and Gloucester in May 1552. In the same month Taylor went to Lincoln. Thus the composition of the bench of bishops was transformed.

Such changes facilitated agreement on changes in liturgy and doctrine that were to be incorporated in the second Book of Common Prayer and in the Forty-Two Articles. Revision of the Prayer Book of 1549 had begun a few months after it was promulgated. No doubt it was never intended as the final word, but the

---

[22] Ibid., i, 24, 22.

[23] Ibid., 23.

[24] Wriothesley, *Chronicle*, ii, 33–4 (deprivation of Bonner); ii, 38 (appointment of Ridley); ii, 45–6 (deprivation of Gardiner and promotion of Ponet).

[25] Edward VI, *Chronicle*, 53.

[26] Ibid., 23.

[27] Ibid., 86.

making of the second Prayer Book can best be understood as a
response to the criticisms – both by radicals and by conservatives –
of the first. Hooper, for instance, wrote in March 1550, that 'I am
so much offended with that book, and that not without abundant
reason, that if it be not corrected, I neither can nor will communicate with the church in the administration of the [Lord's] supper'.[28]
Martin Bucer in particular made pointed comments about its inad-
equacies, criticisms strengthened by Bishop Gardiner's willingness
to endorse some parts of it as 'not distant from the catholic faith'.
Bucer, who had became regius professor of divinity in Cambridge,
was to have a strong impact on the English Church, particularly on
Cranmer himself. He was deeply interested in liturgical matters, and
found some aspects of the 1549 Prayer Book very unsatisfactory,
although he understood the reasons for them; with Paul Fagius, he
wrote a letter on 26 April 1549 saying

> We hear that some concessions have been made both to a respect
> for antiquity and to the infirmity of the present age, such, for
> instance, as the vestments commonly used in the sacrament of the
> eucharist, and the use of candles; so also in regard to the com-
> memoration of the dead, and the use of chrism.... They affirm
> that there is no superstition in these things, and that they are to
> be retained only for a time, lest the people, not having yet learned
> Christ, should be deterred by too extensive innovations from
> embracing his religion.[29]

He also, later, wrote a much longer commentary on the Book,
known as the *Censura*, and it is noteworthy that many of the
elements that he picked out for criticism were altered in the subsequent revision. Bucer rejected the concept of blessing things, epiclesis, manual acts accompanying words of institution, the sign of
the cross in baptism, exorcism and chrism in baptism, chrism in vis-
itations of the sick, mass vestments, the use of the chancel, wafer
bread and its being placed in the mouth of communicants, all
prayers for the dead: he wanted more homilies instead. Of these, all
except the rejection of the sign of the cross in baptism were incorporated into the revised Prayer Book in 1552. In the funeral rite, for
example, the eucharist was no longer celebrated, there were no

[28] Robinson, ed., *Original Letters*, i, 79 (27 March 1550).
[29] Ibid., ii, 535–6.

prayers for the dead, and the priest no longer directly addressed the corpse, as he had done in the earlier service, commending the soul of the departed to God. Praise for Mary and the saints was omitted. In certain respects, the second Prayer Book went beyond Bucer's suggested revisions. Most notably, any phrasing in the first Prayer Book that could be interpreted by conservatives such as Gardiner as endorsing the real presence of Christ in the eucharist was now removed.[30] The new liturgy set out in the second Prayer Book was authorized by an Act of Uniformity in the spring of 1552 and came into effect the following November, only eight months before Edward's death. Theologically, the second Prayer Book took major strides towards the goal of the reformers, though it did not go all the way. But it should again be emphasized that for the majority of the laity the most obvious changes and the most intense shocks in religion had already come in 1549, with the introduction of services in English and with the removal of images.

Popular lay reaction, in the short space of time between the introduction of the new service and Edward's death, was muted. There was, however, a short but fierce debate among the clergy on the matter of kneeling at communion, which was enjoined by the new Prayer Book. The Scots preacher, John Knox, who had been taken up by Northumberland, denounced the practice in a sermon before the king. The council ordered printing of the Prayer Book to cease while it debated the matter. Cranmer counter-attacked by linking Knox's ideas with those of the Anabaptists, and the council agreed to preserve the injunction about kneeling while adding the clauses known as the 'black rubric' to affirm that no adoration was intended to the bread and wine, which remained 'in their very natural substances'. The outcome was a triumph for Cranmer and for the authority of the Church.[31]

Alongside the Prayer Book, Cranmer had for some time been preparing a statement of doctrine for the Church. This was issued by the council in May 1553 as the Forty-Two Articles. Justification by faith alone (xi) and 'predestination unto life' (xvii) were firmly asserted; transubstantiation and 'sacrifices of masses' were equally

---

[30] Hopf, *Martin Bucer*, 55–98; E.C. Whittaker, *Martin Bucer and the Book of Common Prayer* (Alcuin Club Collections, lv, Great Wakering, 1974), contains an edition of Bucer's *Censura*, with Latin text and English translation: see esp. 23–4, 126–8.
[31] MacCulloch, *Cranmer*, 525–8.

firmly denied (xxix and xxx). The articles condemned Anabaptism as unequivocally as they condemned popery.

Cranmer was also much set on revising canon law. The process began with the appointment of a commission in December 1551. Interestingly, this contained two distinguished foreign reformers, John à Lasco and Peter Martyr. Work proceeded slowly. By early 1553 the *Reformatio legum ecclesiasticarum* was ready for presentation to parliament. Had it been enacted, it would profoundly have affected the balance of authority between clerical and secular elements in the Church, and indeed within society as a whole. Moral rules, especially sexual rules, would have been tightened and the authority of the clergy over the laity increased. It was, however, presented at an inauspicious moment. The higher clergy were indignant at the confiscation of church lands by the council and powerful laymen. Privy councillors responded angrily to inflammatory sermons. Relations between Cranmer and Northumberland became particularly strained, partly over church lands, partly over the latter's support for Knox in the debate about kneeling. In the summer Northumberland blocked the passage of the *Reformatio* in the House of Lords. It was never revived.

Promulgation of the second Prayer Book was followed by a final order for the confiscation of church goods: plate, money and robes. This was the culmination of a process of expropriation begun at the start of the reign. Images had mostly been removed or destroyed under Somerset. In 1547, and again in 1549, the council had ordered inventories to be made of church goods. In 1550 Ridley, bishop of London, ordered that the altars in his diocese should be replaced by communion tables placed in the middle of churches; other bishops followed his lead. In the following year the council ordered that further inventories be made of plate and valuables, prior to their confiscation to the king's use. By the time that the confiscation itself was finally ordered in January 1553, much of the plate had disappeared, sold by parish authorities to raise money or hidden away in the hope that better times might return. The edict of 1553 was, in practice, less significant than it might seem; and only six months remained for its operation.

Much, then, had changed during the reign as a whole: the doctrines and liturgy of the Church, the appearance of churches. Chantries and religious guilds had been dissolved. It had seemed towards the end of the reign that the system of church courts might be fundamentally changed. But one institution remained unchallenged, with lasting consequences for the Church of England, namely the office of bishop. Episcopacy survived in England, and it even survived with an intact apostolic succession. Perhaps this was not surprising. No proposals for the abolition of episcopacy were made at this time. The dispute over Hooper's vestments centred on the terms of his ordination: neither Hooper nor those foreign Protestants who supported him abhorred the office of bishop as such. The stranger churches established in England owed an enormous amount to the favour of certain bishops, above all Cranmer. And yet the fact remains that in continental Europe, where the Protestant Reformation had been established, episcopacy had very often been abolished. In Elizabeth's England, there would be repeated efforts to replace episcopacy with a presbyterian system of church government. The stranger churches – that born in 1550 at Austin Friars in London to welcome the German and Dutch congregations, and the French Church in Threadneedle Street – visibly displayed what might be seen as the virtues of an alternative system of ecclesiastical organization. It is noteworthy that they expressly appointed 'superintendents', rather than bishops. Yet, ultimately, the example of the stranger churches appears to have had remarkably little impact on the structure and organization of the Edwardian Church. The Dutch and German Church was to have 'a much more profound influence on the Reformed church in the Netherlands than on the English church', its historian has written,[32] while the distinctive characteristics of the French Church, in particular its emphasis on 'discipline', were also conspicuously absent from the Church of England. But that this would be the outcome was not immediately clear, and many Edwardian churchmen, including some of relatively radical views, such as Nicholas Ridley, who succeeded Bonner as bishop of London, worried about the possible impact of the stranger churches on religious and political stability: indeed, George van Parris, one of the two people burnt for heresy in Edward's reign, came from the Dutch Church.[33]

Certainly, as soon as they arrived, the strangers showed considerable hostility to the bishops. In January 1550 Peter Martyr reported that 'the perverseness of the bishops is incredible; they oppose us with all their might', while Jan Utenhove noted the following year that the bishops were 'far more solicitous for their own glory than

---

[32] A.D.M. Pettegree, 'The Strangers and their Churches in London', University of Oxford D.Phil. thesis, 1983, 76.
[33] Edward VI, *Chronicle*, 58. The other was Joan Butcher, burnt in May 1550.

that of the Lord Christ'.[34] Such remarks were not directed against episcopacy in general. They were provoked in part by those Protestant bishops who placed order above reform, and in part by those conservative bishops in England who were extremely critical about the policies of Edwardian governments. The most notable of those conservative bishops were Stephen Gardiner, bishop of Winchester, and Cuthbert Tunstall, bishop of Durham, from the two richest dioceses in the country, as well as Nicholas Heath, bishop of Worcester, and Edmund Bonner, bishop of London. As we saw earlier, these bishops would ultimately suffer deprivation, as did George Day, bishop of Chichester. Their successors were very different.

Much more importantly, many Englishmen had always severely criticized the way in which bishops carried out their duties. Such criticisms were common in Lollard preaching, and they revived with vigour in the 1520s and 1530s.[35] Robert Barnes and William Tyndale then asserted that there was no scriptural authority that could justify the possession of such vast temporal wealth by churchmen, and that according to divine law the bishops had no secular authority; they declared that the bishops had been as greedy as Judas, receiving from the devil the wealth and pomp that Christ had refused. Pamphlets such as *The Practyse of Prelates* and *The Image of a Very Chrysten Bysshop and of a Counterfayte Bysshop* were secretly circulated, as were the licentious attacks of John Bale.

Nor was there any insistence, on the English side, on *de iure divino* episcopacy. English thinkers at the time seem in general to have considered the episcopate as an administratively practical arrangement, and to have seen the division between bishops and lower clergy 'as a distinction of rank rather than of order'.[36] Bishops would be regarded, as John Jewel, bishop of Salisbury at the beginning of Elizabeth's reign, would put it, as 'pastores, operosos, vigiles'.[37] Most English churchmen would have agreed with Bucer's teaching that 'presbyterorum atque episcoporum unum idemque officium ac munus esse.'[38]

But practical arrangements are there to be changed. Indeed, in the second half of Edward's reign the general political and financial

---

[34] Robinson, ed., *Original Letters*, ii, 479, 585.
[35] W. Clebsch, *England's Earliest Protestants* (New Haven, 1964), 45–6.
[36] P. Collinson, *Godly People* (London, 1983), 157–8, 164–5.
[37] H. Robinson, ed., *Epistolae Tigurinae* (Parker Society 1842), 29.
[38] Collinson, *Godly People*, 27: 'The duty and remuneration of both minister and bishop should be one and the same.'

situation was such that a large-scale attack on the institution of episcopacy, with the foreign theologians playing a leading part in justifying it as a welcome reform, would not have been at all surprising.
The government was interested in bishops and their property for
more mundane reasons than theological ones. The vast cost of
Somerset's wars had been financed in part, as those of Henry VIII
had been, by confiscated church property, including that of the
chantries and religious guilds dissolved under a 1547 statute. Over
a quarter of a million pounds was derived by the government during
the reign from the sale of chantry lands, while land worth £47,000
was given away.[39] But that was not the end: church plate, bells, vestments and church fittings were added to the royal coffers. Still the
government needed money – in 1552 it could scarcely pay its bills.
Monastic wealth had already been seized, and spent. Chantries and
guilds had been dissolved, the silverware belonging to churches,
together with their bells, would soon be confiscated; even lead from
roofs had been taken away. Now greedy eyes looked with interest at
the great wealth of the bishops.[40] When new bishops were elected to
fill the seats from which the conservatives had been ejected, they
therefore found themselves forced to hand over substantial parts of
their landed wealth. They did not do this without protest: Nicholas
Ridley lamented that his position was so deplorable that if the whole
nation got to hear about it, everyone 'would lament and weep at the
idea of so dreadful a fall'.[41] Cranmer thought it necessary to defend
himself and all his colleagues against the accusation of excessive
greed,[42] and a Latin treatise on the illegality of the transfer of the
property of the Church to secular use was prepared.[43]

The abolition of the episcopacy would obviously have facilitated
the confiscation of bishops' lands. It would have been more acceptable if it could have been justified in terms of doctrine. In its attack
on episcopal wealth, the council could have looked for support to
the foreign protestants, who would have been well placed to supply
a justification. Their sympathies undoubtedly lay with those who
sought to diminish episcopal wealth and power. Why did this not
happen?

In the first place, the links between those members of the council

[39] W.K. Jordan, *Edward VI: The Threshold of Power* (London, 1970), 200.
[40] F. Heal, *Of Prelates and Princes* (Cambridge, 1980), 141–8.
[41] PRO, SP10/13, no. 44.
[42] Cranmer, *Writings and Letters*, 437.
[43] PRO, SP10/15, no. 77.

who wanted to seize episcopal wealth and the strangers who might have justified such action by appealing to doctrine were not strong. Like many exiles, the strangers tended to turn back on themselves, constantly complaining about English food and weather (Edward VI gave Bucer money to buy a stove). [44] The death, at Cambridge, of Paul Fagius, followed by that of Bucer himself, increased their sense of isolation. Peter Martyr lamented: 'as long as Bucer was in England...I never thought myself to be in exile'; now, he felt alone.[45] They began to quarrel bitterly among themselves, and wrote venomous letters to their colleagues who had stayed at home.[46]

If they formed a compact group, it was in part because they found it difficult to communicate with the English around them. Few Englishmen spoke Italian, French or German, and few of the exiles spoke English. That did not pose a great problem to those who held posts at the universities, where they preached and delivered lectures in Latin,[47] but all the same, in such a situation, it meant that the possibility of informal contacts was limited. Peter Martyr, we know, gave private lectures in Italian in his house at Oxford to which sympathetic members of the university came, but the number of those who could profit in this way was small.[48] Moreover, as Martyr remarked, the lack of good popular preachers in England could not be compensated for 'by the aid of the foreigners, by reason of their want of acquaintance with the English language'.[49]

The linguistic barrier also limited the weight of the contacts which the strangers had with those who wielded political authority. Some noblemen looked favourably upon the strangers and tried to come to their aid and offer support, but they were few in number. The same names keep recurring – Henry Grey, marquess of Dorset and later duke of Suffolk, with the rest of his family; William Parr, marquess of Northampton; John Cheke, secretary to the council. Protector Somerset was sympathetic, but he lost his effective power in October 1549. John Dudley, duke of Northumberland, who

[44] Robinson, ed., *Original Letters*, ii, 550–1, 723.
[45] Ibid., 491.
[46] Ibid., 575.
[47] Gorham, *Gleanings*, 124.
[48] T. Harding, *A Reiondre to M. Iewels Replie* (Antwerp, 1566), sig. CCC3. See also J. Loach, 'Reformation Controversies', in J. McConica, ed., *The History of the University of Oxford, III* (Oxford, 1986), 369.
[49] Robinson, ed., *Original Letters*, ii, 485.

replaced him as the head of the government, was also a sympathizer at the beginning – and in March and June 1550 was even described by Hooper as 'that most faithful and intrepid soldier of Christ' and as 'a most holy and fearless instrument of the word of God'.[50] But this sympathy does not seem to have produced anything very remarkable. Why not? It is worth considering further, since Northumberland could easily have led the offensive against the bishops.

As president of the king's council, Northumberland was well aware of the desperate financial plight of the government. In the attack on episcopal wealth, he was a prime mover. It was he who dissolved the great medieval liberty of Durham, giving parts of its estates to the crown, and keeping part for himself.[51] But by the latter part of the reign he appears to have been on bad terms with Cranmer, whose influence in government circles was, in the last months of Edward's life, small. According to the imperial ambassador, Northumberland, in the last parliament of the reign, launched a scathing attack in the House of Lords on the bishops, who, he said, wanted more power with which to chastise the laity without being willing to put their own house in order.[52] Why did not Northumberland make use of someone like John à Lasco, leader of the German stranger church, a fervent opponent of the English bishops, to support the suppression of the episcopate on grounds of theological principles? One part of the response was that it was very difficult for Northumberland to communicate with the strangers without an intermediary. But above all relations between the council of which Northumberland was president and Lasco and the stranger churches had been seriously damaged by the Hooper affair over vestments.[53]

That episode had perhaps saved the episcopacy in which Cranmer so much believed. It brought home both to Northumberland and to many reform-minded bishops, most notably Ridley, the risks if radical churchmen were freed from political control. Had Northumberland and the foreign Protestants

[50] Ibid., i, 82 (27 March 1550).
[51] H.R. Trevor-Roper, 'The Bishopric of Durham and the Capitalist Revolution', *Durham University Journal*, new series, vii (1946).
[52] J. Gairdner, *Lollardy and the Reformation* (4 vols, London, 1908–13), iv, 400–1.
[53] Robinson, ed., *Original Letters*, ii, 566–8; see the account in Pettegree, *Foreign Protestant Communities*, 37–43.

been able to make common cause in the early 1550s, the whole shape of the English Church thereafter would have been different.

As the details of his responses to Hooper and Ridley in their dispute over the ordination of bishops suggest, Edward seems around this time to have become firmer in his manifestations of Protestantism. It is interesting that in July 1550 the council went to see the king before deciding to proceed with stern measures against the bishop of Winchester.[54] The imperial ambassador, van der Delft, noted that the king 'changes his mind from day to day' in response to the vagaries of those hostile to the old religion; so that

> in the court there is no bishop, and no man of learning so ready to argue in support of the new doctrine as the King, according to what his masters tell him, and he learns from his preachers, whose sermons he often writes with his own hand before everybody; and this seems to be a source of pride to his courtiers that the King should dictate the very words of the sermons and choose for himself who shall preach.[55]

However, the clearest evidence of Edward's increasing intervention in matters religious came in the controversy over his sister Mary, and her refusal to conform to the 1549 Prayer Book. Intermittent negotiations for a marriage between the princess and the Infante Don Luis of Portugal proved inconclusive; disheartened, she wrote to the imperial ambassador in March 1550 asking if he would help her to flee from England.[56] A fortnight later the emperor instructed the ambassador to get an assurance from the council – or, even, from the king himself – that Mary 'should be permitted to continue in her observance of the ancient religion, and in the enjoyment of the same liberty that was hers' at her father's death.[57] The council's response was to say that Mary alone (with two or three of her women) could hear mass in her chamber, whilst her household must conform to the statutes.[58] Van der Delft told his master that there was no point in trying to speak to the king in person since 'he will only say what he is told to say'; there was no one about him or amongst the gentlemen of the privy chamber 'except

[54] *APC*, iii, 84.
[55] *CSP, Spanish*, x, 63.
[56] Ibid., 47.
[57] Ibid., 56–7.
[58] Ibid., 68–9.

those well-known as partisans and instigators of the new doctrines'.[59] By early May Mary was frantic, and van der Delft convinced that she should be rescued.[60]

In mid-July a rescue party arrived, but it failed to take Mary away. The account of what happened contains farcical elements – a meeting with the Princess's comptroller, Rochester, in a churchyard, complicated negotiations over the corn that the ships had imported as a decoy, Mary's refusal (which exasperated her would-be rescuers) to leave without most of her personal possessions, adverse winds, and the rest.[61] For the remainder of the year Mary was bullied and harassed,[62] and finally, in December, some of her chaplains were arrested.[63] This provoked an angry letter from the princess to the council, repeating her belief that promises had been made to her in the past giving her and her household freedom to have the mass celebrated and to attend other ceremonies performed in the manner used in Henry VIII's time. These promises were now being denied. Mary had been surprised when Edward had told her that he had heard a rumour that she habitually heard mass, and wept when she saw how he had been counselled against her. On seeing Mary's tears, Edward wept himself.[64] But Edward then replied to his sister in an angry letter claiming that

you, our nearest sister, in whom by nature we should place reliance and our highest esteem, wish to break our laws and set them aside deliberately and of your own free will; and moreover sustain and encourage others to commit a like offence.

Quoting the Scriptures, Edward declared himself willing to listen to Mary as her brother rather than her 'sovereign king and lord'. In a postscript written in his own hand, the king added that he was determined to see his laws obeyed, 'and those who break them shall be watched and denounced'.[65] To this Mary replied in pained tones.[66] The meeting offered by the king took place on 17 March 1551. It

[59] Ibid., 69–70.
[60] Ibid., 80–6.
[61] Ibid., 124–35.
[62] Edward VI, *Chronicle*, 41–4.
[63] Ibid., 50; *APC*, iii, 171.
[64] *CSP, Spanish*, x, 205–9. For the council's initial response see *APC*, iii, 177.
[65] *CSP, Spanish*, x, 209–12.
[66] Ibid., 212–13.

started amicably enough, with Mary apologizing that her illness had prevented her from visiting the king earlier, and Edward replying that 'God had sent him health, and to the princess illness'. But then the councillors intervened, and the discussion became acrimonious. Mary spoke of the harsh letter sent earlier by the council, of which the king denied any knowledge, saying that 'he had only taken a share in affairs during the last year'. The councillors responded to the princess's taunt that in that case the changes in religion had not been instigated by the king himself, saying that everyone was required to follow the religion established. Both Mary and Edward seem to have come near to losing their tempers, for the princess told her brother that 'riper age and experience would teach him much more yet', to which he replied that 'she also might still have something to learn, for no one was too old for that'. The councillors again intervened, and the meeting ended with Mary declaring that God should have her soul, but the king owned her body, and might take away her life if he so wished. Edward replied that 'he wished for no such sacrifice'.[67] At this point Scheyfve, the new imperial ambassador, attended the council and read out letters from the emperor threatening war unless Mary be granted freedom to worship in her accustomed way. Probably this was an idle threat since Charles was in no position to carry it out. Nevertheless, the council took it seriously. According to Richard Morison, then English ambassador to the emperor, but writing in exile after Mary's accession, they wished to persuade Edward to give way, and having no success themselves, called in Cranmer and Ridley to urge him that although 'licence to sin was sin, to suffer and wink at it for a time might be borne...'. In spite of their persuasions, Edward, according to Morison, remained resolute, not only standing his ground, but insisting in an eloquent and emotional speech that whatever the circumstances God's commands must be obeyed. Morison's account leaves the rest of the story somewhat in the air, but the implication is that Edward, under renewed pressure from the council, gave way.[68] It is far from easy to know what to make of this. If Morison is taken literally, then Edward emerges as learned in the Scriptures and more determined to follow God's way than his councillors and

---

[67] Ibid., 258–60. See also Edward VI, *Chronicle*, 55, an incoherent entry that suggests something of the king's agitation.

[68] Ibid., 55–6; *CSP, Spanish*, x, 251–61; Nichols, *Literary Remains*, i, ccxxiv–ccxxxiv.

the two prelates. But Morison was not in England while these events were supposedly taking place, and having been recalled at this time from his embassy by the council, had reason to feel angry with Northumberland, whom he painted as the villain of the piece. Probably Edward did remain stubborn about giving Mary freedom; that fits the general pattern of his behaviour. But it seems unlikely that he was capable, at the age of thirteen (Morison mistakenly says sixteen) of delivering an oration which could confound two prelates as well as the councillors.

However that may be, two days later 'serjeant Morgan' appeared before the council accused of hearing mass two or three days earlier in the princess's house.[69] Three days after that Sir Anthony Browne was questioned about the same offence, and sent to the Fleet, and Mary's comptroller, Robert Rochester, was issued with a warrant.[70] Later, one of Mary's chaplains, Dr Mallet, was arrested and put in the Tower. The princess again protested, but the council defended itself robustly.[71] In August 1551, the council resolved that Mary's household should be forbidden to hear mass;[72] this message was given to Mary's comptroller, Rochester, and to Edward Waldegrave and Sir Francis Englefield; they returned from a visit to Mary with a letter from her again protesting that she must obey her conscience.[73] The council dispatched three of its members (Lord Rich, the Lord Chancellor, Sir William Petre and Sir Anthony Wingfield) to reason with the Princess.[74] In September, her comptroller and two other gentlemen were summoned before the council. Again, Mary herself and the imperial ambassador protested. Warwick told Scheyfve that the council would have to consult the king, who now 'wished to concern himself with all the public affairs of the kingdom', and later declared that 'he held the King to be as much of age as if he were forty'.[75]

What emerges from these pressures on Mary is how much Edward resented her determination to break what he saw as his laws: 'in our estate it is most grievous to suffer that so high a subject should disregard our laws'. It set a dangerous example. A regal desire for obe-

[69] *APC*, iii. 239.
[70] Ibid., 239–40.
[71] *CSP, Spanish*, x, 287–8.
[72] *APC*, iii. 329–30.
[73] Ibid., 333–4, 336–40.
[74] Ibid., 341–6. Mary's response is iii, 348–52.
[75] *CSP, Spanish*, x, 356–64, esp. 361.

dience is what characterizes Edward's letter to Mary, including the concluding paragraph in his own hand, of 28 January 1551.[76] Again the emphasis in Mary's interview with king and council on 17 March was on her disobedience: the king intended to have the ordinances and statutes of the realm inviolably obeyed by everyone.[77] But there is little hint of any attempt at religious conversion. Edward's hostility to Catholic masses and ceremonies is palpable in his letter to Barnaby Fitzpatrick, then at the court of Henry II in France, on 29 December 1551, but again his emphasis is on obedience: if Fitzpatrick was pressed to go on pilgrimage, he should say that 'with sauf conscience you can not doe any such thing, being brought up with me and bounden to obey my lawes'.[78] Edward's part in the pressure placed on Mary shows his increasing prominence in matters of state, but only in a limited way does it illustrate his own religious convictions. How far Edward deserves his reputation as 'the godly imp' is a question that can best be considered in the course of study of his court: that will offer an appropriate context in which to judge the extent and depth of his religious convictions.

[76] Ibid., 209–12.
[77] Ibid., 250–61, esp. 260.
[78] Nichols, *Literary Remains*, i, 69–70

Chapter 11

EDWARD'S COURT

One of the most famous portrayals of Edward VI, and one that has profoundly influenced the way in which he has since been perceived, is an illustration from Foxe's *Acts and Monuments*, in which the young king is depicted listening attentively to a sermon preached before him by Hugh Latimer. Flanked by Protector Somerset and other councillors, Edward looks earnestly out from a casement window on to the privy garden at Whitehall which is thronged with soberly dressed courtiers listening attentively to Latimer's sermon. The preacher, delivering what was almost certainly one of the Lenten sermons of 1549, stands in a newly constructed and severely classical pulpit, at the foot of which sits a woman following the references in her bible. Here is the image that has dominated all subsequent writing about the boy-king and his entourage.[1]

Edward was both pious and well versed in religious matters, yet the image is misleading if it is seen as a full picture of the young king and his interests. He inherited a lavish and well-established court and he played an enthusiastic role in its activities.

Henry VIII built and accumulated more than any other English king: 55 houses,[2] 2,000 pieces of tapestry, more than 150 panel paintings, over 2,000 pieces of plate, scores of books, and a mass of other possessions.[3]

---

[1] For a discussion of this woodcut, see J.N. King, *Tudor Royal Iconography: Literature and Art in an Age of Religious Crisis* (Princeton, 1989), esp. 164, 95; cf. illus. 52. The cut first appeared in Day's 1562 edition of Latimer's sermon (*RSTC* 15276, sig. D 7). See Plate 13, and below, 188.

[2] D. Starkey, 'The Legacy of Henry VIII', in D. Starkey, ed., *A European Court in England* (London, 1981), 8; H.M. Colvin, ed., *The History of the King's Works, Vol. IV (1485–1660, Part II)*, (London, 1982), 3.

[3] BL, Add. MS 46348; Society of Antiquaries, MS 123 (D. Starkey, ed., *The Inventory of King Henry VIII, Vol. I: The Transcript*, (London, 1998)); W.A. Shaw, *Three Inventories of Pictures in the Collections of Henry VIII and Edward VI* (London, 1937); *LP*, XII, ii, 754.

Most of Henry's wealth was inherited by his son, who even took
over his father's fool, Will Somers.[4] The financial needs of government led to some dispersals during the reign, and Edward's age and
relative poverty precluded him from collecting on his father's scale,
but he lived in great splendour, surrounded by beautiful things.
Henry's taste had been for the magnificent, and even the vulgar.
The first impressions of the young Edward must have been of food
served to the sound of trumpets and hautbois on vessels of gold and
silver gilt set with precious and semiprecious stones, of walls hung
with Flemish tapestries depicting biblical and classical scenes that
Henry had seized from Wolsey, of garments made from cloth of
gold and tissue embroidered with silver, of necklaces, collars and
even the covers of books sparkling with jewels and precious metals.

No complete inventory of Edward's possessions survives, but a list
of his jewellery at the time of his death suggests that this environment had shaped his own taste. Amongst his belongings was a book
cover of enamelled gold clasped with a ruby, one side decorated
with a cross set with diamonds, and the other with a fleur-de-lys set
with diamonds and rubies, the whole finished by a pendant of white
sapphire; the cover hung on a chain garnished with rubies and
emeralds.[5] Edward also owned a dagger of gold and some green
stone, speckled with red, its sheath decorated with rubies, diamonds
and emeralds, and the blade, wrought with 'moorish work', with
small rubies; this had a gold tassel and hung from ropes of pearl.[6]
Amongst Edward's possessions delivered to Jane Grey at his death
was a sable skin, 'with a head of gold, containing in it a clock, with
a collar of gold, enamelled black, set with four diamonds, and four
rubies, and two pearls hanging at the ears, and two rubies in the
ears, the same skin having feet of gold, the claws thereof being sapphires...and with a diamond upon the clock'.[7]

Not all the king's belongings were quite so ostentatious. Amongst
the items of plate lost or stolen during his reign were a gilt cup with
a cover, chased with branches and leaves, with twelve antiques and
sylphs, and a rose on the top, and a pair of gilt flagons, engraved
with leaves, and with 'Great and small chains' held by antique
women's heads: these items together were worth £112.[8] However,

[4] PRO, E101/426/8.
[5] BL, Harleian MS 7376, fo. 37v.
[6] Ibid., fo. 34.
[7] HMC, Salisbury, i, 129.
[8] PRO, E351/1952.

simplicity was rare. For example, when a looking-glass was broken, it was described as being garnished all round with silver, and the cover decorated with roses and fleurs-de-lys, and it stood upon three pomegranates.[9] The king was able to 'lend' Sir Andrew Dudley a 'fair tablet of gold', which opened at the back, 'made like a castle, garnished with xxvij diamonds, eight rubies and four sapphires, cut lozenge-wise, with a picture of a woman' and an agate figure 'holding a small diamond in her hand, like a glass'.[10] When the king's library was purged in February 1551 of 'all superstitiouse bookes, as masse bookes, legendes and suche like', substantial quantities of gold and silver were retrieved from their 'garnytures'.[11]

Edward thus maintained all his father's magnificence. When he had a new close stool made it was covered with crimson velvet, embroidered, and decorated with silk and gold. A new bed was commissioned, and sent to Oatlands: it was surmounted by a crown of cloth of gold, cased in silk and velvet, and gilded.[12] He bought more jewels to add to Henry's substantial collection: in May 1551, for example, he purchased from Jacob Fugger the great Burgundian jewel known as 'The Three Brothers', an ornament that remained in the royal collection until pawned by Charles I in 1626.[13] This 'very fair jewel of. . .four rubies marvelous big, one orient and great diamond, and one great pearl', as Edward gloatingly described it in his journal,[14] cost 100,000 English crowns, a sum so large that it had to be paid in instalments.[15] The young king also bought from Erasmus Skette, a merchant of Antwerp, 'a faire great ring of gold' with a table diamond set in coloured enamel.[16] He clearly enjoyed wearing such things, and on a journey from Titchfield to Southampton in 1553 lost the great diamond, pearl and ruby pen-

[9] Ibid.
[10] *HMC Salisbury*, i, 131.
[11] *APC*, iii. 224.
[12] PRO, E101/426/8.
[13] R. Lightbown, 'The King's Regalia, Insignia and Jewellery', in A. MacGregor, ed., *The Late King's Goods: Collections, Possessions and Patronage of Charles I in the Light of the Commonwealth Sale Inventories* (London, 1989), 269–70; R. Strong, *Lost Treasures of Britain* (London, 1990), 84–5.
[14] Edward VI, *Chronicle*, 60.
[15] *CSP, Spanish*, x, 282.
[16] BL, Harleian MS 7376, fo. 33v. See also PRO, SP10/15, no. 41. Sketes, in early 1551, was supplying the English government with gunpowder (*APC*, iii. 252).

dant which hung from the gold and enamel chain set with pearls, diamonds and rubies round his neck.[17] (It was subsequently recovered.)

The king's clothes, on public occasions at least, shone with gold, silver and precious stones. François de Scépeaux, later maréchal de Vieilleville, visited England twice in Edward's reign, and left a vivid account of what he saw.[18] After his visit to Hampton Court in 1551 he reported that Edward's garments were covered in diamonds, rubies, pearls, emeralds, and sapphires, 'si bien appropriez, que toute la salle en reluysoit [sparkled]'.[19] Certainly the new caps Edward had made for the French visit were heavily decorated with gems: one white velvet cap was garnished with forty-eight rubies and innumerable pearls and pieces of gold, and had pinned to it a brooch decorated with the figure of a man and two antiques, embellished with thirteen diamonds and three rubies. Another cap, this time of black velvet, was decorated with diamonds, pearl love-knots and gold beads: in this the king wore a brooch with a cross made of diamonds.[20]

Overall, the young king seems to have been as enthusiastic about personal display as his father had been. His buttons and aglets (tags on the end of laces) were, we know from the account books, made of gold, and even his napkins were garnished with gold and silver.[21] Amongst the king's personal possessions on his deathbed was a coffer containing a purple velvet cap embroidered with damask thread and garnished with diamonds, rubies and pearls;[22] he also owned a black velvet cap 'with a little square table ruby', and a black leather case containing a black velvet 'muffler', which was 'striped with small chains of gold', garnished with pearls, rubies and diamonds, 'the same muffler being furred with sables, and having thereat a chain of gold enamelled green, garnished with certain pearls'.[23] A Florentine visitor, Petruccio Ubaldini, noted that Edward was usually dressed in red, white and violet, embroidered

[17] BL, Add. MS 46348, fo. 152.
[18] Scépeaux, *Mémoires*, ii, chs 2–4; iii, chs 28–9.
[19] Ibid., i, 341.
[20] BL, Add. MS 46348, fo. 217.
[21] PRO, E101/426/6, fo. 31v; E101/426/8; E351/2932.
[22] BL, Harleian MS 7376, fo. 25.
[23] *HMC, Salisbury*, i, 129.

with gold, silver thread and pearls, and 'nobody would venture to wear a hat of that colour'.[24]

Although, then, the Edwardian court was a court that revolved around a child, and that child was a man – indeed, his father – in miniature, there was nothing simple or childish about his appearance or his surroundings. The tone of his court remained, as it had been in Henry's day, cosmopolitan and worldly.

Edward's court was organized much as his father's had been. The 'downstairs' provision of food, laundry and other physical necessities was controlled by the lord great master, the 'upstairs', and more public, aspects of the court were looked after by the lord chamberlain. The great master – initially Paulet, succeeded in 1550 by Warwick – was assisted by the treasurer, Sir Thomas Cheyne, a Kentish gentleman who had held the post since 1539 and had become a privy councillor; by the comptroller, William Paget until 1549, then Sir Anthony Wingfield, a Suffolk man promoted from the post of vice-chamberlain, who had been sent by the council in London to arrest Somerset in October 1549, and finally, from August 1552, Sir Richard Cotton of Warblington, Hampshire, one of Prince Edward's councillors before 1547 and a close associate of Warwick;[25] by the cofferer, briefly Sir Edmund Peckham, treasurer of the Royal Mints from 1544,[26] followed in March 1547 by John Ryther, an Essex man who had been cofferer to Edward when he was prince,[27] and finally by Thomas Weldon, a Berkshire landowner whose career in the court had begun in 1520 as clerk to the cofferer.[28] Below these officials was a steadily rising number of other royal servants – 269 by 1553.[29] The chamberlain, the earl of Arundel, who was succeeded by Thomas, Lord Wentworth, and then by Darcy, controlled the king's near servants, and the vice-chamberlain – Wingfield, Darcy and then, in 1551, Sir John Gates – controlled the gentlemen pensioners and Yeomen of the Guard, who

[24] BL, Add. MS 10169, fo. 56v, an eyewitness account of England in 1551. The translation is taken from F. von Raume, *The Political History of England* (1837), 115.

[25] S.T. Bindoff, *The House of Commons, 1509–58* (3 vols, London, 1982), i, 711–12.

[26] Ibid., iii, 78–9.

[27] Ibid., 240–1.

[28] Ibid., 571–2.

[29] R.C. Braddock, 'The Royal Household, 1540–1560: a Study of Officeholding in Tudor England', Northwestern University Ph.D., 1971, 74, 214.

provided for the king's security. (Briefly, between February 1551 and the autumn of 1552 these guards were supplemented by about 850 mounted cavalry, or 'gendarmes'.)[30]

The most significant part of the chamberlain's empire was the privy chamber, for the eighteen gentlemen of the chamber looked after all the monarch's personal needs, and also controlled access to him. Their position gave them considerable patronage and much political influence, and the personnel of the chamber therefore fluctuated with the twists of political fortune. Some of those who first served Edward had, like Sir Anthony Denny and Sir William Herbert, also served his father. Others were adherents of Somerset, such as the groom of the chamber, John Fowler, and the 'first gentleman' of the chamber, who was Somerset's brother-in-law, Sir Michael Stanhope. Stanhope stayed physically close to the king, had a key to the privy chamber suite, and controlled access to it.[31] But Fowler was to prove a weak link in the barrier Somerset had tried to construct around his nephew. The threat came from very near at hand, from Somerset's brother, Thomas, who had been aggrieved since the time of Henry's death by his elder brother's pre-eminence, and who used Fowler and other chamber officials to win Edward's favour.[32]

Perhaps surprisingly, the fall of Seymour in January 1549 did not produce any major changes in the personnel of the chamber – even Fowler, after a brief imprisonment in the Tower,[33] retained his position. However, when Somerset himself fell from power in the autumn of 1549, there was considerable reorganization of the chamber, to ensure that Edward was surrounded by men loyal to Warwick.

The privy chamber did not merely control access to the king, it also controlled a great deal of money. In the last five years of Henry VIII's reign £243,423 had passed through the hands of Sir Anthony Denny, most of it being spent on buildings, 'engines of war', clothes, plate and jewels.[34] The accounts of Sir Michael Stanhope, who as groom of the stole controlled the privy purse in the first two years of

[30] D.E. Hoak, 'The King's Privy Chamber, 1547–1553', in D. Guth and J. McKenna eds, *Tudor Rule and Revolution* (Cambridge, 1982), 92. See above, 95.

[31] Hoak, 'The King's Privy Chamber', 105–6.

[32] For a full account see G.W. Bernard, 'The Downfall of Sir Thomas Seymour', in G.W. Bernard, ed., *The Tudor Nobility* (Manchester, 1992), 212–40.

[33] Bindoff, *House of Commons, 1509–58*, ii, 166.

[34] BL, Lansdowne MS, Roll 14. The money came to Denny in his capacity as keeper of the palace of Westminster, a position in which he was succeeded by

Edward's reign, are not as full, and the young king's complaints about how short of money the protector kept him certainly suggest a more frugal administration: it was, for example, from Thomas Seymour that Edward received money with which to reward his schoolmaster, Cheke, and his French master, Belmain.[35] Although Stanhope's extant accounts show the king spending money on fabrics, clothes and small personal items, they suggest that payments for building and warfare were not at this time coming from the privy purse.[36] However, this may merely reflect a change in accounting procedures, rather than any greater stringency over expenditure: during the same period the expenditure of the court of augmentations sanctioned by royal warrant was unusually high.[37] By August 1551 the privy purse account was certainly again being used for non-personal expenses, this time for repairs to Farnham castle.[38] In 1552–3, the next year for which full privy purse accounts survive, we find nearly £40,000 being spent on fortifications and equipping ships as well as on rewards and more obviously personal expenditure.[39] By then, the four principal gentlemen of the privy chamber, who controlled the privy purse after Somerset's fall, had a full-time clerk, Peter Osborne, to assist them.

Most wages were paid by the treasurer of the chamber, Sir William Cavendish, who in the year ending in September 1549 spent nearly £17,000 on alms, gifts and salaries. Moreover, the number of courtiers and retainers paid for by the crown substantially increased over the reign. The staff of the chamber, for instance, rose from twenty-six at Edward's accession to thirty-seven at his death.[40] The bakehouse, which had employed thirteen people at Henry's death, held seventeen in 1553. Even the spicery, which had managed in Henry's reign with a staff of three, rose to four under Edward.

Edward's year had a certain, fixed shape. New Year was spent in a variety of palaces – in 1548 it was Hampton Court, but thereafter it was usually Whitehall. After Epiphany, the king might either stay at Whitehall, or go to Greenwich, returning to London whenever

Sir Andrew Dudley (W.C. Richardson, *History of the Court of Augmentations, 1536–1554*, Baton Rouge, Louisiana, 1961, 355–6).
[35] BL, Harleian MS 249, fo. 31v.
[36] PRO, E351/2932.
[37] Richardson, *Court of Augmentations*, 345.
[38] *APC*, iii. 346.
[39] Richardson, *Court of Augmentations*, 365.
[40] Braddock, 'The Royal Household', 75.

needs of state – a session of parliament, or a visit from a foreign envoy – required. (When in London, he stayed at Whitehall, or, more rarely, St James's). Easter was spent at Greenwich, although the king would usually be in London for Maundy Thursday. In July he went to Hampton Court, where he would remain until the middle of August, when he often visited Oatlands, in Surrey. From 1550 Edward undertook a summer progress through parts of southern England. In the early autumn he went to Windsor, or back to Hampton Court. Christmas was spent at either Hampton Court or Whitehall.

As this itinerary suggests, Edward had an immense range of accommodation available. Although a number of Henry's houses were alienated in his son's reign – Hunsdon to the Princess Mary Enfield to Elizabeth, and others, like Westhanger and Syon, to royal servants, Edward rarely imposed himself on others, even during the great progress of 1552.

However, little more than necessary maintenance and repairs was carried out on these houses during Edward's reign; it was left to courtiers, and in particular to Protector Somerset, to maintain the interest in building that had been so marked in the second part of Henry's reign. Although he described Halnaker House, in Sussex, which he visited in 1552 as 'pretty',[41] Edward does not appear to have taken any great interest in domestic architecture. Indeed, he seems to have preferred the moated, gabled Oatlands to the smarter Nonsuch, which Henry had remodelled on his birth; he visited Nonsuch only once, and that briefly.[42] It is interesting to note that James I provided his eldest son, Henry, with an establishment at Oatlands, and that both he and Charles I later gave it to their consorts.[43] Oatlands's comparative lack of grandeur and its attractive park may have been particularly appealing to the young Edward, who complained in 1549 about Windsor, where there were no galleries or gardens to walk in.

Whatever the architectural setting, the impact made by the court on visitors was always impressive. When Gaspard de Coligny, seigneur de Châtillon, first visited England in May 1550 for the signing of the peace treaty with France, he was lavishly entertained with jousting, hunting at Hampton Court, a Garter ceremony and a

---

[41] Colvin, *King's Works*, IV, 126.
[42] Ibid., 202.
[43] Ibid., 213.

supper given by the duke of Somerset to the accompaniment of various water festivities.[44] Edward and Coligny, as head of the mission, took communion together on Whit Sunday, to establish the peace, and the king also had the delegation to dinner at Greenwich, and watched with them 'a pastime of ten against ten at the ring'.[45] Later Coligny asked for a portrait of the young king.[46] In April 1551 Henry II was elected a knight of the Garter, and Edward VI was in return elected to the French order of St Michel. The order was bestowed in July by Maréchal St André and a number of other nobles, including Scépeaux. The celebrations were spectacular,[47] including the construction in Hyde Park of the kind of temporary 'banqueting houses' last built in 1527,[48] and clearly much enjoyed by the young king. Edward joked with the French ambassador, Boisdauphin, about English food, which, he said, was causing the (very substantial) Frenchman to lose weight, and received the order 'avec un visage riant et très joyaux'.[49] (On the next Michaelmas Day, the king wore his robes to mark the festival,[50] and invited the French ambassador to dine with him in his privy chamber.)[51] Scépeaux much admired Edward's establishment: he especially remarked on the costumes of the Yeomen of the Guard, who had 'E's and imperial crowns embroidered in gold thread on the back of their coats,[52] the guards themselves, who were all blond and of the same height, and the liveries of the horsemen who accompanied the French party from Hampton Court to Windsor. No bemused provincial, but an *habitué* of one of the most elegant courts in Europe, Scépeaux found Edward's establishment both lavish and tasteful; however, like other foreign observers, he was uncertain whether or not he approved of the way in which the English courtiers knelt to

[44] Edward VI, *Chronicle*, 26, 31–2; Wriothesley, *Chronicle*, i, 38–40.

[45] Bodleian Library, Oxford, Ashmole MS 861, fo. 341; Edward VI, *Chronicle*, 31.

[46] J. Delaborde, *Gaspard de Coligny* (Paris, 1879), 87.

[47] Edward VI, *Chronicle*, 72–5.

[48] *HMC, Salisbury*, i, 92–3; S. Thurley, 'The Banqueting and Disguising Houses of 1527', in D. Starkey, ed., *Henry VIII: A European Court in England* (London, 1991), 64–7.

[49] Scépeaux, *Mémoires*, i, 340.

[50] Edward VI, *Chronicle*, 84; BL, Cotton MS, Vitellius B v, fo. 4v; J.G. Nichols, ed., *The Diary of Henry Machyn* (Camden Society, 1st series, xlii, 1848), 9.

[51] *CSP, Foreign, 1547–1553* (London, 1861), 175.

[52] In September 1551 £200 was paid out 'for certain spangles. . .for the coates of the garde, fotemen and messingers' (*APC*, ii. 355).

serve the king at dinner. Ubaldini had similar doubts: noting that even the king's sisters were not allowed to dine with him under the canopy of state, but were required to sit some distance away on a simple stool, he described the rituals used as ridiculous: he had seen Elizabeth, he writes, 'kneel down before her brother five times before she sat down'.[53]

When the French left after this visit they were given very substantial presents, which were, the English ruefully noted, much more generous than those given by Henry II to the English delegation.[54] Edward gave St André a diamond ring from his finger 'worth by estimation £150 for [his] pain and [the king's] memory', and, later, 'three thousand pounds in gold of current money', plus other large sums to members of his suite.[55] In addition, the French were presented with various gold items, including spice plates decorated with scallop shells (the symbol of the order of St Michel) to Châtillon.[56] Sir Anthony Aucher, the master of the jewel house, had earlier been given £2,000 with which to purchase plate for the ambassadors, £3,000 'to be employed in golde and plate for the rewarde of the Frenche Ambassadours', and £3,200 towards 'the byeng of certein silver plate'.[57] The year before, nearly £2,000 had been given as rewards to the peace envoys.[58] Very large quantities of gold were handed out in the course of the reign; amongst other presents, collars of gold were given to the duke of Brunswick,[59] and the young count of Rangona,[60] gold cups worth £327 to the French ambassador, and gilt basins, goblets, flagons and salts to the imperial ambassador.[61]

Foreign ambassadors and visitors were also often given portraits of the king, partly in order to facilitate the various marriage negotiations of the period. Edward received a portrait from Henry II of

---

[53] Von Raume, *Political History*, 115.

[54] *CSP, Spanish*, x, 346.

[55] Edward VI, *Chronicle*, 75.

[56] PRO, E351/1951.

[57] *APC*, iii. 312, 319, 323.

[58] Ibid., 39.

[59] Presumably this was Otho, duke of Brunswick and Lunenburg, to whom the king granted a pension in 1549 (*CSP, Foreign*, 47).

[60] *APC*, iii. 7, explains that the young count, the son of 'a noble man of Italie', resided at court and received a pension of 1,000 crowns a year. His father was governor of Milan (*APC*, iii. 77). The chain cost over £70 (ibid., 207–8). See also *CSP, Foreign*, 171.

[61] PRO, E351/1951.

France, for example, and sent one back. A number of painters were retained to undertake this task. William Scrots (or Screets), who succeeded Holbein as king's painter, continued throughout the reign to be paid the high salary of £62 per annum.[62] Other painters 'on the establishment' in Edward's reign included a Florentine, Bartholomew Penni, another Italian, Nicholas Bellin (usually known as Nicholas da Modena), who had earlier worked at Fontainebleau, and a pupil of Ghirlandaio, Anthony Toto, who held the office of serjeant painter from 1543 until his death ten years later.[63] Edward inherited from his father a 'paintrix', Lavinia Terling,[64] who, in October 1551 was sent to paint Elizabeth's likeness.[65] She would go on to serve both Mary and Elizabeth in turn when they succeeded to the throne.

These painters were mainly employed in producing heraldic devices for royal funerals and coronations, and – like Inigo Jones seventy years later – in painting scenery for court festivities. Nicholas da Modena, for example, was responsible for the great mound made for the coronation interludes.[66] Such festivities were elaborate and expensive. The extant accounts from the Office of Revels, Tents and Toils – the department responsible for the provision of costumes and 'props' for such entertainments – make it possible to construct a detailed picture of much of what Edward saw.

Court festivities followed a fairly fixed formula, being provided regularly at what the French ambassador described as 'mardy gras', the period immediately before Lent, at Christmas and at the New Year. There were often outdoor celebrations on May Day and in the succeeding weeks. Extra entertainments were, of course, provided for important foreign guests. Entertainments were produced both by the king's own troupe of players, and by 'players of interludes'[67] and the many bands maintained by members of the nobil-

[62] W.C. Richardson, ed., *The Report of the Royal Commission of 1552* (Morgantown, WV, 1974), 89. See below, appendix.

[63] Richardson, *Royal Commission of 1552*, 122; J.P. Collier, ed., *Trevelyan Papers prior to AD 1558* (Camden Society, lxvii, 1857), 195. See also E. Auerbach, *Tudor Artists* (London, 1954). See below, appendix.

[64] Collier, ed., *Trevelyan Papers prior to AD 1558*, 195, BL, Stowe MS 571, fo. 28v; R. Strong, *Artists of the Tudor Court* (Catalogue of the portrait miniatures at the Victoria and Albert Museum) (London, 1983), 52–7. See below, appendix.

[65] *APC*, iii. 376; Auerbach, *Tudor Artists*, 75. See below, appendix.

[66] See above, 38.

[67] J.P. Collier, ed., *Trevelyan Papers 1446–1643* (Camden Society, lxxxiv, 1862), 17, 18.

ity;[68] between 1550 and 1552 the king rewarded for their efforts
the players of the duchess of Suffolk, and those of the duke of
Somerset and the marquis of Northampton.[69]

If we look at the entertainments in one year – 1550 – we find the
accustomed masques at Shrovetide. Late May was taken up with the
entertainment of the French peace negotiators, who, as well as a
great deal of hunting and jousting, also saw 'wildfire cast out of
boats and many pretty conceits'.[70] The following month, one of the
French hostages who remained in England provided 'a great
supper', with 'divers masques and other conceits'.[71] Later that
month, Lord Clinton, recently appointed lord admiral, entertained
Edward at Deptford with what the young king happily recorded as
men standing 'upon the end of a boat without hold of anything',
until they fell into the river. After dinner there was something more
elaborate: 'a fort made upon a great lighter on the Thames, which
had three walls and a watch-tower in the midst', defended by a
yellow galley and soldiers in yellow and black against four pinnaces
manned by troops dressed in white.[72] At Christmas, masques were
provided that included, for Twelfth Night, 'Irishmen', a bagpipe
player and a masque of Moors. Edward himself joined in these last
with great alacrity, both acting in and altering the plays to his own
taste.[73]

As the king grew older, the festivities became more elaborate and
more expensive.[74] The visit of the French in 1551 to present the
order of St Michel led to the construction in Hyde Park of a temporary 'banqueting house'; this banqueting house, which was 62
feet by 21 feet, and the various 'standings' there and in Marylebone
Park, together with their furnishings, cost £450.[75] In October of that

[68] S.R. Westfall, *Patrons and Performance: Early Tudor Household Revels* (Oxford,
1990), esp. 122–51, 216–41.
[69] W.R. Streitberger, 'Financing Court Entertainments, 1509–58', *Research
Opportunities in Renaissance Drama*, xxvii (1984), 36, transcribing PRO,
E101/426/8.
[70] Edward VI, *Chronicle*, 32.
[71] Ibid., 33–4.
[72] Ibid., 36.
[73] A.W. Feuillerat, *Documents Relating to the Revels at Court in the Time of King
Edward VI and Queen Mary* (Louvain, 1914), 47.
[74] For figures, see S. Anglo, *Spectacle, Pageantry and Early Tudor Policy* (Oxford,
2nd edn, 1997), 302.
[75] *HMC Salisbury*, i, 92–3; Thurley, 'Banqueting and Disguising Houses',
64–7.

year Mary of Guise, the dowager queen of Scotland, was given an escort of 120 gentlemen when she visited the king at Hampton Court. She later dined with the king in great state, two great services of plate, one gold and the other silver, being put out on display;[76] in the previous June four parcels of plate 'of the best sorte and guilte that can be founde' had been ordered, worth, in all, £3,700.[77] In January 1552 the custom of appointing a lord of misrule, 'which had not been done for fifteen or sixteen years',[78] was revived, to the apparent delight not only of the courtiers who were involved but also of the Londoners who witnessed the lord of misrule's ceremonial entry into the capital.[79] George Ferrers, master of the king's revels, acting the part of the lord, was provided with three pages, and eight 'councillors', whose costumes had to be remade as they were of the quality that men such as Sir Robert Stafford and Thomas Wyndham had a right to expect.[80] The following year Ferrers was again appointed lord of misrule.[81] This time the festivities included a play at night, between Youth and Riches 'fought two to two at barriers in the hall', then by another contest between two courtiers dressed as Germans, two as friars. It was all very elaborate, with 'many jousts, tourneys and other sports...for his majesty's pleasure and recreation'.[82] Again, the city of London shared fully in these festivities, with the king's lord of misrule and that of the lord mayor competing over the splendour of their costumes and the generosity of their alms.[83] There were masques, one of men, one of women, and a banquet of 120 dishes to mark, the king noted in his diary, 'the end of christmas'.[84]

Unfortunately, few texts are extant for those plays.[85] However, from the lists of costumes provided for the masques and plays of the reign

[76] Edward VI, *Chronicle*, 89–94.

[77] *APC*, iii. 288. For similar displays of plate at an earlier period, see P. Glanville, 'Cardinal Wolsey and the Goldsmiths', in S.J. Gunn and P. Lindley, eds, *Cardinal Wolsey* (Cambridge, 1991), 131–48.

[78] *CSP, Spanish*, x, 444.

[79] Machyn, *Diary*, 13–14; Bodleian, Ashmole MS 861, fos 342–3.

[80] *APC*, iii. 508; Feuillerat, *Revels*, 57–94; Anglo, *Spectacle, Pageantry and Early Tudor Policy*, 301–9.

[81] *APC*, iv. 181.

[82] *CSP, Spanish*, x, 443.

[83] Machyn, *Diary*, 28–9. See also 157.

[84] Edward VI, *Chronicle*, 105.

[85] For an attempt to date some extant works to Edward's reign, see J.N. King, *English Reformation Literature: The Tudor Origins of the Protestant Tradition* (Princeton, 1982), ch. 6.

it is clear that many of them involved, as did those of the 1530s, anti-papal polemic. The Shrovetide celebrations immediately after Edward's succession required costumes for friars, cardinals and pilgrims,[86] while the Revels Office accounts record the making of 'Crownes and Crosse for the poope'. Shrovetide 1549 saw the office making costumes for hermits and a dragon with seven heads,[87] and that Christmas there were costumes for 'palmers', hermits and friars. The revival at the beginning of 1552 of the ceremonies associated with the lord of misrule led to a great outburst of anti-Catholicism. The imperial ambassador was very shocked when describing a religious procession of priests and bishops. Parading through the court they carried, under an infamous tabernacle, a representation of the holy sacrament in its monstrance, which they wetted and perfumed in most strange fashion, with great ridicule of the ecclesiastical state.[88]

Many of these court festivities were performed to the sound of music. Henry VIII had left a substantial music establishment; amongst those provided with liveries for his funeral were eighteen trumpeters, seven minstrels, five 'musicians', four sackbut players, eight players of the viols, five flautists, a 'fyffer', a drummer, a harper and a bagpipe player.[89] (This was in addition to the thirty or so singers of the chapel royal.) Edward, in the first years of his reign, paid wages to a harper, two lute-players, a flautist, two singing-men, one bagpipe-player, eight minstrels, a virginals player, John Heywood, one rebec player, viols and sackbut players, a drummer, and the musicians of the chapel royal.[90] Indeed, he even added to the establishment the 'newe ministrelles who was with his grace when he was prince'[91] and engaged 'Newe Sagbuttes'.[92] By 1552 he had two harpers instead of one, two extra drummers and virginal players, and another flautist.[93] This musical establishment war-

[86] Anglo, *Spectacle, Pageantry and Early Tudor Policy*, 296.

[87] Ibid.

[88] *CSP, Spanish*, x, 444.

[89] PRO, LC2/2, fos 40v, 64v, 80v, 83v–84. In 1529, Henry had maintained sixteen trumpeters, nine sackbuts, two viols, four lute-players, three players of the rebec (a stringed instrument), three drummers and a harper (Collier, ed., *Trevelyan Papers prior to AD 1558*, 138–9), and in 1545 seventeen trumpeters, four sackbuts, eight viols, six flutes, and three harpers (H. Cole, 'Gentlemen and Players', *Country Life*, clxxxv (xli), October 1991, 90).

[90] Collier, ed., *Trevelyan Papers 1446–1643*, 14–15, 18–19, 23–4, 30.

[91] Collier, ed., *Trevelyan Papers to AD 1558*, 191–204.

[92] Collier, ed., *Trevelyan Papers 1446–1643*, 19–20.

[93] BL, Stowe MS 571, fos 29–29v. See also Richardson, *The Royal Commission of 1552*, 18, 114–17.

ranted the appointment, at £10 a year, of an instrument tuner, an organ maker and maker of 'regalles',[94] and a tuner for them,[95] an organ maker, and a 'song-pricker'.[96] There were also at court a number of 'musician strangers', including the five Bassano brothers.[97]

The purpose of this establishment was functional rather than purely aesthetic; trumpeters, in particular, were used for a number of ceremonial tasks, and the serjeant trumpeter was closely associated with the College of Arms;[98] early in Edward's reign the trumpeters were rewarded for playing at the coronation and at 'the Justs holden at the palais of Westminster'.[99] Trumpets and hautbois were also used to herald the arrival of food at feasts.

Kings and nobles routinely took with them on their travels a considerable musical assemblage; in 1520, for example, both the king of England and the king of France brought the musicians of their chapels royal to their meeting at the Field of the Cloth of Gold.[100] On their peace-making mission in 1550 the French were accompanied by Henry II's own minstrels, as well as those of the dauphin, whilst Châtillon brought musicians, trumpeters, drum and fife. All were rewarded by Edward.[101] The deputation which brought the king the French order of St Michel in 1551 was accompanied by trumpeters, a cornet-player, flutes, shaums and sackbuts,[102] and when the order was handed over trumpets and hautbois sounded.[103]

The main function of the chapel royal, which by 1552 consisted of forty men and 'the children',[104] was to provide the king with choral services on principal and major feast days – under Henry VII,

[94]BL, Stowe MS 571, fo. 29v. 'Regalles' are small portable organs.

[95] Calendar of Patent Rolls, Edward VI, ii. 338.

[96]Collier, ed., Trevelyan Papers 1446–1643, 18, 25.

[97]BL, Stowe MS 571, fo. 29v. Richardson, Royal Commission of 1552, 21. For the Bassano family, see P. Holman, 'Music at the Court of Henry VIII', in Starkey, ed., Henry VIII: A European Court in England, 104–6, and Westfall, Patrons and Performance, 87.

[98]Bodleian Library, Ashmole MS 861, fos 285–7.

[99] Trevelyan Papers to AD 1558, 202.

[100]J. Jacquot, ed., Fêtes et cérémonies au temps de Charles Quint (2 vols, Paris, 1960), ii, 135–60.

[101]Streitberger, 'Financing Court Entertainments', 36, transcribing PRO, E101/426/8.

[102]Ibid., 37.

[103]Scépeaux, Mémoires, i, 343.

[104]BL, Stowe MS 571, fo. 36v.

all Sundays, Christmas, Easter, Whit Sunday, and forty other feasts of the year.[105]

The chapel royal also took part in court masques and plays.[106] The children of the chapel royal were occasionally summoned to sing to the king in his own room; on All Saints' Day in 1547 and 1548 they sang to him 'Audivi vocem', and at Christmas 'Gloria in excelsis'.[107] Edward here, as so often, was following the example of his father, who had heard the same pieces on the same days in 1543, and of his grandfather;[108] moreover, he continued to reward the children on All Saints' Day until the end of his reign.[109] In 1547, as in the previous reign, the children entertained the king on St Nicholas's Day.[110]

The religious changes of the reign, and the demand of many reformers for musical settings which enhanced but did not obscure the words of the liturgy, made this a period of some difficulty for church musicians. Despite this, amongst the gentlemen of the chapel royal in Edward's reign were Thomas Tallis and John Sheppard,[111] both of whom grappled effectively with the requirements of new liturgies and services. Tallis composed a *Te Deum* for the 1549 Prayer Book,[112] a short service and a number of anthems, including 'Hear the voice and prayer', and 'If ye love me';[113]

[105]P. Le Huray, *Music and the Reformation in England 1549–1660* (London, 1967), 57–89; F. Kisby, 'Courtiers in the Community: the Private and Professional Activities of the Members of Henry VII's Royal Household Chapel', unpublished paper, 3, 9.

[106]For a general account of this function of household chapels, see Westfall, *Patrons and Performance*, ch. 1.

[107]PRO, E101/426/5, fos 49v, 50v, and E101/426/6, fos 17v, 20v, transcribed in part by Streitberger, 'Financing Court Entertainments', 32–4. Did Edward hear the versions written by Taverner for boys' voices as settings of the Sarum Use two decades earlier? (The Sarum Use was the medieval modification of the Roman liturgy, so termed because it was developed at Salisbury Cathedral.) For the Taverner pieces, see J. Caldwell, *The Oxford History of English Music* (Oxford, 1991), i, 236–7.

[108]Streitberger, 'Financing Court Entertainments', 31; Kisby, 'Courtiers in the Community', 11.

[109]Richardson, *Royal Commission of 1552*, 129.

[110]PRO, E101/426/6, fo. 20v.

[111]For Tallis, see PRO, LC2/2, fo. 33 (Henry VIII's funeral list), BL, Stowe MS 571, fo. 36v (a household list of 1552), and PRO, E101/427/6, fo. 17 (Edward's funeral list). Sheppard is on the 1552 and 1553 lists. For an enthusiastic account of Sheppard, see D. Wulstan, *Tudor Music* (London and Melbourne, 1985), 271–7.

[112]Caldwell, *English Music*, i, 276–8.

[113]Bodleian Library, MS Mus. Sch. e.420–2.

Sheppard provided anthems and other service music.[114] Another of
the gentlemen of the chapel royal, Christopher Tye,[115] was respon-
sible for various anthems, including a setting of the 1552 version of
'Christ rising again',[116] and music for his own verse translation of
the Acts of the Apostles. Thomas Causton, a yeoman of the
chapel,[117] was the principal contributor to *Mornyng and Euenyng
Prayer and Communion, Set Forthe in Foure Partes* . . ., published by John
Day in 1565, but prepared before the appearance of the 1552
Prayer Book.[118] Another member of the chapel royal, William
Hunnis,[119] produced in 1550 *Certayne Psalmes Chosen out of the Psalter
of Dauid, and Drawen into Englysh Meter*,[120] and, like his colleague,
Richard Farrant,[121] either at this time or in the very early years of
Elizabeth, a number of short services and anthems.[122]

Two other composers who contributed significantly to the devel-
opment of church music during this period were also closely
attached to the court: Thomas Sternhold, one of the gentlemen of
Edward's privy chamber,[123] and John Marbeck, the organist of St
George's Chapel, Windsor, who in 1550 produced *The Booke of
Common Praier Noted*.[124] Marbeck wrote various prose works, including *A Concorda[n]ce, That Is To Saie, a Worke Wherein Ye Maie Finde any
Worde Conteigned in the Whole Bible*, which he dedicated to Edward.[125]
In this, he explained that a childhood spent in the study of singing
and the organ had left him almost illiterate but that his desire to
study the Scriptures was so burning that he had worked hard to
remedy his deficiencies; now he wanted to help others in a similar
situation. Marbeck's clear assertion of his reformed views is almost

---

[114]Anthem 'Haste thee, O God' to 1549 setting: first service 1549; *The New
Grove Dictionary of Music and Musicians* (London, 1980), vii, 250–1.

[115]Tye is on neither the 1547 nor the 1553 funeral list, nor the 1552 household list. On the other hand, he describes himself on the frontispiece of his
1553 *Actes of the Apostles* (*RSTC* 2984) as a gentleman of the chapel royal, and
it would have been distinctly odd to claim such a distinction in work dedicated
to someone as conversant with the court as Francis Russell if it were untrue.

[116]Wulstan, *Tudor Music*, 287–8.

[117]BL, Stowe MS 571, fo. 36v, and PRO, E101/427/6, fo. 17.

[118]*RSTC* 6419; Caldwell, *English Music*, i, 283.

[119]BL, Stowe MS 571, fo. 36v, and PRO, E101/427/6, fo. 28.

[120]London: *RSTC* 2727.

[121]PRO, E101/427/6, fo. 17.

[122]Caldwell, *English Music*, i, 292–3, 285–6.

[123]See below, 152.

[124]Printed by the royal printer, Richard Grafton. *RSTC* 16441.

[125]*RSTC* 17300.

unique, for most musicians at Edward's court, including Tallis and Sheppard, subsequently served his Catholic sister with apparently equal devotion.[126]

There is some evidence to suggest that Edward, like his father, actively enjoyed music, as well as accepting it as a necessary background to many of his activities. While flattering phrases used by those with careers to advance must always be regarded with suspicion, the words of Thomas Sternhold in 1549, when he dedicated to the king his version of the metrical Psalms, have about them a ring of truth: Sternhold, 'grome of the Kynges maiesties Robes',[127] was obviously in a position to know something of the king's tastes:

Seyng furdre that your tender and godlye zeale doeth more delight in the holy songes of veritie than in any fayned rymes of vanitie; I am encouraged to travayle furdre in the said boke of psalmes. Trustyng that as your grace taketh pleasure to hear them sung sumtimes of me, so ye wil also delight to command them to be sung to you of others, that as ye haue the Psalme it selfe in youre mynde, so ye may judge myne endeuoure by your eare.[128]

Throughout the reign Edward took part in masques and plays. In March 1547 the accounts record the making of 'pleyers garments for the Kinges person, the duke of suffolke and my lord Strange',[129] and there are several subsequent entries which make it clear that Edward was enthusiastic about participating in court festivities, even though, for some years, his costumes had to be made particularly small.[130] In this he followed the precedent set by his father, for it was not until his time that the English aristocracy had begun to take part in person in such entertainments.[131] Indeed, Edward went further: the Revels accounts for Christmas 1551 show the king not only performing but also directing, as the 'plaies and pastimes' are

[126]Tye was ordained at the beginning of Elizabeth's reign, but that should not be taken as a certain indication of Protestantism, since it was at that time far from clear what form the English Church would take.

[127]Collier, ed., *Trevelyan Papers prior to AD 1558*, 201.

[128]*Certayne Psalmes* ... (London, n.d., *RSTC* 2419), sig. A 4.

[129]Feuillerat, *Revels*, 24.

[130]Ibid., 33, 47, 191, 236, 296, 297.

[131]Westfall, *Patrons and Performance*, 57.

described as having been frequently altered 'to serve his maiesties plasure and determinacion'.[132]

Edward enjoyed watching tumblers, jugglers and tightrope walkers. In 1548 Fowler gave 40 shillings to 'certayn tumblers that played, his grace loking out vpon them', and another privy purse payment was made later in the reign to Frenchmen who 'Dawnsed on the Rope and vaulted and a boie that tombled before the Kinges maiestie'.[133] One of the last masques of the reign was described as being 'of tumblers goinge upon theyre handes with theyr feete vpward'.[134] In January 1552 the king even snubbed the imperial ambassador, who wanted to discuss the important matter of Princess Mary's liberty to hear mass, by moving to one side whilst he was speaking so that he could see 'some games' at the same time.[135]

He participated, too, in a wide range of physical activities and sporting interests. This is hardly surprising, given his environment. At Whitehall there was a cockpit, a 'tennis-play' and a bowling alley; during Edward's reign both the tiltyard and the tennis-play were improved.[136] At Greenwich there was a tilt-yard, an armoury, a tennis-play, an elaborate octagonal cockpit decorated with heraldic beasts, archery butts and a hawk mews.[137] A new tennis court was built at Hampton Court in 1532–3 to link up with an earlier court put in by Wolsey, and a tiltyard was constructed there during the late 1530s.[138] There were three bowling alleys at Hampton Court at Edward's accession, as well as a 'house' for turning new bowls.[139]

Edward appears to have made regular use of the archery butts. One of his archers gave him bowstrings at New Year in both the years, 1548 and 1549, for which records exist,[140] and one John Bateman did the same later in the reign.[141] A number of privy purse payments were made to the king's bowmakers and his fletcher.[142]

---

[132]Feuillerat, *Revels*, 47.

[133]BL, Harleian MS 246, fo. 31v; PRO, E101/426/8, fo. 37.

[134]Feuillerat, *Revels*, 145; W.R. Streitberger, 'The Revels at Court from 1541 to 1559', *Research Opportunities in Renaissance Drama*, xxix (1986–7), 25–46, at 38.

[135]*CSP, Spanish*, x, 438.

[136]Colvin, *King's Works*, iv, 312–16.

[137]Ibid., 106.

[138]S. Thurley, *The Royal Palaces of Tudor England* (London, 1993), 186–7, 181.

[139]Ibid., 189.

[140]PRO, E101/426/8.

[141]Ibid., fo. 66.

[142]PRO, E101/426/8.

The keeper 'of the lyons and other beasts in the Tower of London' received, in 1551–2, the large annual sum of £36 14s 6d.[143] The king also maintained falconers, and keepers of ostringers (a kind of goshawk), hawks, spaniels, bears,[144] mastiffs and hares.[145] In the 1552 household list separate entries covered 'harte hounds', 'buck hounds', and 'other hounds'.[146] These were not the only dogs at court: there were also 'harriers' and greyhounds.[147] Sir Anthony Kingston gave the king a pair of greyhounds as a New Year's gift,[148] and the king's reading matter even included a book about them.[149] The Italian riding masters who had taught 'haute école', an early form of dressage, at the court of Henry VIII,[150] remained 'on the establishment',[151] and presumably gave instruction to Edward. He also paid for an Italian 'studman', Matthew de Mantua,[152] and a number of stud farms.[153] He was given 'a courser Mare' by the master of the horse of one of the French hostages, and, at various times, Irish saddles.[154]

As this establishment suggests, hunting was a major activity of the Edwardian court. It was, for instance, a constant element in the entertainment of foreign guests – the French envoys were entertained in 1547 by hunting, 'the baiting of the bears and bulls',[155] and dog-fights.[156] There was more hunting in 1551 for St André and his train, whilst the dowager queen of Scotland watched the 'coursing of deer'.[157] The king himself hunted – unfortunately, so routine was this that it only occasionally prompted a special payment that

[143]Richardson, *Royal Commission of 1552*, 17.
[144]*Trevelyan Papers 1446–1643*, 18; Streitberger, 'Financing Court Entertainments', 35.
[145]Collier, ed., *Trevelyan Papers prior to AD 1558*, 195. One of the most enjoyable payments to those in Edward's funeral train was to one John Beadle, the king's dog–keeper.
[146]BL, Stowe MS 571, fo. 26.
[147]Richardson, *Royal Commission of 1552*, 5–6.
[148]PRO, E191/426/6, fo. 31v.
[149]Ibid., 37.
[150]G. Worsley, 'Henry's Flying Horses', *Country Life*, clxxxv (xli), October 1991, 85.
[151]PRO, E101/426/6, fo. 63.
[152]Ibid., fo. 27.
[153]*APC*, ii. 86; Richardson, *Royal Commission of 1552*, 49, 107.
[154]PRO, E101/426/8.
[155]Edward VI, *Chronicle*, 32.
[156]Scépeaux, *Mémoires*, i, 161–2. Scépeaux was delighted when the English presented them with fighting dogs to take back to France.
[157]Edward VI, *Chronicle*, 92.

appears in the records.[158] (The dismantling of the chase at Hampton Court early in Edward's reign is sometimes used as evidence for the young king's lack of interest in or ability for hunting; in fact, the Privy Council memoranda simply note that whereas Henry, in a sick old age, was not able to go the short distance from Hampton Court to Windsor to use the facilities there, his son could.)[159] In 1552 the parish priest of Barkham, Berkshire, noted that the king had hunted 'in the bear wood in the forest of Windsor and there did his grace kill a great buck'.[160] In August that year Edward informed Barnaby Fitzpatrick how 'we have ben occupied in killing of wild bestes' and had 'good hunting'.[161] Towards the end of Edward's reign an Italian observer noted that the king 'delights in hunting, and he does it so as to have an excuse to ride, because his men, out of fear for his life, often seem to keep rather a tight rein on him in this area'.[162]

Edward was, in short, very much his father's son, interested in sport and in warfare. He enjoyed hearing about martial exploits. Amongst the most lively passages in his *Chronicle* are those describing fighting and jousting, and almost all the longer descriptive sections of the *Chronicle* relate to matters military. This surely reveals something of the boy's own tastes and interests.[163] The *Chronicle* also shows Edward interested in fortification and preoccupied by the problems of the defence of the French possessions.[164] He rewarded from the privy purse the surveyor of Calais who drew 'a plate' of Calais and the Marches.[165] When he made a visit to Portsmouth in August 1552 he particularly noted that the defences were not good, telling Barnaby Fitzpatrick in a letter that the bulwarks were 'il facioned, il flanked, and set in unmete places, the toune weake in comparison of what it ought to be'; and so he had devised 'two strong castellis on either side of the Haven at the mouth thereof'.[166]

[158]PRO, E101/426/8 records a reward given 'by his graces specyasll commaundement when his grace went out hunting by thandes of Mr blounte'.

[159]*APC*, ii. 190–2.

[160]Noted by John Longbridge on his copy of *The Mirror of the Blessed Life of Christ*, according to W.K. Jordan, *Edward VI: The Threshold of Power* (London, 1970), 403.

[161]Nichols, *Literary Remains*, i, 80–1.

[162]BL, Add. MS 10169, fos 1–125.

[163]See above, Ch. 5.

[164]Edward VI, *Chronicle*, 35, 55.

[165]PRO, E101/426/8.

[166]Nichols, *Literary Remains*, i, 81.

The notes in Edward's hand relating to the occupation of France in the reign of Henry VI (consisting of details of the military administration in 1427–8, Sir John Fastolf's counsel against accepting terms offered by the French at Arras, and articles devised by Richard, duke of York, for the governance of France) are perhaps also revealing of the king's martial interests.[167]

Edward enjoyed watching tournaments and jousts, and, later, participating in them. There were several days of jousting after the coronation,[168] and in 1548 'a castle or fort of turves', costing £108, was constructed in the park at Greenwich and 'beseiged and assaulted to shew the king the manner of wars, wherein he had great pleasure'.[169] When John Fowler described the sums that Thomas Seymour gave him at this time to pass on to Edward they included four payments to 'my lord privie seales trumpet at hampton court when his highnes skirmissed in the garden'.[170] The visit of the French peace negotiators in 1550 was marked by a variety of events; one was 'a pastime of ten against ten at the ring', one side being dressed in yellow and the other in blue. A month later, at Shene to celebrate the Dudley–Seymour wedding, the king sat in a chamber made of boughs to watch a number of courses, and a tilt and tourney on foot.

In 1551 the king himself, then aged fourteen, took part in a contest at Greenwich; Edward records that he, 'with sixteen of my chamber', challenged 'any seventeen of my servants, gentlemen in the court', to 'run at base, shoot, and run at ring'. He noted proudly that on 1 April, 'the first day of the challenge at base, or running, the King won', but on 6 April his side lost the challenge 'of shooting at rounds and won at rovers'.[171] A month later Edward was again involved in a challenge of running at the ring at Greenwich. The king, sixteen footmen and ten horsemen, all dressed 'in black silk coats pulled out with white silk taffata' competed in 120 courses against their rivals, who were clad in yellow taffeta.[172] The king's side lost. In April 1551 he 'mounted his horse in full armour, rode two or three miles each time, and also charged the target to exercise and show himself to the people'.[173]

As the imperial ambasssador reported in May, the king was

[167]Ibid., ii, 555–60.
[168]BL, Egerton MS 3026, fos 30–1: coronation jousts.
[169]PRO, E351/3326.
[170]BL, Harleian MS 249, fo. 31v.
[171]Edward VI, *Chronicle*, 57.
[172]Ibid., 61.
[173] *CSP, Spanish*, x, 266.

'beginning to exercise himself in the use of arms, and enjoys it heartily'. When there was tilting at the buckler and sword play at Greenwich the king 'tried his skill five or six times with the other young lords'.[174] Soranzo says Edward soon commenced 'arming and tilting, managing horses and delighting in every sort of exercise, drawing the bow, playing rackets, hunting and so forth, indefatigably, though he never neglected his studies'.[175] The French ambassador told the king that he 'had borne himself right well, and shown great dexterity. The king replied that it was a small beginning, and as time passed he hoped to do his duty better.'[176] A few days later, Edward watched a muster of the guard, and an archery display. In July he rode from Greenwich Park to Blackheath with his nobles and the guard in twos, while trumpets played.[177] At Blackheath he ran at the ring before supping at Deptford on board a ship.

The visit of St André in July 1551 provided the opportunity for a number of sporting displays. On 19 July the king saw 'some courses', and the next day he and his guard put on an archery display for their visitors. On 27 July St André 'came to me a-hunting', and on the next day to Hyde Park, 'where there was a fair house made for him, and he saw the coursing there'.[178]

There were several tilts at the beginning of 1552, including one presided over by the lord of misrule.[179] In May the king rode with his guard from Greenwich to Blackheath, and then joined in running at the ring.[180] At Greenwich four days later he watched a massive muster of noblemen and their retainers, with 'ther standards, and ther cottes in brodery of yche lords còlers, and ther speyres coloryd lyke, and ther fott-men';[181] the imperial ambassador thought that about 1,200 men were assembled.[182]

Edward's court, like that of his father, was extremely cosmopolitan. In addition to foreign members of the household – Italians, Spaniards – and visiting envoys, there were a number of long-term visitors. Girolamo Cardano, Italian doctor and mathematician, met Edward in autumn 1552 and left an encomium and elegiac verses.[183]

[174] Ibid., 293.
[175] CSP, Venetian (9 vols, London, 1864–98), v, 535.
[176] CSP, Spanish, x, 293.
[177] Machyn, Diary, 6–7.
[178] Edward VI, Chronicle, 75.
[179] Ibid., 103, 105, 106; Machyn, Diary, 13–14.
[180] BL, Cotton MS Vitellius F v, fo. 9; Machyn, Diary, 18.
[181] Machyn, Diary, 18–20.
[182] CSP, Spanish, x, 525.
[183] Nichols, Literary Remains, i, ccviii–ccx.

If Henry VIII looked down from heaven upon his young son he would surely have found nothing in his surroundings or in his pastimes to surprise him. Like Henry in his youth, Edward enjoyed the martial pursuits proper to his status, and courtiers, recognizing this, presented him with suitable gifts such as falcons, donated on two occasions by the marquis of Brandenburg,[184] or the pair of greyhounds given by Sir Anthony Kingston.[185] Few gifts more obviously pleased the king than the twelve horses and two mules sent by Henry II of France in January 1552.[186]

Like his grandfather[187] and his father, the young king enjoyed tennis, cards and games of chance. It is significant that when in 1552 the king devised a design for new five-shilling coins, the form of the numeral five was to be the same as that on a pack of cards.[188] He frequently gambled, losing large sums at 'shotinge, tennys, Cardes, Tables, Chesse and other plaies',[189] and 'by makinge of Wagers'.[190]

Alongside Foxe's image of the young Josias, listening attentively to Latimer's sermon, must then go another, of the young king in the tiltyard or – elaborately costumed – taking his part in a masque. Indeed, we may note, it is the masques and the jousts that are recorded in Edward's *Chronicle*, not who preached before him or what was said. None of the great series of Lenten sermons – Latimer in 1549, Hooper in 1550 – is mentioned. True, in the preface written by the Jacobean bishop of Winchester, James Montagu, to the collected works of James I, Montagu listed among the writings of Edward VI 'the notes of the most of the sermons he heard...under his owne hand', but that manuscript is no longer extant. Montagu states that in it Edward recorded 'the preacher's name, the time and all other circumstances', but not the sermons' contents. It would be unwise to deduce from this any deep or informed interest in Protestant theology.[191] Foxe's image, so profound in its subsequent impact, may be no more than the product of his own wishful thinking.

---

[184] *CSP, Foreign*, 187.

[185] PRO, E101/426/6, fo. 31v.

[186] Edward VI, *Chronicle*, 108.

[187] S.J. Gunn, 'The Courtiers of Henry VII', *English Historical Review*, cviii (1993), 25.

[188] C.E. Challis, 'Presidential Address', *British Numismatic Journal*, lxiii (1993), 175–6.

[189] PRO, E101/426/8.

[190] PRO, E351/2932.

[191] Nichols, *Literary Remains*, i, pp. i, xx

Chapter 12

EDWARD'S ILLNESS AND DEATH

In early February 1553 the king contracted a feverish cold.[1] He did not throw off the infection with his customary speed, and on 1 March he was forced to open the new parliament with a ceremony in the great chamber at Whitehall instead of going, as was customary, to Westminster.[2] On the 17th, he was described as being still confined to his room, and looking 'very weak and thin'.[3] He did not go to Greenwich, as he had intended, for Easter, according to the imperial ambassadors because 'he is not entirely recovered yet, and is still troubled by catarrh and a cough'.[4] However, Edward subsequently began to take the air in the park at Westminster whenever the weather was good, although both this exercise and his diet were still carefully monitored by his doctors and physicians.[5]

On 11 April the king felt well enough to move to Greenwich: he travelled by water to the sound of gun salutes from the Tower and from the three ships about to set off on the Newfoundland expedition.[6] But he remained weak, and appeared in public only once during the remainder of April, 'in the gardens, the day after his arrival'.[7] Ominously, Scheyfve, the imperial ambassador heard from what he described as 'a trustworthy source' that the king was 'becoming weaker as time passes and wasting away. The matter he ejects from his mouth is sometimes coloured a greenish yellow and black, sometimes pink, like the colour of blood.'

The doctors were, Scheyfve's informant declared, perplexed by

---

[1] *CSP, Spanish*, xi, 9. He had not been ill earlier, for on 10 January he received his elder sister, Mary, formally at Westminster (J.G. Nichols, ed., *The Diary of Henry Machyn*, Camden Society, xlii, 1848, 301).

[2] Machyn, *Diary*, 32.

[3] *CSP, Spanish*, xi, 17.

[4] Ibid., xi, 22.

[5] Ibid., 32.

[6] Machyn, *Diary*, 33–4.

[7] *CSP, Spanish*, xi, 35.

the king's illness.[8] A week later, according to Scheyfve, they met in conference 'as the King's life was in great danger': the ambassador added that 'the king is declining from day to day so rapidly that he cannot last long'.[9] Although letters written on 7 May by the councillor, William Petre, and by the duke of Northumberland himself, suggested the king's health was improving and that he would soon be able 'to take the air',[10] things did not progress well. On 12 May the imperial ambassador wrote that

> the physicians are now all agreed that [the king] is suffering from a suppurating tumour [apostème] on the lung, or at least his lung is attacked. He is beginning to break out in ulcers; he is vexed by a harsh, continuous cough, his body is dry and burning, his belly is swollen, he has a slow fever upon him that never leaves him. [11]

Although on 17 May the king was able to receive the French ambassadors, they found him weak, and still troubled by a cough.[12] By the end of the month Edward was reported to be 'wasting away daily.... He cannot rest except by means of medicines and external applications; and his body has begun to swell, especially his head and feet. His hair is to be shaved off and plasters are going to be put on his head.'[13] What was going on?

Few contemporaries attempted any diagnosis beyond the customary one of poison:[14] it was a rare royal death in the sixteenth century that was not accompanied by such rumours, which should surely all be discounted. Scheyfve claimed that Edward was suffering from the same disease as that which had killed Henry VIII's illegitimate son, Henry Fitzroy, duke of Richmond, in 1536;[15] it is not, however, known what Richmond suffered from, although rumours of poisoning again abounded. Early in Mary's reign the Venetian ambassa-

---

[8] Ibid.

[9] Ibid., 37.

[10] HMC Salisbury, i, 121; BL, Lansdowne MS 3, fo. 23.

[11] CSP, Spanish, xi, 40.

[12] M. l'abbé de Vertot, ed., Ambassades de Messieurs de Noailles en Angleterre (5 vols, Leyden, 1763), ii, 26–7. See also CSP, Spanish, xi, 44–5.

[13] CSP, Spanish, xi, 45.

[14] See, for example, Machyn, Diary, 35; H. Robinson, ed., Original Letters Relative to the English Reformation (Parker Society, 1846–7), i, 365 (Julius Terentianus); ii. 684 (John Burcher). Burcher claims that the body was so disfigured that another, murdered, youth was substituted for the lying–in-state.

[15] CSP, Spanish, xi, 45.

dor, Soranzo, was to report that Edward had been 'seized with a malady, which the physicians knew to be consumption (fu conosciuta essere da etico)',[16] and this suggestion has been accepted by many later historians.[17] But any diagnosis of tuberculosis rests on a number of questionable assumptions. One of these is the oft-repeated, but quite erroneous belief, that the king had for years suffered from chronic ill health: whatever it was that afflicted Edward, it was not in evidence before early 1553. Tuberculosis progresses comparatively slowly, over a number of years and usually with periods of remission, whereas Edward declined rapidly.[18] Moreover, although there are many accounts of Edward coughing, and descriptions of his sputum, there is hardly any mention of the copious blood that would undoubtedly have been coughed up by a consumptive. But the long descriptions that the imperial ambassadors produced in June offer valuable clues. On 15th they noted that Edward

> is never free from fever, but on the 11th...he was attacked by a violent hot fever, which lasted over 24 hours, and left him weak and still feverish, though not so much so as at first. On the 14th, the fever returned more violent than before...he is at present without the strength necessary to rid him of certain humours which, when he does succeed in ejecting them, give forth a stench. Since the 11th, he has been unable to keep anything in his stomach, so he lives entirely on restoratives and obtains hardly any repose. His legs are swelling, and he has to lie flat on his back.[19]

Four days later they reported that 'the king himself has given up hope, and says he feels so weak that he can resist no longer'.[20] On 24 June Scheyfve told the emperor that Edward

---

[16] *CSP, Venetian*, v, 536.

[17] See, for example, B.L. Beer, *Northumberland: The Political Career of John Dudley, Earl of Warwick and Duke of Northumberland* (Kent, Ohio, 1973), 149; C.E. Challis, 'Presidential Address', *British Numismatic Journal*, lxiii (1993), 173.

[18] Edward's reported symptoms do not match those of miliary tuberculosis, a primary infection, with a 'snowstorm' of foci in the lungs, or generalized throughout the body, which would have proved fatal much more rapidly.

[19] *CSP, Spanish*, xi, 54.

[20] Ibid., 75.

has not the strength to stir, and can hardly breathe. His body no
longer performs its functions, his nails and hair are dropping off,
and all his person is scabby.[21]

All these accounts mention fever, and suggest that the king was
coughing up infected matter that had a foul smell. These symptoms
strongly suggest that Edward developed a chronic infectious disease
in the chest, in technical terms a suppurating pulmonary infection.
Beginning with a 'feverish cold', the infection developed into acute
bilateral bronchopneumonia, almost incapable of treatment in the
days before antibiotics. Now such drugs swiftly control the infection;
but formerly the illness was protracted, commonly damaging the
bronchi and the lungs. The weakened bronchi dilate and fill with
pus and secretions, giving rise to bronchiectasis. As the inflamma-
tion spreads into the lungs, abscesses develop, and from these, foul
purulent sputum is coughed up. Extension into the pleural cavity
causes empyaemia, producing a fluctuating fever, loss of weight and
yet more thick and purulent sputum – all symptoms described in
this case. General septicaemia is the fatal complication of such infec-
tions: the bacteria, and the toxins they produce, attack other vital
organs. By this stage a range of bacteria are involved. The reports of
swelling in the lower body perhaps indicate that during June the
infection caused renal failure. And Scheyfve's accounts can here be
supplemented by a story repeated by the king's first biographer,
Hayward. Hayward said that a 'wise woman' had declared that she
could cure the king, but that Edward had deteriorated in her care:

> his vitall parts were mortally stuffed, which brought him to a diffi-
> cultie of speech and breath, his legs swelled, his pulse failed, his skin
> changed colour, and many other horrid symptomes appeared.[22]

Once infection had spread as widely as this, no one could save the
king: he was to die of a suppurating pulmonary infection which,
within five months, had led to generalized septicaemia with renal
failure.[23]

[21] Ibid., 66.
[22] J. Hayward, *The Life and Raigne of King Edward the Sixth*, ed. B.L. Beer (Kent,
Ohio, 1993), 177.
[23] I am very grateful to Professor Paul Beeson, formerly Nuffield Professor of
Clinical Medicine in the University of Oxford, and to Trevor Hughes for very
valuable advice on these symptoms.

According to the Succession Act of 1544, and to the provisions of Henry VIII's will, the crown was to descend to the Princess Mary if Edward died childless; if Mary died without heir, her half-sister, Elizabeth, was to succeed. Mary's accession would, of course, deal a bitter blow to the duke of Northumberland, and to the Protestant cause, for Mary was fully committed to the old faith, as her vigorous defence of her right to worship according to traditional rites had indicated. The king therefore produced some time in the late spring or early summer – probably soon after the dissolution of his second parliament on 31 March – what he called 'my deuise for the succession', a document that excluded both his half-sisters from the throne, and vested the succession in the descendants of Henry VIII's younger sister, Mary; these descendants were defined initially as the heirs male of Mary's daughter, Frances, duchess of Suffolk, and then the heirs male of her three daughters, the Ladies Jane, Catherine and Mary Grey, and then, failing such issue, to the heirs male of Jane, Catherine and Mary's daughters.[24] However, neither the duchess nor her daughters had any sons at the time when the 'deuise' was written, but this illogical and possibly illegal document, which totally ignored the strong claims of the Scottish line, was soon rendered even more bizarre: by the striking out of one letter and the insertion of two words, the succession was vested, after the non-existent heirs male of the duchess of Suffolk, directly in Jane Grey and her heirs male. It seems likely that this alteration was made after Jane Grey's marriage to Northumberland's son, Lord Guildford Dudley, on 21 May.

It is customary to see Northumberland as the prime mover in all this, since he had too much to lose by Mary's accession, and his daughter-in-law was the main beneficiary. Many contemporaries stressed the extent to which Edward was influenced by the duke, and one French commentator at least was certain that Northumberland, through his 'creatures' in the chamber, had persuaded the king into doing what he wished. The same observer also reported that the 'Precepteur maistre' – probably Cheke – and the bishop of Ely, Thomas Goodrich, who received the king's last confession, also urged him on.[25]

---

[24] Inner Temple, London, Petyt MS, vol. 47, fo. 317. On this, see S.T. Bindoff, 'A Kingdom at Stake, 1553', *History Today*, iii (1953), 642–8. The words 'Lady Janes heirs male' were altered, to 'Lady Jane and her heirs male'. See Plate 24.

[25] BN, Paris, Fonds français 15888, 'Relation de plusieurs particularités d'Angleterre du temps de Henry VIII et d'Edouard son filz tant du faict de la Religion que régime politique', fo. 225.

However, there seems no reason to believe that the king was an unwilling participant in the diversion of the succession. He, too, believed in the Protestant cause, and he had better reason than most to know how firm was Mary's Catholicism. Cranmer later told Mary that the duke had never spoken to him about the scheme, and that it was the king himself and other members of the council who sought to persuade him.[26]

On 12 June the judges were summoned to a meeting with privy councillors at which the planned alteration to the succession was discussed. The judges asked for a few days in which to consult but, finally, the lord chief justice, Montagu, declared that the whole question of the succession was so momentous that the judges dared not become involved 'for the danger of treason'; at this, he later reported, Northumberland 'fell into a great anger and rage, and called [him] traitor before all the Council, and said that in the quarrel of that matter he would fight in his shirt with any man living'.[27] According to Scheyfve, the judges then joined some of the council in suggesting that a better solution would be to allow Mary to succeed only if she promised to make no religious changes, and to retain existing ministers, but this compromise did not command much support.[28]

On 15 June the judges were called before the king, and commanded by him 'with sharp words and angry countenance' to obey his request that they should help him to draw up a will. According to Robert Wingfield, writing only a couple of years later, the king explained why he wished to disinherit Mary, whose accession would bring to an end 'the religion whose fair foundation we have laid', and Elizabeth, the daughter of the adulterous Anne Boleyn; he also praised Jane and Guildford Dudley.[29] The judges then submitted. Their change of heart persuaded others: Archbishop Cranmer, for instance, was later to tell Mary that he had agreed to sign the 'devise' only after he had heard the opinions 'of the Judges and others [the king's] learned counsel in the laws of this realm'.[30]

[26] T. Cranmer, *Miscellaneous Writings and Letters*, ed. J.E. Cox (Parker Society, Cambridge, 1846), 443–4.
[27] *HMC, Report on the MSS of Lord Montagu of Beaulieu* (London, 1900), 4. See also D. MacCulloch, ed., 'The *Vita Mariae Angliae Reginae* of Robert Wingfield of Brantham' (Camden Society, 4th series, xxix, 1984), 248–9 [henceforward: Wingfield, '*Vita Mariae*'].
[28] *CSP, Spanish*, xi, 57.
[29] Wingfield, '*Vita Mariae*', 248–9.
[30] R.W. Heinze, 'I Pray God to Grant that I may Endure to the End', in P. Ayris and D. Selwyn, eds, *Thomas Cranmer: Churchman and Scholar* (Woodbridge, 1993), 263.

Wingfield believed that Montagu's submission was dependent on a personal grant of a general pardon under the great seal, and upon the summoning of parliament to give the 'devise' the authority of statute law.[31] He was probably correct, for on 19 June chancery began to prepare writs for a new parliament to meet on 18 September.

Meanwhile, letters-patent giving effect to the provisions of the 'devise' were drawn up and, between 15 and 21 June, signed by most of the major figures in the government, by judges and legal officials and by a number of prominent London citizens. Later, many of the signatories, including William Cecil, explained at length that they had been bullied by Northumberland into signing both the letters-patent and a separate document undertaking that they would uphold the succession as altered by the king, but few of them gave any clear indication of reluctance at the time. However, one of the judges, Sir James Hales, refused to sign, although he was a committed Protestant,[32] and another, John Gosnold, who had 'put his hand to the royal will, and copied a proclamation for the so-called Queen Jane', very soon repented of his action.[33] The crypto-Catholic earl of Arundel would not sign the undertaking, although he signed the letters-patent. On 4 July the imperial ambassador reported that Shrewsbury, Paulet, Cheyne, Bedford and Arundel had also raised objections to the letters-patent.[34]

Northumberland reinforced his position by a lavish bestowal of lands and titles on those whose support was crucial; thus, the earls of Huntingdon, Bedford, Pembroke, Shrewsbury and Clinton all received substantial grants of land during the month of June.[35] The Tower and other strongholds were secured, soldiers and armaments amassed, and a substantial fleet assembled.[36]

---

[31] Wingfield, 'Vita Mariae', 249. Montagu himself claimed that Northumberland refused to allow the pardon to be sealed (ibid., 294).

[32] G. Burnet, History of the Reformation of the Church of England, ed. N. Pocock (7 vols, 1865), ii, 369–70.

[33] Wingfield, 'Vita Mariae', 248. It is probable that Gosnold, a Suffolk man, was Wingfield's informant (ibid., 294).

[34] CSP, Spanish, xi, 70.

[35] See J. Loach, Parliament and the Crown in the Reign of Mary Tudor (Oxford, 1986), ch. 1 for further details.

[36] See, for example, CSP, Spanish, xi, 72, 99. The French ambassadors offered help at the meeting with the council on 7 July: E.H. Harbison, Rival Ambassadors at the Court of Queen Mary (London, 1940), 45.

Northumberland also made common cause with the French.[37] A special delegation from France was received at court on 28 May, which the imperial ambassadors correctly regarded as sinister.[38] We do not know what was discussed at this meeting since the envoys returned immediately to report in person to the French king, but the very guarded correspondence between the French court and its new ambassador, Noailles, suggests that some plan had been agreed upon.[39] Noailles wanted to speak to Northumberland in person, but the duke was cautious about being seen too often in the company of the French. However, on 26 June, when the king was clearly failing, Northumberland took the extraordinary step of travelling up from Greenwich to visit Noailles secretly at home, and spending a good two hours with him.[40] The duke told the ambassador that Mary had no prospect of succeeding her brother, that the council was in agreement on the change in the succession, and that there was no call for Henry II to feel any anxiety. Such machinations could not be kept secret. On 4 July the imperial ambassador reported that it was being generally suggested that the duke wished to hand England to the French, with whom he was 'negotiating a great deal … in order to make sure of his support and strike terror into the adversaries'.[41]

During these weeks, Edward seems to have been cared for primarily by the chief gentlemen of the privy chamber, Sir Thomas Wroth and Sir Henry Sidney, and by a favoured groom of the chamber, Christopher Salmon.[42] How he spent his time we do not know, although the fact that in a little desk he kept with him were both counters and a silver-gilt box for ink suggests that he and his gentlemen sometimes played board games.[43] On 19 June *A Prayer Sayd in the Kingess Chappell in the Time of his Sicknes, and Mete to be Vsed of all*

---

[37] For a fuller account, see J. Loach, '"A Close League with the King of France": Lady Jane Grey's Proclamation in French and its Part in a Planned Betrayal', *Proceedings of the Huguenot Society*, xxv (1991), 234–43.

[38] For an account of these diplomatic manoeuvres, see Harbison, *Rival Ambassadors*, chs 1–2.

[39] PRO, PRO 31/3/20.

[40] Ibid., Noailles's report of 28 June. Harbison, in his otherwise excellent account of these events, argues that Northumberland was much less enthusiastic about an agreement than were the French (*Rival Ambassadors*, 43–4). Northumberland's visit in itself is enough to invalidate this view.

[41] *CSP, Spanish*, xi, 71.

[42] *APC*, iv. 83, 183.

[43] BL, Harleian MS 1376, fo. 30v.

the Kinges Subiects was published.[44] On 27 June the king showed himself at a window, no doubt to dispel the widespread rumours that he was already dead, but his appearance was 'so thin and wasted' that few observers were cheered.[45] Crowds gathered again on 2 and 3 July at rumours that he would appear, but on the latter day a gentleman of the bedchamber came out and declared that 'the air was too chill'.[46] Finally, between eight and nine o'clock on the evening of 6 July, Edward died in the presence of Wroth, Sidney and Salmon. His doctors, Dr Owen and Dr Wendy, were also present. According to a later French source, it was Goodrich, the reforming bishop of Ely, who received Edward's last confession.[47] *The Prayer of Kynge Edwarde ... Thre Houres afore his Death* was later published.[48] Legend has it that he died in Sidney's arms, and that his last words were, 'I am faint: Lord have mercy upon me, and take my spirit.'[49]

Edward's death was kept secret, just as Henry's had been. The reasons for the secrecy in 1553 were more compelling, since the ground had to be prepared for announcement of the changed succession. Only on 10 July was Jane proclaimed in London.[50] By then Mary, told by some well-wisher of her brother's death, had fled to East Anglia and was gathering troops.[51]

The dramatic events that followed, culminating in Mary's proclamation as queen on 19 July, meant that Edward's funeral did not take place until 8 August. In style the funeral closely followed that provided for Henry VIII, save in the choice of Westminster rather than Windsor as a place of burial.[52] The procession, led by 'a grett company of chylderyn in ther surples', with singing clerks, and twelve of Henry VIII's bedesmen,[53] was watched by Londoners 'wepyng and lamentyng'.[54] Two heralds followed the children, then

---

[44] *RSTC* 7508.
[45] *CSP, Spanish*, xi, 70.
[46] Ibid.
[47] BN, fonds français, 15888, fo. 225.
[48] *RSTC* 7509.
[49] Foxe, vi, 352. For a legend of Edward after his death, see M.E. Cornford, 'A Legend concerning Edward VI', *English Historical Review*, xxiii (1908), 286–90.
[50] Machyn, *Diary*, 35.
[51] See next chapter.
[52] For Henry VIII's funeral, see J. Loach, 'The Function of Ceremonial in the Reign of Henry VIII', *Past and Present*, cxlii (1994), 56–66.
[53] PRO, LC2/41, printed in *Archaeologia*, xii (1796), 334–96, at 393.
[54] Machyn, *Diary*, 39.

a standard with a dragon, the badge of Owen Tudor.[55] A great number of the king's former servants, wearing black, were followed by another standard, this time with a greyhound, a Lancastrian emblem.[56] More officers and heralds followed, and then a third standard, that of a lion,[57] a standard Henry VIII had adopted for his own use. Norroy, king of arms, carried the king's helmet and crest, Clarencieux his target or shield, garter and sword, 'gorgyusly and ryche', and Garter his coat armour.[58] Then came a chariot with 'grett horsses trapyd with velvet to the grond', ridden by nine henchmen dressed in black,[59] each carrying a banner, whilst the horses wore escutcheons. The funeral chariot which followed was covered with cloth of gold and pulled by seven horses.[60] On it, as was customary, lay an effigy, made by Nicholas Bellin of Modena, of the young king, wearing a crown and a great collar, with a sceptre and his Garter ribbon round the leg.[61] Round the coffin were four standards: the Garter, the red rose, Jane Seymour's standard, and one described as that 'of the queen's mother'. A canopy of blue velvet was carried above the coffin.[62] After the chariot came the chief mourner, the lord treasurer, Winchester, on a horse trapped in black velvet, another horse, trapped to the ground in cloth of gold, bearing the master of the horse, and a third horse bearing a man in a suit of armour: the armour and the horse would later be offered to the Church. They were followed by nine hooded henchmen on horses trapped in black velvet.

At Westminster a great hearse,[63] draped in 72 yards of black velvet, had been prepared, 'of eight panes, and thirteen principals';[64] Henry VII's hearse had had only nine principals.[65] No full

---

[55] On the use of the dragon by Tudor kings see S. Anglo, *Images of Tudor Kingship* (London, 1992), 56–60.

[56] H.S. London, *Royal Beasts* (East Knoyle, 1956), 38–41.

[57] PRO, LC2/41.

[58] Machyn, *Diary*, 40.

[59] PRO, LC389.

[60] *Archaeologia*, xii, 391.

[61] PRO, LC2/41, fo. 4v; E101/427/6, fo. 5v.

[62] PRO, LC2/41 (*Archaeologia*, xii, 334–96, esp. 339). There are also warrants for the issue of quantities of cloth in PRO, E101/427/6.

[63] For a note on the meaning of the term 'hearse' at this period, see Machyn, *Diary*, xxix.

[64] Principal: 'An upright pillar or stem having branches to bear tapers'; Pane: 'A piece, width, or strip of cloth' (*OED*).

[65] Bodleian Library, Ashmole MS 857, fo. 431.

contemporary account of the funeral survives, but it appears to have been conducted according to Reformed rites.[66] Mary had commanded 'that the night before the funeral the service for the dead should be said in her chapel in Latin, as is the custom in Rome', and Foxe reports that at the same time a requiem mass, conducted by Gardiner, was held in the Tower, at which the queen was present.[67] It is not certain which cleric preached at the funeral, although many sources mention George Day, bishop of Chichester.[68] Edward's body was afterwards placed in a white marble vault beneath the altar made by Pietro Torrigiano for Henry VII's tomb; the altar was destroyed by Puritans in 1644, but the vault was discovered in 1685 by workmen searching for a suitable site for the burial of Charles II.[69] Not until 1573 do any serious plans seem to have been made for a tomb: then, William Cure of Amsterdam produced a Franco-Italianate monument in marble and bronze incorporating crowns imperial, Tudor roses and fleur-de-lys, to be built, rather surprisingly, next to that of Henry VIII at Windsor. In the event, Henry's tomb (originally constructed for Wolsey) was never finished, and Edward's never begun.[70]

[66] Was Mary persuaded to allow this by Charles V? (*CSP Spanish*, xi, 156).
[67] A. de Guaras, *The Accession of Queen Mary*, ed. R. Garnett (1892), 101. Wingfield, 'Vita Mariae', 272, says that 'a mass for the dead' was said on the day of the funeral. According to Julius Terentianus (Hastings Robinson, ed., *Original Letters Relative to the English Reformation* (Parker Society, Cambridge, 1846), i, 368), and to Foxe (vi, 537) this service was conducted by Stephen Gardiner.
[68] See for instance Foxe, vi, 537. However, in November 1553 Julius Terentianus declared firmly that Cranmer had performed the funeral service (Robinson, ed., *Original Letters*, i, 367–8).
[69] D. Hoak, 'The Iconography of the Crown Imperial', in D. Hoak, ed., *Tudor Political Culture* (Cambridge, 1995), 93.
[70] Ibid., 96–8.

Chapter 13

QUEEN JANE AND QUEEN MARY

At Edward's death on 6 July 1553, Mary seemed an isolated figure, her cause hopeless. Northumberland controlled the capital, with substantial troops at his disposal and the hope of more, should they be needed, from the French king. Most of the privy councillors, many household officials, the mayor and aldermen of London, twenty-two peers, several judges, leading merchants, and the sheriffs of Middlesex, Surrey and Kent had all given their consent to Edward's 'devise'. Yet on 19 July, amidst bonfires and the ringing of bells, Mary herself was proclaimed queen and Edward's wishes were dashed in an astonishing change of fortune.

Mary was transformed from refugee to ruler by the action of gentlemen and nobles in the provinces – in East Anglia, Oxfordshire, Buckinghamshire and the Thames Valley. Hers was a triumph of the counties against the centre; perhaps, as one commentator has put it, the last occasion before 1640 on which a local ruling establishment would 'so unambiguously set itself up against Westminster'.[1] It was made possible by an astonishing omission of Northumberland's: although the government had sought to conceal from the public the fact of Edward's critical illness, and, later, his death, no steps had been taken to secure the person of the princess, who was, according to the statute of 1544 and to Henry's will, his heir. Northumberland and the council were clearly startled when, on 4 July, just before Edward's death, Mary suddenly left her residence, Hunsdon in Hertfordshire,[2] and travelled via Sawston Hall, Cambridgeshire, and Hengrave Hall, Suffolk, to a former Howard property in Norfolk, Kenninghall.[3] There she learned of

[1] D. MacCulloch, 'Introduction', in D. MacCulloch, ed., 'The *Vita Mariae Angliae Reginae* of Robert Wingfield of Brantham' (Camden Society, 4th series, xxix, 1984), 190–1 [henceforward: Wingfield, '*Vita Mariae*'].
[2] A. de Guaras, *The Accession of Queen Mary*, ed. R. Garnett (1892).
[3] S. Haynes, ed., *A Collection of State Papers ... left by William Cecil, Lord Burghley* (1740), 118; *CSP, Spanish*, xi, 70.

Edward's death. On 8 July she summoned to her assistance Sir George Somerset, Sir William Waldegrave and Clement Heigham.[4] The next day she wrote to the council in London formally claiming the throne, and also to Sir Edward Hastings, ordering him to support her in Middlesex and Buckinghamshire.[5] Waldegrave and Heigham arrived, presumably in response to her letters, and so did Sir John Mordaunt, John Sulyard, Sir William Drury and John Bourchier, earl of Bath, the stepfather of young Thomas Kitson, whose hospitality she had enjoyed at Hengrave.[6] The party then moved on to another, and better fortified, Howard property, Framlingham in Suffolk. On 14 July Robert Brown, a baron of the exchequer, arrived at Framlingham with Sir Henry Bedingfield, and they were joined the next day by the earl of Sussex, who had been persuaded by his second son, Henry, to assist Mary, by Sir Nicholas Hare, Sir John Shelton, and a serjeant-at-law, Richard Morgan.[7]

Meanwhile, on 10 July, Jane Grey had been proclaimed in London. Some other towns followed the lead of the capital, but many local authorities appear to have been reluctant to commit themselves in what was rapidly becoming a confused situation: in some towns, such as Ipswich and Coventry, both candidates were proclaimed by rival groups.[8] Northumberland's plan had presumably always assumed that it would be easy to secure Mary's person: her departure from Hunsdon had been a shock. Robert Dudley, sent after Mary, failed to seize her and on 14 July Northumberland himself left London with an army in pursuit.[9] At Ware, the duke met his sons and about 500 men-at-arms: Jane was proclaimed and Mary declared a bastard.[10] A total force of about 3,000 men moved to Cambridge, sacking Sawston Hall on the way.[11] At Cambridge the duke summoned the vice-chancellor of the university, Edwin Sandys, and ordered him to preach a sermon justifying Jane's acces-

[4] BL, Lansdowne MS 1236, fo. 29.
[5] Foxe, vi, 385; J. Strype, *Ecclesiastical Memorials* (London, 1721), III, ii, 1.
[6] J.G. Nichols, ed., *The Chronicle of Queen Jane and Two Years of Queen Mary* (Camden Society, old series, liii, 1852), 4–5; Wingfield, 'Vita Mariae', 254–5.
[7] *APC*, iv. 429–32.
[8] Nichols, *Queen Jane and Queen Mary*, 8, 111; *Victoria County History of Warwickshire*, ii. 442; Wingfield, 'Vita Mariae', 255–6.
[9] *HMC, Third Report* (Bedingfield Papers, London, 1872), appendix 237.
[10] *Calendar of Patent Rolls 1554–5*, 42–3: the pardon of Sir Andrew Dudley.
[11] F. Madden, 'The Narrative of Richard Troughton', *Archaeologia*, xxiii (1831), 41.

sion, which Sandys did the following day.[12] But events were overtaking Northumberland. In Buckinghamshire, Sir Edward Hastings had proclaimed Mary queen, and Sir John Williams did the same in Oxfordshire;[13] by 16 July the situation in these counties was considered by the council to be so grave that troops were dispatched.[14] In East Anglia there appears to have been little enthusiasm for the duke's cause. He set out for Framlingham on 18 July, but grew discouraged.[15] There was a retreat to Bury St Edmunds, where Jane was again publicly declared queen.[16] Northumberland himself returned to Cambridge, where he learned on 19 July that the councillors in London had proclaimed Mary.[17]

Two factors explain Mary's triumph. One is the behaviour of the Privy Council after Northumberland's departure from London. The other is the support that Mary received in both East Anglia, and, a fact less often noticed, in the Thames Valley, for it was the assistance that Mary found amongst provincial nobles and gentry that persuaded the council to abandon Northumberland. After Mary's triumph most councillors claimed that they had always had their doubts about the legality and justice of Northumberland's proceedings, but they had all nevertheless signed the letters-patent bestowing the crown on Jane Grey and all of them except the earl of Arundel had signed an additional engagement promising to keep faith: they clearly believed at the time of Edward's death that Northumberland would be successful. The arrival on 11 July of Mary's letter claiming the throne shook their confidence,[18] which was further undermined the next day by the erroneous rumour that Robert Dudley had been defeated by Mary in battle.[19] The news that the crews of several ships at Ipswich had been persuaded by Henry Jerningham to defect to Mary also worried the council; the Tower chronicler reports that at this information 'eche man then began to pluck in his hornes'.[20] On

---

[12] Foxe, viii, 590.

[13] Nichols, *Queen Jane and Queen Mary*, 8–9.

[14] Ibid., 108.

[15] *Calendar of Patent Rolls, 1553–4* (pardon of Francis Jobson); Madden, 'Narrative of Richard Troughton', 32.

[16] *Calendar of Patent Rolls, 1553–4*, 42.

[17] Wingfield, '*Vita Mariae*', 266.

[18] *CSP, Spanish*, xi, 82.

[19] Ibid., 86.

[20] Nichols, *Queen Jane and Queen Mary*, 8–9, which says the ships were off Yarmouth; *APC*, iv. 295; Wingfield, '*Vita Mariae*', 258 states that the ships were off Ipswich.

14 July certain of the council asked for an interview with the imperial envoys at which they adopted a far more conciliatory line than they had before.[21] The council's letters to the counties suggest a growing despair at the size of the revolt.[22] The first councillor to crack entirely may have been Paulet, who was fetched from his house at midnight on 16 July and escorted into the Tower.[23] But within a few days everything changed. On 19 July Shrewsbury, Bedford, Pembroke, Arundel, Cheyne, Cheke, Paulet, Paget, Mason and other councillors proclaimed Mary.[24] The imperial ambassadors subsequently reported that the councillors had been moved by 'the popular rising, the increase of the Lady Mary's forces and the fact. . .that seven of the best warships had surrendered to her'.[25] The plot to seize the Tower for Mary also seems to have played a part in the change of heart.[26] Thus, it was the information that reached the council about Mary's support in the provinces that persuaded councillors to desert Northumberland.

The behaviour of Arundel is illuminating here.[27] He had protested against the provisions of the letters-patent, having, he said, no desire to see perpetuated the power of a man who had earlier imprisoned and fined him; but in the end he signed. When Northumberland left London in his attempt to capture Mary the earl was said to have expressed his regret at not being able to go with him, 'in whose presence he coulde fynde in his harte to spende his bloode, even at his foote'.[28] Ten days later, however, it was Arundel who came to Cambridge to arrest the duke, replying to Northumberland's valid complaint that whatever he had done had been with the consent of the council only, with the cold observation that 'my lorde . . . ye shoulde have sought for mercy sooner; I must do according to my commandment'.[29] Thus Arundel had been willing to be conciliated as long as Mary appeared powerless, but when he realized that her cause was not a lost one he turned

[21] CSP, Spanish, xi, 88.
[22] Nichols, Queen Jane and Queen Mary, 107–9; APC, iv. 295.
[23] Nichols, Queen Jane and Queen Mary, 9.
[24] Ibid., 11–12; J.G. Nichols, ed., The Diary of Henry Machyn (Camden Society, old series, lxxvii, 1859), 37.
[25] CSP, Spanish, xi, 96.
[26] Nichols, Queen Jane and Queen Mary, 8, 119.
[27] J.G. Nichols, ed., 'The Life of Henry Fitz Allan, Last Earle of Arundell', Gentleman's Magazine, civ (1833), 118–21.
[28] Nichols, Queen Jane and Queen Mary, 7.
[29] Ibid., 10.

with relief to a monarch more likely to be sympathetic to his desires.

The important questions therefore are who supported Mary in the counties and why. To this various answers have been given. Some contemporaries believed that popular support for Mary – 'the popular rising', in the imperial ambassador's words – swayed the county leaders and frightened the council in London.[30] But that does not justify Diarmaid MacCulloch's claim that Mary was carried to victory by a 'groundswell of popular support'.[31] Robert Wingfield in his account of Mary's success uses the terms 'populus', 'plebs', 'vulgus' in a fairly loose way to mean 'non-noble': he was not concerned about sociological exactitude. A study of East Anglian towns shows that court links and self-interest provided some urban support for Northumberland, but that there was nothing resembling a popular movement in support of Mary.[32] The mutiny of the ships' crews sent to Ipswich to arrest Mary was taken by the council as a sign of popular support for her and may well have helped to undermine support for Northumberland; but recently discovered documents reveal that the mutiny resulted from poor conditions in the ships and lack of pay; the crews went over to Mary when they were persuaded to it by Henry Jerningham, a leading member of Mary's household.[33]

The key role in Mary's coup seems, as that last detail suggests, to have been played by noblemen and gentlemen in the counties. The traditional explanation for their behaviour has been that they were profoundly disturbed by any tampering with the established line of the succession and that in any case they much disliked Northumberland's government. But there is little to suggest that Northumberland's government was detested. As we have seen, his methods had been careful, conscientious and conciliatory, making it difficult to see why the 'nation' should have turned against him in 1553. The lower orders had been kept in their places – which appeased the propertied classes – yet had been handled in a traditional but not uncharitable way. If we were to try to see

[30] *CSP, Spanish*, xi, 96.
[31] MacCulloch, 'Introduction', 188.
[32] R. Tittler and S.L. Battley, 'The Local Community and the Crown in 1553: the Accession of Mary Tudor Re-visited', *Bulletin of the Institute of Historical Research*, lvii (1984), 131–9.
[33] J.D. Alsop, 'A Regime at Sea: the Navy and the 1553 Succession Crisis', *Albion*, xxiv (1992), 577–90; Nichols, *Queen Jane and Queen Mary*, 8–9.

Northumberland as his contemporaries saw him in the spring and early summer of 1553, that is before the recantation on the scaffold that so alienated his Protestant friends, we should surely see a charismatic and powerful figure, and one likely to attract support. Of course, no regime can embrace everyone, and certainly some of those who supported Mary may have done so because they were out of favour with Northumberland. This is probably true of Sir Edmund Peckham, whose appearance on the council in Edward's reign had been humiliatingly brief,[34] and of Sir John Williams, whose career in the court of augmentations had ended with accusations of peculation and debt.[35] But others amongst Mary's supporters had prospered under Northumberland. Sir Leonard Chamberlain, for instance, had held high office at the Tower, yet with Peckham he proclaimed Mary and was involved in the plan to march on London and seize the armaments in the palace of Westminster.[36] Thomas Boys had been appointed captain of Deal castle in 1550.[37] Sir William Drury and Sir Henry Bedingfield were amongst the earliest to join Mary, and yet only three months before they had both been recommended by Northumberland's Privy Council as knights of the shire for Suffolk.[38] At a different level, several of Mary's supporters were simply country gentlemen, such as Huddleston – whose house sheltered Mary on her way to Norfolk and was then burnt by Northumberland's troops – who had little interest in advancement at court. Huddleston was rewarded by a place on the Privy Council, as was another of Mary's earliest supporters, the obscure Norfolk squire Sir John Shelton. There is no evidence that either actually attended a meeting. Mary's supporters were not, then, merely the 'outs' of the previous regime, and they were not men who had nothing to lose by a rash attempt to stop Northumberland. Indeed all those involved must have shuddered at the risk they were running of total political and social upheaval: the great success of Northumberland's government had, after all, been the re-establishment of order. Clearly, too, some men did resent the interference with what had been decided by statute and by Henry

---

[34] *Dictionary of National Biography*; D. Hoak, *The King's Council in the Reign of Edward VI* (Cambridge, 1976).

[35] W.C. Richardson, *History of the Court of Augmentations 1534–1554* (Baton Rouge, Louisiana, 1961).

[36] *Dictionary of National Biography*; APC, iv. 293.

[37] *Calendar of Patent Rolls, 1551–2*, 36.

[38] BL, Lansdowne MS 3, fo. 36.

VIII's will, a document for which contemporaries had considerable reverence. Sir John Harington of Exton, Rutland, is said to have gone into his parlour after dinner one day during the crisis, and got out a statute book, which he laid open on the table 'that every man myghte rede hit; and had noted the substaunce of the statute for the declaracion of the Quenes Maiesties ryght to the Crowne of Englond, after the deathe of Kynge Edward'.[39] Arundel, when persuading his colleagues to change sides, is reported to have declared, 'you knowe that by right of succession this Crowne discends upon Mary'.[40] None the less, Harington did not give Mary any active support, and Arundel changed sides not because of Mary's legitimacy but because of the behaviour of the gentlemen in the counties.

It was not, in fact, primarily in terms of legitimacy and legality that contemporaries saw the struggle. The politicians and preachers who presented Jane's cause to the people did so in religious terms. Edward himself, and then Northumberland and Jane, had been at pains to emphasize that support for Jane meant support for Protestantism, whereas support for Mary was support for Catholicism. Even before Edward's death the London preachers were reported to have been harping on such matters 'with a view to make the people ill-disposed towards the Princess',[41] whilst the explanation given by the dying king for his plan to supplant his sister was that if she were 'to possess the kingdome (which almighty God prevent), it would be all over for the religion whose fair foundation we have laid'.[42] Jane's first proclamation argued that Mary, if she were queen, would aim to bring 'this noble, free realm into the tyranny and servitude of the bishop of Rome'.[43] Ridley, in a sermon at Paul's Cross, declared not only that Mary and Elizabeth were bastards but also that Mary wished to subvert 'the true religion'.[44] Northumberland's last words to his colleagues when he left London were a reminder that they were fighting for 'Goddes cause ... the perferment of his worde and the feare of papestry's re-entrance': this, he declared, had been 'the oryginall grounde' of their undertaking.[45] Letters sent by the council into the counties declared that

---

[39] Madden, 'Narrative of Richard Troughton', 31.
[40] Nichols, 'Life of Arundell', 118.
[41] *CSP, Spanish*, xi, 65.
[42] Wingfield, '*Vita Mariae*', 247.
[43] The Queen's College, Oxford: Select cases b228(1).
[44] Foxe, vi, 389.
[45] Nichols, *Queen Jane and Queen Mary*, 6–7.

Mary was stirring up rebellion 'to the great parell and daunger of the utter subversyon of Godes holye worde and of the hole state of this realme' and that Mary's accession would have been followed by 'the bondage of this Realme to the old servitude of the Antichriste of Rome, the subversion of the true preaching of Goddes worde, and of thauncient lawes, usages, and liberties of this realme'.[46] They went on to argue that Mary 'through the counsell of a nombre of obstinate papistes ... forsaketh as by her seditious proclamations may appere the just title of supremacie annexed to thimperial Crowne of this Realme'.[47]

So it is no surprise to find that it was the Catholic gentry of East Anglia and the Thames Valley who actively supported Mary: Protestants, whatever their doubts about Northumberland's behaviour or their convictions about the validity of her title, seldom spontaneously joined her. In Norfolk, where fourteen established magnate families have been identified at the accession of Elizabeth,[48] it was the two most firmly Catholic families who sent representatives to aid her in the shape of Sir Henry Bedingfield of Oxborough, afterwards Elizabeth's gaoler at Woodstock, and Sir Richard Southwell of Wood Rising, whose vehement outburst against heretics later in the reign – 'to the rack with them, one of these knaves is able to undo a whole city'[49] – is an indication of where his religious sympathies lay, despite a career as surveyor of the court of augmentations. Bedingfields and Southwells were to provide support for the old religion for many decades to come. But families such as the Heydons of Baconsthorpe and the L'Estranges of Hunstanton, who had protestant sympathies, did not help Mary.[50] In Norfolk there is nothing to suggest that those who supported her were moved by anything other than religious considerations. The same is true of the Suffolk gentlemen who arrived at Kenninghall and Framlingham: Foxe later described Clement Heigham and John Sulyard as amongst the most violent persecutors of Protestantism in

---

[46] *HMC, Manuscripts of A.J. Finch* (London, 1913), i, 2 ; *HMC Seventh Report* (More–Molyneux Papers, London, 1879), app., 609.

[47] Guildford Museum and Muniment Room, Loseley Correspondence 3/3.

[48] A. Hassell Smith, *County and Court: Government and Politics in Norfolk 1558–1603* (Oxford, 1974), 52.

[49] Foxe, *Acts and Monuments*, vi, 596; vii, 151; viii, 585.

[50] BL, Lansdowne MS 156 is a list of annuities given by Mary for service at Framlingham: those local families whose names do not appear may be presumed not to have helped Mary.

the county.[51] Sir Thomas Cornwallis of Brome was to retire entirely from public life at Elizabeth's accession, whilst Richard Freston had been in trouble for his religious views since 1538.[52]

The list of those swearing loyalty to Mary during those early days, like the list of those receiving rewards for service at Kenninghall and Framlingham, contains Catholic name after Catholic name: William Dormer of Wing, whose daughter became the countess of Feria and who was himself described in 1564 as 'a hinderer of religion',[53] Francis Allen, Gardiner's secretary,[54] Anthony Browne, later Viscount Montagu, and so on.[55] Indeed, when in 1561 Dr Sanders composed a list of Catholic gentlemen who were suffering as a result of the accession of a Protestant monarch it bore an uncanny resemblance to the earlier list of those rewarded in 1553: Browne, Waldegrave, Hastings, Sir Thomas Wharton and Sir Thomas Mordaunt.[56] No nobleman sympathetic to Protestantism supported Mary, and most of those who came to her aid were committed Catholics. The earl of Derby, for example, had opposed the religious changes of Edward's reign.[57] Lord Dacre, who marched south to join Mary, had voted against the 1549 Prayer Book in the House of Lords and was to remain a catholic in Elizabeth's reign,[58] and Lord Windsor, who assisted Hastings in proclaiming Mary in Buckinghamshire,[59] had persistently voted against the religious innovations of the previous reign. Thomas West, Lord Delaware, had opposed both Edwardian Prayer Books as he had earlier opposed the dissolution of the monasteries.[60] The earl of Bath, although he played little part in public affairs in Edward's reign, had voted against the bill for the marriage of priests.[61]

Mary's early support was drawn almost exclusively from the

[51] Foxe, viii, 493, 497, 630.
[52] A. Simpson, *The Wealth of the Gentry* (Cambridge, 1961); *LP*, XIII, i. 964.
[53] *Calendar of Patent Rolls 1554–5*, 181, 211; M. Bateson, ed., 'A Collection of Original Letters from the Bishops to the Privy Council, 1564' (Camden Society, *Camden Miscellany*, London, ix, 1895), 32.
[54] *Calendar of Patent Rolls, 1554–5*, 189.
[55] Ibid., 314.
[56] Catholic Record Society, *Miscellanea*, i (1905), 44–5.
[57] *Lords' Journals*, 5 Jan. 1549, 25 Jan. 1550, 6 Apr. 1552; *HMC, Bedingfield*, iii, 297.
[58] *Lords' Journals*, 15 Jan. 1549; *Camden Miscellany*, ix, 50; *CSP, Spanish*, ix, 107; *APC*, iv. 301.
[59] Nichols, *Queen Jane and Queen Mary*, 8; Wingfield, '*Vita Mariae*', 260.
[60] *Dictionary of National Biography*; *Calendar of Patent Rolls, 1553–4*, 82.
[61] *Lords' Journals*, 10 Feb. 1552.

catholic and the conservative. Given this, it is difficult to argue that those who assisted her did so for any other reason than because they wanted a Catholic ruler. If the appeal of her cause had lain primarily in her legitimacy, or even in her opposition to Northumberland, the religious views of those who helped her would surely have been much more varied. Her opponents had made sure that everyone realized where Mary's sympathies lay. Their propaganda had been effective, for the news of Mary's triumph was often greeted by the restoration of elements of the old faith: Richard Troughton recorded that at Grantham the proclamation of 21 July was accompanied by the singing of a *Te Deum*,[62] as it had been in London. Robert Parkyn in Chester-le-Street noted that when the news of Mary's accession reached Yorkshire 'preastes was commandyde by lordes and knyghttes catholique to say masse in Lattin withe consecration and elevation of the bodie and bloode of Christ under forme of breade and wyne'.[63] Politically aware men knew what the consequences of Mary's accession would be: the error that Northumberland's propagandists had made was to believe that, knowing those consequences, the governing classes would oppose her.

Thus Mary was not making the fatal error of which historians usually accuse her when she assumed that her triumph had proved that Catholicism was still a political force. She may have mistakenly taken the behaviour of certain men in some areas as more typical of the whole country than it actually was, but her conviction that many noblemen and gentlemen would support the restoration of the old religion was not mistaken. She may have overlooked the possibility that men might still be sympathetic to Protestantism, even though they did not actively support Northumberland in his hour of need, but their lack of action in a crisis which both sides had seen as a religious struggle was surely encouraging to her. For Edward the outcome was doubly tragic. Not only had he died young, but his attempt to control the affairs of the kingdom after his death by diverting the succession had come to nothing.

[62] Madden, 'The Narrative of Richard Troughton', 44.
[63] A.G. Dickens, 'Robert Parkyn's Narrative of the Reformation', in *Reformation Studies* (London, 1982), 308.

Chapter 14

ASSESSMENT

For Protestant historians of the sixteenth century, such as John Foxe, Edward VI's reign was a time of lost opportunities. Later historians – A.F. Pollard, Sir John Neale and Sir Geoffrey Elton, for instance – saw Edward's reign, and Mary's too, as a rather uninteresting interlude between the dramatic triumphs of the reigns of Henry VIII and Elizabeth I. The past generation has seen a growing interest in the middle years of the century and the reigns of Edward VI and Mary have begun to be reassessed on their own terms. This book is intended as a contribution to that process.

Edward VI has here emerged rather differently from the picture of him painted by earlier biographers, who saw him primarily as a sickly but pious child, infected with tuberculosis, awaiting his removal to a better and higher place, and dominated by a rigid Protestant faith. Edward was portrayed by his ministers and propagandists as the young Solomon, son of Henry VIII as David, whose task was to complete the rebuilding of the temple of Jerusalem, or the spiritual temple of Christianity in England. Edward was, in the words of Thomas Becon, 'the true Josias, that earnest destroyer of false religion, that fervent setter-up of God's true honour...'[1] Historians have taken the reformer's clarion call as a valid description of Edward's intentions. John Foxe and his publisher, John Day, seeking at the beginning of Elizabeth's reign to describe what they saw as England's inevitable, and triumphant, progress towards Protestantism, continued the imagery of the young Josias and his virtuous land. It was a startlingly successful portrayal: Foxe's *Acts and Monuments*, first printed in English in 1563, and including the famous woodcut of Edward listening closely to Latimer's sermon, was expanded in 1570, and there were fresh editions in 1576, 1583, 1593, 1610 and 1632. It had an immense impact: many in the later

---

[1] J.N. King, *Tudor Royal Iconography: Literature and Art in an Age of Religious Crisis* (Princeton, 1989), 93.

sixteenth and seventeenth centuries mentioned the Bible and Foxe's book in the same breath. The *Book of Martyrs* went with the Pilgrim Fathers to New England, and became part of the American cultural heritage as it already was part of the English. It has over-shadowed all our thinking about Edward and his reign.

But there was a very different side to Edward: far from being sickly until stricken by fatal illness in the last months of his life, he was his father's son, keen on sport and on display, fascinated by tourna-ments and warfare, concerned about his inadequate pocket money. He was a typical aristocratic youth of the sixteenth century. His *Chronicle* records nothing of his religious views, which casts doubts on the depth of his supposed zeal. No sermon – not even that preached by Latimer and immortalized in Foxe's *Actes and Monuments* – is mentioned in it. It is much harder than the conven-tional view has it to document his Protestantism. He supported Hooper in his quarrel with Ridley over his consecration, apparently writing a letter to Cranmer urging that Hooper might be conse-crated without superstition, but if he did intervene, it was not with complete success. He reprimanded his sister Mary for her continued adherence to the mass, and was determined to prevent her from succeeding him as ruler. How far that reflected informed religious conviction rather than a regal desire to be obeyed is, however, more uncertain than the traditional portrait allows. If, as has been argued above, the decisive religious changes in the reign came early, with the removal of images and ornaments, the dissolution of chantries and colleges, and the introduction of a new liturgy in English, then Edward, just nine years old on his accession, cannot have been directly involved in the making of those policies. And if, as he grew older, he clearly associated himself with what we might call the Protestant cause, notably in seeking to exclude Mary from the throne, that perhaps reflects an adolescent's attachment to what he grew up with, to what for him would have been familiar institutions, and to well-loved pastors, notably Archbishop Cranmer. If we do not need to throw away entirely the image of Edward listening with such interest to a sermon, we do need to add to it the image of a boy boasting and showing off about his exploits on a horse, a boy who read books about greyhounds as well as the Scriptures and the clas-sics, a boy who copied out notes about Henry VI's military occu-pation of Normandy. If Edward's commitment to the Protestant cause is seen together with his interest in military matters, perhaps what we have is not so much a godly imp as a 'guerrier de Dieu' in the making.

Edward's youth meant that others had to rule in his name, and
Edward's involvement in government, while beginning to increase,
was never very great. A history of his reign must inevitably be in
large part a history of the government provided by the *de facto* rulers,
Protector Somerset and the duke of Northumberland. War and
financial difficulties were an unenviable inheritance and backcloth
to the reign. An enormous amount of crown land was distributed
amongst the crown's ministers and chief servants during this period:
nearly £0.5 million-worth in the course of the reign. Selected bene-
ficiaries were allowed to bring to the Mint specified amounts of bul-
lion in the form of silver and plate and have it coined into money:
the profits could be enormous. The absence of an ultimate authority meant that periodic disputes occurred between councillors
and noblemen over who should rule. In 1549 large-scale rebellions
in the south-west and in East Anglia seriously weakened Somerset's
government. And in 1553 an attempt was made – which came close
to success – to divert the succession from Mary.

Edward VI's reign was a time of religious change. Archbishop
Cranmer, other bishops, and the foreign refugees exploited the new
opportunities for driving forward religious reform. The changes set
out in the Prayer Books, the dissolution of the chantries, and a series
of instructions to dismantle images and roods, together resulted in
a very radical break, visually and orally, with traditional religion.
Theological developments under Edward would provide a vital reference point in the reign of his sister Elizabeth. Reform from the
top there undoubtedly was. But was that reform implemented? The
work of a generation of Reformation historians – work often done
on a county or diocesan basis – has shown that Edward's Protestant
regime failed to have the total, devastating, impact that previous
generations of historians had assumed: the whole of England did
not, by any means, become Protestant under Edward. The religious
changes of the reign were undoubtedly welcomed by a number of
reforming zealots, especially in London, in other of the larger
towns, and in Kent and Essex, where Protestant enthusiasm was considerable. But elsewhere, especially but not only in the north and
south-west, in the Thames Valley and even in Sussex, many
remained attached to the old religion, conforming outwardly, but,
it may be supposed, not in their hearts. Moreover Edward VI's advisers, like those of Henry VIII, saw the Church primarily as an important source of funding for the state: chantries, church goods,
bishops' lands, the metal from which church bells were cast, and
eventually even the lead from church roofs – all were taken. Under

Edward VI, the boy hailed by reformers as the young Josias and the
new David, the English Church was systematically impoverished and
threatened. This had, of course, important consequences for the
quality of the service it could provide. Despite promises made at the
time of their dissolution, the property of the chantries was not used
to improve low clerical stipends, and pluralism and non-residence
remained rife: many parishes were without the regular, sustained
preaching and instruction that mass conversion required. More
serious still was the drop in the numbers of suitable candidates
coming forward for ordination, which had begun in the 1530s, for
that made it impossible to purge the Church of clergy opposed to
change, or even of men such as those whose woeful ignorance of the
Ten Commandments and the Lord's Prayer was revealed by Bishop
Hooper's visitation of Gloucester in 1551. Moreover, without following in their entirety the romantic notions of pre-Reformation
Catholicism offered to us by Eamon Duffy, I should also suggest that
what Protestantism stood for in the eyes of many parishioners by
1553 must have been looting and sacking, and the stripping by the
state of the objects of beauty which bound them to their locality and
to its past. It is not surprising that so many of them were very ready
to accept the Marian restoration.

The reign of Edward VI, together with that of his sister Mary, has
usually been seen as a time of upheaval, 'the mid-Tudor crisis'.
Faction fighting between ambitious and greedy men supposedly led
to fluctuations of policy that threatened the security of the realm,
or, on another account, saw the triumph of evil (the capitalistic,
hard-faced egocentric Northumberland) over good (the liberal,
compassionate Somerset). But while there were undoubtedly difficulties, the thrust of this book has been to emphasize the more positive features. The political struggles of the reign – Somerset's
elevation in 1547, the fall of Sir Thomas Seymour, the toppling of
Somerset, the emergence of the future duke of Northumberland –
did not degenerate into lasting factional conflicts and, unlike the
mid-fifteenth-century minority of Henry VI, tensions between politicians at the centre never merged with noble and gentry rivalries in
the localities. Arguably the fall of Somerset was evidence not of the
instability of politics at this time, but rather of the stability of a
system that could effectively replace a weak and incompetent ruler
by a strong and competent one. The country's governors, while
doing well for themselves, at the same time strove to do their best to
cope with a myriad social problems. There were fewer fluctuations
in policy than a view of the reign as beset by faction fighting would

suggest: politicians struggled manfully with very similar problems, and came up with very similar solutions. Nationally and locally, in Church and state, there was a remarkable continuity of personnel. The rebellions of 1549, while undoubtedly dangerous, and ultimately bloodily defeated, never turned into endemic *jacqueries*. Religious divisions, though often sharply voiced, never festered into the violent feuds that would characterize later sixteenth-century France. Of course, a measure of good fortune is not the least of the explanation. But those who ruled in Edward's reign, however much they have rightly been criticized, deserve some credit too.

No sound interpretation of the reign can be based on an examination of the period 1547–53 alone: we must look back at the last years of Henry VIII's reign, and forward to Mary's reign and even to the first years of Elizabeth's. The striking impression then is of continuity in the structures and methods of government. That is hardly surprising given the stability of personnel, both at the level of the council, and further down. There were also continuities in the priorities of government – law and order, foreign policies; above all war, with all its consequences in deaths and injuries. The picture of Edward's reign that should be remembered is, then, a rather lurid one: neither white nor black nor grey, but splashed with the crimson of blood spilled in war. It is the picture of a political world preoccupied with the needs of war – armaments, horses, provisioning – and with the costs of war. My picture of Edward himself, above all, is a picture not of the young Josias purifying the Church and destroying idolatry, but of a conventional upper-class youth, delighting in warfare, castle building and in the substitute for war that tournaments provided.

APPENDIX: THE PORTRAITS OF EDWARD VI[1]

BY PENRY WILLIAMS

Several portraits of Edward were painted before he succeeded to the throne, reflecting perhaps the interest shown in him as the heir. The earliest picture of Edward must be the drawing done at his christening; but it can hardly be called a portrait (Plate 2).[2] The first true portrait of him was painted by Holbein and presented by him to Henry VIII on 1 January 1539 (Plate 3).[3] Edward was fortunate in being born in time to be painted by one of the greatest portraitists of the century. The young prince is shown wearing a cap with a feather, one hand pointing to his right, the other holding a rattle. Latin verses written by Richard Morison at the bottom urge him to 'emulate thy father and be the heir of his virtue; the earth contains nothing greater...'. Another copy of this portrait belonged to the earl of Yarborough and was sold in 1929; a third, the property of the duke of Northumberland, is at Syon House. All three versions were probably based upon a drawing by Holbein now at Windsor (Plate 4).[4] Another, slightly later, drawing at Windsor has been attributed to Holbein but is at best doubtful: it shows Edward aged five or six looking straight ahead: on it is based a half-length picture, now in the National Portrait Gallery.[5] There is a third Windsor drawing, certainly not by Holbein but probably of Edward, in profile aged about six, looking to the viewer's left.[6] Various painted portraits seem to be based upon this drawing: there are versions at Wilton and at Woburn and two in the National Portrait Gallery. The first of the latter, showing the prince in half-length holding a flower, is from the

[1] The purpose of this appendix is to provide a general guide rather than a comprehensive list. Such lists exist in J.G. Nichols, *A Catalogue of the Portraits of Edward VI* (London, 1859), L. Surry, *The Portraits of Edward VI* (Portsmouth, 1925), R. Strong, *Tudor and Jacobean Portraits* (2 vols, London, 1969), i, 87–94, R. Ormond, M. Rogers and A. Davies, *Dictionary of English Portraiture* (4 vols, London, 1979), i.
[2] College of Arms MS M6.
[3] Now in the National Library of Art, Washington, DC, Andrew Mellon Collection. I am grateful to Susan Foister for the translation.
[4] K.T. Parker, *The Drawings of Hans Holbein* (Oxford and London, 1945), 49, pl. 46.
[5] Ibid., 55, pl. 71. NPG 1132. Strong, *Tudor and Jacobean Portraits*, ii, pl. 165.
[6] Parker, *Drawings of Holbein*, 58, pl. 65.

studio of William Scrots and is similar to several other versions.[7] The
second of the Portrait Gallery versions is the remarkable anamorphosis by
Scrots, Holbein's successor as King's Painter (Plate 5). [8] Seen from the
front, the head is heavily distorted with an elongated nose, but viewed from
the proper angle through a small hole in an iron bar it becomes a recog-
nizable portrait.

The prototype for portraits of Edward as king was actually painted by an
unknown artist, just before he came to the throne (Plate 6). [9] It was plainly
influenced by Holbein's great portrait for Whitehall Palace of Henry VII,
Henry VIII, Elizabeth of York and Jane Seymour. Edward is shown very
much in his father's pose and image, looking straight at the viewer with his
left hand grasping a dagger. The principal portraits of Edward when king
are by Scrots and are similarly linked to the Whitehall picture but more
heavily influenced by the artistic world of the Habsburg court. In March
1552 Scrots was paid for two of these which were sent to the English ambassadors in France, presumably in connection with marriage negotiations
(Plate 7). [10] Many copies of the Scrots portrait exist, in country houses and
in college collections as well as overseas. Among four unique marble busts
of Tudor monarchs made for Lord Lumley and recorded in an inventory of
1590 is one of Edward as a young man, perhaps copied from the coronation
medallion of 1547. It was certainly carved after the accession of Elizabeth.[11]

Several group portraits show Edward as a member of the Tudor family.
The earliest, painted around 1545, usually known as *The Family of Henry
VIII*, depicts Henry, Jane Seymour and the young Edward seated in a room
in Whitehall Palace, with the two princesses, Mary and Elizabeth, each
standing to one side, separated from the central group by pillars (Plate 8).[12]
Linked with this picture in type is the later *Allegory of the Tudor Dynasty*,
painted around 1572, and attributed to Lucas de Heere. Henry again dominates the picture and sits without a queen. Edward is shown kneeling at
Henry's left side, partly obscured by the larger and dominating figure of
Elizabeth, who enters from the right-hand side of the picture hand in hand
with Peace trampling the instruments of war underfoot. Plenty follows
behind with a cornucopia of fruits. On the other side of Henry are Mary
and Philip, with smaller images and accompanied by Mars accoutred for
war (Plate 9). [13] The message is plain.

[7] NPG 442; Strong, *Tudor and Jacobean Portraits*, ii, pl. 168.

[8] NPG 1299; Strong, *Tudor and Jacobean Portraits*, i, 88–90; ibid., ii, pls 169, 170.

[9] It is in the Royal Collection: Strong, *Tudor and Jacobean Portraits*, i, 92; ibid.,
ii, pl. 171, and see also pl. 167.

[10] Ibid., ii, pl. 172. See also pl. 173. Plate 172 is now in the Louvre (see ibid.,
i, 93–4). The left ear in both portraits by Scrots bears a disturbing resemblance
to that of Mr Spock in the TV programme *Star Trek*.

[11] K. Hearn, ed., *Dynasties. Painting in Tudor and Jacobean England 1530–1630*
(London, 1995), 84, pl. 37.

[12] The picture is now in the Royal Collection: C. Lloyd and S. Thurley, *Henry
VIII: Images of a Tudor King* (Oxford, 1990), 36–7, pls 1, 35.

[13] This picture is at Sudeley Castle, Gloucestershire; Lloyd and Thurley, *Henry
VIII*, 40, pl. 55.

A third picture of Edward with his father is more problematic. This is *Edward VI and the Pope*. Henry is propped up on his pillows in an elaborately carved bed, pointing at Edward, who is seated on a throne beneath a cloth of estate. At his feet lies an open book, with a text from Isaiah, and below that the Pope is slumped, with the text 'All Fleshe is Grasse' on his breast. To the right of Edward is a bearded man standing, with several men, presumably councillors, seated at a table. Above them is an inset scene of soldiers pulling down a statue and smashing images (Plate 10).[14] The message of Protestant Reformation, anti-popery and iconoclasm is clear enough; but the problem lies in the date. Until lately it was supposed that the picture was painted shortly after Edward's accession in order to encourage reform. Dr Margaret Aston has, however, argued that the painting contains unmistakable references, in particular a remarkable bedpost, to a print by Maerten van Heemskerck, published in 1564, and proposes that the picture was commissioned in 1567–8, either to remind Elizabeth of the need to take up the cause of true religion or to warn the duke of Norfolk of the dangers to England of his proposed marriage to Mary Queen of Scots.[15] Dr Loach has, however, cast some doubt on this account. There is nothing in the painting to link it with the reign of Elizabeth in general, nor with the Howard family in particular. The identity of many of the councillors in the picture is uncertain – especially those Aston supposes to be Cuthbert Tunstal, bishop of Durham, and Thomas Seymour, Protector Somerset's younger brother – and has to be deduced from other portraits whose own dating and provenance are themselves debatable. The new dating depends entirely upon the identification of the bedpost and a column with the same items in the Heemskerck engraving. While Dr Aston's scholarship and reasoning make an intriguing case, even here some doubts may be voiced: maybe there was a common source for both pictures; maybe it was Heemskerck who was influenced by this painting; or perhaps the picture of Edward was altered after it was first painted. Dr Loach concludes that 'the possibility remains that the picture (or some earlier version of it) was painted, as we have always supposed, early in Edward's reign, and that it was then intended, as the casual observer might assume, to encourage the king and his council in their struggles against the pope and all his works'.[16]

A contemporary picture, *The Coronation of Edward VI*, now exists only in a later copy. The original was executed as a mural at Cowdray House, Sussex, in 1547 or 1548, on the orders of Sir Anthony Browne, Master of the Horse, who accompanied the king in the procession. Cowdray House

[14] NPG, no. 4615.

[15] M. Aston, *The King's Bedpost. Reformation and Iconography in a Tudor Group Portrait* (Cambridge, 1993).

[16] J. Loach, review in *English Historical Review*, cxi (1996), 704–5. R. Strong, *The Tudor and Stuart Monarchy. Pageantry, Painting and Iconography* (3 vols, Woodbridge, 1995), i, 86–7, accepts Aston's re-dating of the picture, placing it a little later, in the 1570s. He considers, however, that most of her other conclusions are conjectural, in particular her suggestions about the purposes of the picture.

was destroyed by fire in 1793 and we have to depend on a drawing by Samuel Hieronymous Grimm in 1785, now owned by the Society of Antiquaries (Plate 11).[17] There is a fine miniature at Windsor of Edward VI at either the opening or closing of parliament in 1553 (Plate 12).[18] Edward is shown seated in majestic isolation on the throne in the House of Lords, with the lord chancellor and the lord treasurer standing bareheaded behind a bench on either side of him. Garter king-of-arms, together with three figures carrying the cap of state, the sword of state and the marshal's gilt rod stand in front of the throne. The chancellor's red woolsack is placed in front of them, vacant while Edward is present. Opposite the chancellor's woolsack the clerks of parliament sit at a table, with the judges and royal councillors on two other woolsacks to their left and right. Behind this group, the bishops are seated to the king's right, with the lay peers on his left; there is a bench facing the king for additional lay peers. The Commons seem to be just edging into the picture at top right.

Finally, among the group pictures, are two showing Edward presenting charters to the London hospitals. They are reminiscent of the better-known picture of Henry VIII giving a royal charter to the Barber-surgeons. The first of these shows the young king handing the lord mayor his grant of the royal palace of Bridewell, the second records the grant of a charter, also presented to the lord mayor, for the three royal hospitals of Christ's, Bridewell and St Thomas's. Both are probably seventeenth-century or later in date.[19]

Several portrait engravings were made of Edward during his reign and many more after his death. The best known of these is probably the picture of Latimer preaching to the court in 1549 from Foxe's *Acts and Monuments*. Edward is shown seated at an open window, listening attentively to the words of the great preacher (Plate 13).[20] Elsewhere in *Acts and Monuments* he is portrayed handing a bible to his bishops. There is a fine engraving of him, taken from the Scrots portrait, in the frontispiece to the 1552 edition of Tyndale's *New Testament* (Plate 14).[21]

Many portraits of Edward have survived on formal documents, such as plea rolls and charters. With a few exceptions these do not attempt any form of likeness and are simply iconic. They contrast sharply with the major painted portraits of Edward as king, which were designed to be sent abroad to foreign rulers and therefore conformed to contemporary continental styles.[22]

---

[17] Lloyd and Thurley, *Henry VIII*, 54–6, pl. 39. Although the picture is known as the Coronation Procession, it actually shows Edward's entry into London from the Tower the previous day. An engraving of this drawing by James Basire was published in 1786.

[18] This is in the *Dethick Register of the Order of the Garter 1551–1558* in the Royal Library, Windsor Castle. See Lloyd and Thurley, *Henry VIII*, 43, fig. 33.

[19] Strong, *Tudor and Jacobean Portraits*, i, 94. See above, 100, for comments on Edward's supposed foundation of Bridewell.

[20] Cf. 135, above, on this plate.

[21] King, *Tudor Royal Iconography*, 96; cf. 97, 99; and Aston, *King's Bedpost*, 132.

[22] E. Auerbach, *Tudor Artists* (London, 1954), ch. 3.

Portraits on medals and coins are more interesting. The lead coronation medal has a fine portrait of Edward, adapted from one of the Windsor drawings. Most of the coins bear a simple head-and-shoulders image in profile, with the king wearing a crown. The gold sovereign of 1551–2 has a half-length image of Edward with the orb and sword of state. Most impressive of all is the silver crown of 1552. In his *Chronicle* for 24 September 1551, Edward records that it had been agreed that the crown and half-crown 'should be a king on horseback armed with a naked sword hard to his breast'. The crown shows that the order was carried out (Plate 15). [23]

Two points stand out after looking at the various portraits of Edward. First, the image presented was closely related to that of his father: the commanding presence dominates the space. Second, in spite of the shortness of the reign, a very large number of portraits survives, the majority from 1558. Portraits of Mary, by contrast, are much fewer. Edward was, so to speak, on the winning side, a builder of the Protestant Reformation in England, and he has been honoured as such.

[23] W.K. Jordan, ed., *The Chronicle and Political Papers of King Edward VI* (London, 1966), 83; C.E. Challis, *The Tudor Coinage* (Manchester, 1978), 213, fig. 40; see also figs 24, 25, 35, 39

BIBLIOGRAPHY

The place of publication is London unless otherwise stated.

I. MANUSCRIPT SOURCES

London, British Library
Additional MSS: 5464; 9000; 10169; 11043; 46348; 48018; 48023; 48126.
Cotton MSS: Nero C. x; Titus B. ii; Vitellius C. x; Vitellius F. v.
Egerton MS: 3026.
Harleian MSS: 246; 249; 523; 2194; 1376; 1419A;1576; 6989; 7376.
Lansdowne MSS: 3; 156; 238; 1236; Lansdowne Roll 14.
Royal MSS: 8 B. vii; 16 E. xxxii; 17 C. x; 20 A. xiv; Appendix 89.
Stowe MSS: 571; 579.

London, College of Arms
MS M6: Edward's Christening.
MS I, 7: Edward's Coronation.

London, Inner Temple
Petyt MS 538, vol. 47: Edward's 'Devise'.

London, Public Record Office
E 101/426/6, 8; 427/ 6: King's Remembrancer, various accounts.
E 23/4/: Henry VIII's Will.
E 351/1951; 2932; 3326: Exchequer, declared accounts (Pipe Office).
LC 2/2; 41: Lord Chamberlain's Department, special events.
SP 10: State Papers, Domestic, Edward VI.
SP 46: State Papers, Domestic, Supplementary.

London, Society of Antiquaries
MS 123: Edward's Coronation.

Oxford, Bodleian Library
Ashmole MS 817: Edward's Coronation.
Ashmole MS 857: Henry VII's Funeral.
Ashmole MS 861: Events at Court, 1550.
MS Mus. Sch. e. 420–2: Chapel Royal.

Oxford, The Queen's College
Select Cases, b228 (1): Proclamation of Queen Jane.

Guildford Museum and Muniment Room
Loseley Correspondence 3/3: Letters from the Council to the counties, 1553.

Paris, Bibliothèque Nationale
Fonds français, 15888: Unknown French Observer on Edward's Court.

II. PRINTED SOURCES

The Acts of the Privy Council of England, ed. J.R. Dasent (46 vols, 1890–1964).
Ambassades en Angleterre de Messieurs de Noailles, ed., R.A.Vertot and C. Villaret (5 vols, Leyden, 1763).
BRINKELOW, H., *The Complaynt of Roderyck Mors*, ed. J. Meadows Cooper (*Early English Text Society*, extra series, xxii, 1874).
Calendar of the Patent Rolls, ed. R.H. Brodie (5 vols, 1924–9).
Calendar of State Papers, Domestic, 1547–1590 (2 vols, 1856–72).
Calendar of State Papers, Domestic, Edward VI, ed. C.S. Knighton (1992).
Calendar of State Papers, Foreign, Edward VI and Mary, ed. W.B. Turnbull (2 vols, 1861).
Calendar of State Papers, Spanish, ed. M.A.S. Hume and R. Tyler, ix–xi (1912, 1914).
Calendar of State Papers ... Venice, v, ed. R. Brown (1873).
CALVIN, J., *An Epistle of Godly Consolacion*, English trans., 1550 (RSTC 4407).
The Chronicle and Political Papers of King Edward VI, ed. W.K. Jordan (1966).
The Chronicle of Queen Jane and Two Years of Queen Mary, ed. J.G. Nichols (Camden Society, liii, 1852).
'A Collection of Original Letters from the Bishops to the Privy Council, 1564', ed. M. Bateson (Camden Society, *Camden Miscellany*, ix, 1895).
A Collection of State Papers ... at Hatfield, ed. S. Haynes (1740).
'"The Commoyson in Norfolk, 1549": A Narrative of Popular Rebellion in Sixteenth-Century England', ed. B.L. Beer, *Journal of Medieval and Renaissance Studies*, vi (1976).
Correspondance Politique de MM de Castillon et de Marillac, ed. J. Kaulek (Paris, 1885).
Correspondance Politique de Odet de Selve, Ambassadeur de France en Angleterre (1546–1549), ed. G. Lefèvre-Pontalis (Paris, 1888).
CRANMER, T., *Miscellaneous Writings and Letters*, ed. J.E. Cox (2 vols, Parker Society, Cambridge, 1844).
DE GUARAS, A.,*The Accession of Mary Tudor*, ed. R. Garnett (1892).
The Diary of Henry Machyn, ed. J.G. Nichols (Camden Society, xlii, 1848).
A Discourse of the Common Weal of this Realm of England, ed. E. Lamond (Cambridge, 1929).
Documents relating to the Revels at Court in the Time of King Edward VI and Queen Mary, ed. A. Feuillerat (Louvain, 1914).

Edward VI and the Book of Common Prayer, ed. A. Gasquet and E. Bishop (revised edn, 1928).

English Coronation Records, ed. L.G. Wickham Legg (1901).

Epistolae Tigurinae, ed. H. Robinson (2 vols, Parker Society, Cambridge, 1842).

FABYAN, R., *Cronycle* (1559).

Fêtes et Cérémonies au Temps de Charles Quint, ed. J. Jacquot (2 vols, Paris, 1960).

Four Supplications, ed. J.M. Cowper (Early English Text Society, extra series, xiii, 1871).

FOXE, J., *The Acts and Monuments*, ed. J. Pratt (8 vols, 1870).

GRAFTON, R., *Chronicle or History of England*, ed. H. Ellis (2 vols, 1809).

HARDING, T., *A Reiondre to M. Iewels Replie* (Antwerp, 1566).

Historical Manuscripts Commission, Calendar of the Manuscripts of the Marquis of Salisbury at Hatfield House (24 vols, 1883–1976).

——, *Calendar of the MSS of the Marquis of Bath at Longleat, iv, Seymour Papers* (1968).

——, *Report on the MSS of Lord Montagu of Beaulieu* (1900).

——, *Report on the Records of the City of Exeter* (1916).

——, *Report on the MSS of A.G. Finch* (1913).

——, *Third Report, Bedingfield Papers* (1872).

——, *Seventh Report*, appendix, *More Molyneux Papers* (1879).

——, *Twelfth Report*, appendix iv, *Calendar of the MSS of the Duke of Rutland at Belvoir Castle* (London, 1888).

——, *Thirteenth Report*, appendix iv, *MSS of the Corporation of Hereford* (1892).

The Inventory of King Henry VIII, I: The Transcript, ed. D. Starkey (1998).

Journals of the House of Lords, beginning anno primo henrici octavo (1771).

LANQUET, T., *An Epitome of Chronicles* (2nd edn, 1559).

LELAND, J., *De Rebus Britannicis Collectanea*, ed. T. Hearne (6 vols, Oxford, 1715).

Letters and Papers, Foreign and Domestic, of the Reign of Henry VIII, ed. J. S. Brewer, J. Gairdner and R.H. Brodie (23 vols, in 38 parts, 1862–1932).

'The Letters of Richard Scudamore to Sir Philip Hoby', ed. S. Brigden (Camden Society, 4th series, xxix, 1990).

Letters of Royal and Illustrious Ladies of Great Britain, ed. M.A.E. Wood (3 vols, 1846).

The Letters of Stephen Gardiner, ed. J.A. Muller (Cambridge, 1933).

'The Letters of William, Lord Paget of Beaudesert, 1547–1563', ed. B.L. Beer and S.N. Jack (Camden Society, 4th series, xiii, 1974).

The Life and Raigne of King Edward the Sixth by John Hayward, ed. B.L. Beer (Kent, OH, 1993).

'The Life of Henry Fitz Allan, last Earl of Arundell', ed. J.G. Nichols, *Gentleman's Magazine*, civ (1833).

The Lisle Letters, ed. M. St C. Byrne (6 vols, Chicago, 1980).

The Literary Remains of King Edward VI, ed. J.G. Nichols (2 vols, 1857).

MEIGRET, L., *Le Tretté de la Grammere Francoeze* (Paris, 1550).

Mémoires de la vie de François de Scépeaux, sire de Vieilleville, xxvi–xxvii of *Collection complète de mémoires relatif à l'histoire de France*, ed. C.-B. Petitot (Paris, 1822).

A Message sent by the Kynges Maiestie to certain of his People assembled in Devonshire (RSTC 7506, 1549).

'The Narrative of Richard Troughton', ed. F. Madden, *Archaeologia*, xxiii (1831).

Original Letters relative to the English Reformation (Zurich Letters), 1537–1558, ed. H. Robinson (2 vols, Cambridge, 1847).

The Report of the Royal Commission of 1552, ed. W.C. Richardson (Morgantown, WV, 1974).

'Robert Parkyn's Narrative of the Reformation', in A.G. Dickens, *Reformation Studies* (1982).

RYMER, T., *Foedera* (3rd edn, 1741).

The Sermons of Hugh Latimer, ed. G.E. Corrie (Parker Society, Cambridge, 1844).

A Short Title Catalogue of Books printed ... 1475–1640, ed. A.W. Pollard and G.R. Redgrave, revised by W.A. Jackson et al. (3 vols, 1976–91).

SOTHERTON, N., *Commoyson*, ed. S. Yaxley (Stibbard, 1987).

State Papers published under the authority of His Majesty's Commissioners, King Henry VIII (11 vols, 1830–52).

Statutes of the Realm, ed. A. Luders et al. (11 vols, 1810–28).

STRYPE, J., *Ecclesiastical Memorials, Relating Chiefly to Religion and the Reformation* (3 vols in 6 parts, Oxford, 1822).

——, ed., *Memorials of Thomas Cranmer* (2 vols, Oxford, 1840).

Trevelyan Papers prior to AD 1558, ed. J.P. Collier (Camden Society, lxvii, 1857).

Trevelyan Papers, 1446–1643, ed. J.P. Collier (Camden Society, lxxxiv, 1862).

Troubles Connected with the Prayer Book of 1549, ed. N. Pocock (Camden Society, new series, xxxvii, 1884).

Tudor Economic Documents, ed. R.H. Tawney and E. Power (3 vols, 1924).

Tudor Royal Proclamations, ed. P.L. Hughes and T.F. Larkin (3 vols, New Haven and London, 1964, 1969).

Two London Chronicles, ed. C.L. Kingsford (Camden Society, 3rd series, xviii, 1910).

'The *Vita Mariae Angliae Reginae* of Robert Wingfield of Brantham', ed. D. MacCulloch (Camden Society, 4th series, xxix, 1984).

WERDMUELLER, O., *A Spyrytuall and Moost Precyouse Pearle*, trans. M. Coverdale (RSTC 25255, 1550).

The Westminster Chronicle, ed. L.C. Hector and B.F. Harvey (Oxford, 1982).

WRIOTHESLEY, C., *A Chronicle of England*, ed. W.D. Hamilton (2 vols, Camden Society, new series, xi, parts i and ii, 1875, 1877).

The Writings of John Bradford, ed. A. Townsend (Parker Society, Cambridge, 1848–53).

III. SECONDARY SOURCES

ADAIR, E.R., 'William Thomas. A Forgotten Clerk of the Privy Council', in *Tudor Studies*, ed. R.W. Seton-Watson (1924).

ALSOP, J.D., 'The Revenue Commission of 1552', *Historical Journal*, xxii (1979).

——, 'A Regime at Sea. The Navy and the 1553 Succession Crisis', *Albion*, xxiv (1992).

ANGLO, S., *Spectacle, Pageantry and Early Tudor Policy* (Oxford, 1969).

——, *Images of Tudor Kingship* (1992).

ASTON, M., *The King's Bedpost: Reformation and Iconography in a Tudor Group Portrait* (Cambridge, 1993).

AUERBACH, E., *Tudor Artists* (1954).

BAILEY, D.S., *Thomas Becon and the Reformation of the Church in England* (Edinburgh, 1952).

BALDWIN, T.W., *Shakespeare's Smalle Latine and Lesse Greeke* (2 vols, Urbana, 1944).

BEER, B.L., *Rebellion and Riot: Popular Disorder in England during the Reign of Edward VI* (Kent, OH, 1982).

——, *Northumberland: The Political Career of John Dudley, Earl of Warwick and Duke of Northumberland* (Kent, OH, 1973).

——, and NASH, J., 'Hugh Latimer and the Lusty Knave of Kent. The Commonwealth Movement of 1549', *Bulletin of the Institute of Historical Research*, lii (1979).

BELLAMY, J., *The Tudor Law of Treason* (1979).

BERKMAN, J., 'Van der Delft's Message. A Reappraisal of the Attack on Protector Somerset', *Bulletin of the Institute of Historical Research*, liii (1980).

BERNARD, G.W., *The Power of the Early Tudor Nobility: A Study of the Fourth and Fifth Earls of Shrewsbury* (Brighton, 1985).

——, 'The Fall of Anne Boleyn', *EHR*, cvi (1991).

——, ed., *The Tudor Nobility* (Manchester, 1992).

——, 'The Downfall of Sir Thomas Seymour', in *The Tudor Nobility*, ed. G.W. Bernard (Manchester, 1992).

BINDOFF, S.T., *Kett's Rebellion* (1949).

——, ed., *The History of Parliament. The House of Commons, 1509–1558* (3 vols, 1982).

BIRRELL, T.A., *English Monarchs and their Books from Henry VIII to Charles II* (1987).

BLOMEFIELD, F., *An Essay towards a Topographical History of the County of Norfolk* (Norwich, 1745).

BRADDOCK, R.C., 'The Royal Household, 1540–1560: A Study of Office-Holding in Tudor England' (PhD thesis, Northwestern University, 1971).

BRENCHLEY, W., *England as seen by Foreigners in the Days of Elizabeth and James* (1865).

BRENNAN, G., and STATHAM, E.P., eds, *The House of Howard* (2 vols, 1907).

BRIGDEN, S., *London and the Reformation* (Oxford, 1989).

——, 'Henry Howard, Earl of Surrey, and the "Conjured League"', *Historical Journal*, xxxvii (1994).

BROOKS, C.W., *Pettyfoggers and Vipers of the Commonwealth: The 'Lower Branch' of the Legal Profession in Early Modern England* (Cambridge, 1986).

BUISSERET, D., ed., *Monarchs, Ministers and Maps* (Chicago and London, 1992).

BURNET, G., *History of the Reformation of the Church of England*, ed. N. Pocock (7 vols, 1865).

BUSH, M.L., *The Government Policy of Protector Somerset* (1975).

——, 'The Lisle-Seymour Land Disputes', *Historical Journal*, ix (1966).

——, 'Tax Reform and Rebellion in Early Tudor England', *History*, lxxvi (1991).

CALDWELL, J., *The Oxford History of English Music* (Oxford, 1991).

CHALLIS, C.E., *The Tudor Coinage* (Manchester, 1978).

——, 'Presidential Address', *British Numismatical Journal*, lxiii (1993).

CHAPMAN, H., *The Last Tudor King: A Study of Edward VI* (Bath, 1958).

CLARK, P., *English Provincial Society from the Reformation to the Revolution: Religion, Politics and Society in Kent, 1500–1640* (Hassocks, 1977).

CLEBSCH, W., *England's Earliest Protestants* (New Haven, 1964).

COLEMAN, C., and STARKEY, D., eds, *Revolution Reassessed* (Oxford, 1986).

COLLINS, A.J., *Jewels and Plate of Queen Elizabeth I* (1956).

COLLINSON, P., *Godly People* (1983).

COLVIN, H.M., *The History of the King's Works, Vol. IV: 1485–1660* (1982).

CORNFORD, M.E., 'A Legend concerning Edward VI', *EHR*, xxiii (1908).

CORNWALL, J., *Revolt of the Peasantry* (1977).

COWELL, H.J., 'The French Walloon Church at Glastonbury, 1550–1553', *Proceedings of the Huguenot Society*, xiii (1928).

CROSS, C., 'Oxford and the Tudor State, 1509–1558', in *The History of the University of Oxford*, iii, ed. J. McConica (Oxford, 1986).

DAVIES, C.S.L., 'Slavery and Protector Somerset: the Vagrancy Act of 1547', *Economic History Review*, second series, xix (1966).

DELABORDE, J., *Gaspard de Coligny* (3 vols, Paris, 1879).

de MOLEN, R.L., 'The Birth of Edward VI and the Death of Queen Jane', *Renaissance Studies*, iv (1990).

DEWAR, M., *Sir Thomas Smith: A Tudor Intellectual in Politics* (1964).

DORMER, E.W., *Gray of Reading* (Reading, 1923).

DOWLING, M., *Humanism in the Age of Henry VIII* (Beckenham, 1986).

DUFFY, E., *The Stripping of the Altars: Traditional Religion in England, c.1400– c.1580* (New Haven and London, 1992).

ELTON, G.R., *England under the Tudors* (1955).

——, *Policy and Police* (Cambridge, 1972).

——, 'Reform and the "Commonwealthmen" of Edward VI's Reign', in *The English Commonwealth, 1547–1640,* ed. P. Clark et al. (Leicester, 1979).

——, 'Tudor Government: the Points of Contact: I, Parliament', *Transactions of the Royal Historical Society,* fifth series, xxiv (1974), reprinted in id., *Studies in Tudor and Stuart Politics and Government,* (4 vols, Cambridge, 1974–83) iii.

FISHER, F.J., 'Commercial Trends and Policy in Sixteenth-Century England', *Economic History Review,* x (1940).

GAIRDNER, J., *Lollardy and the Reformation* (4 vols, London, 1908–13).

GORHAM, G.C., *Gleanings of a Few Scattered Ears* (1857).

GOULD, J.D., *The Great Debasement* (Oxford, 1970).

GUNDESHEIMER, W. L., *Life and Works of Louis le Roy* (Geneva, 1966).

GUNN, S.J., 'The Courtiers of Henry VII', *EHR,* cviii (1993).

GUY, J., *Tudor England* (Oxford, 1988).

HAMILTON, D., 'The Household of Queen Katherine Parr' (University of Oxford DPhil. thesis, 1992).

HARBISON, E.H., *Rival Ambassadors at the Court of Queen Mary* (1940).

HASSELL SMITH, A., *County and Court: Government and Politics in Norfolk, 1558–1603* (Oxford, 1974).

HEAL, F., *Of Prelates and Princes: A Study of the Economic and Social Position of the Tudor Episcopate* (Cambridge, 1980).

HEARN, K., ed., *Dynasties: Painting in Tudor and Jacobean England, 1530–1630* (1995).

HEINZE, R.W., *The Royal Proclamations of the Tudor Kings* (Cambridge, 1976).

——, 'I pray to God that I may endure to the end', in *Thomas Cranmer, Churchman and Scholar,* ed. P. Ayris and D. Selwyn (Woodbridge, 1993).

HOAK, D.E., *The King's Council in the Reign of Edward VI* (Cambridge, 1976).

——, 'Rehabilitating the Duke of Northumberland: Politics and Political Control, 1549–1553', in *The Mid-Tudor Polity,* ed. J. Loach and R. Tittler (1980).

——, 'The King's Privy Chamber, 1547–1553', in *Tudor Rule and Revolution,* ed. D. Guth and J. McKenna (Cambridge, 1982).

——, ed., *Tudor Political Culture* (Cambridge, 1995).

——, 'The Iconography of the Crown Imperial', in *Tudor Political Culture,* ed. Hoak (Cambridge, 1995).

HOLMES, M.A, 'New Light on St Edward's Crown', *Archaeologia,* xcvii (1959).

——, 'The Crowns of England', *Archaeologia,* lxxxvi (1936).

HOPF, C., 'Bishop Hooper's Notes to the King's Council', *Journal of Theological Studies,* xliv (1943).

——, *Martin Bucer and the English Reformation* (Oxford, 1946).

HOULBROOKE, R.A., 'Henry VIII's Wills: a Comment', *Historical Journal,* xxxvii (1994).

HURSTFIELD, J., 'Corruption and Reform under Edward VI and Mary: The Example of Wardship', *EHR,* lxviii (1953).

IVES, E.W., *Anne Boleyn* (Oxford, 1986).

——, 'The Common Lawyers in Pre-Reformation England', *Transactions of the Royal Historical Society*, fifth series, xviii (1968).

——, 'Henry VIII's Will: a Forensic Conundrum', *Historical Journal*, xxxv (1992).

——, 'The Protectorate Provisions of 1546-7, *Historical Journal*, xxxvii (1994).

JAMES, H., 'The Aftermath of the 1549 Coup and the Earl of Warwick's Intentions', *Bulletin of the Institute of Historical Research*, lxii (1989).

JONES, W.R.D., *The Mid-Tudor Crisis, 1539–1563* (1973).

——, *The Tudor Commonwealth, 1529–1559* (1970).

——, *William Turner: Tudor Naturalist, Physician and Divine* (1988).

JORDAN, W.K., *Edward VI: the Young King* (1968).

——, *Edward VI: the Threshold of Power* (1970).

KERRIDGE, E., *Agrarian Problems in the Sixteenth Century and After* (1969).

——, 'Returns of the Inquisitions of Depopulation', *EHR*, lxx (1955).

KING, J.N., *English Reformation Literature: The Tudor Origins of the Protestant Tradition* (Princeton, 1982).

——, *Tudor Royal Iconography: Literature and Art in an Age of Religious Crisis* (Princeton, 1989).

——, 'Protector Somerset, Patron of the English Renaissance', *Papers of the Bibliographical Society of America*, lxx (1976).

——, 'Freedom of the Press, Protestant Propaganda and Protector Somerset', *Huntington Library Quarterly*, xl (1976).

KREIDER, A., *English Chantries: The Road to Dissolution* (Cambridge, Mass., 1979).

LAMBLEY, K., *The Teaching and Cultivation of French during Tudor and Stuart Times* (Manchester, 1920).

LEADAM, I.S., 'The Security of Copyholders in Fifteenth- and Sixteenth-Century England', *EHR*, viii (1893).

——, *The Domesday of Inclosures, 1517–1518* (1897).

LE HURAY, *Music and the Reformation in England 1549–1660* (1967).

LLOYD, C., and THURLEY, S., *Henry VIII: Images of a Tudor King* (Oxford, 1990).

LOACH, J., 'Opposition to the Crown in Parliament, 1553–1558' (University of Oxford D.Phil. thesis, 1974).

—— , and TITTLER, R., eds, *The Mid-Tudor Polity* (1980).

——, *Parliament and the Crown in the Reign of Mary Tudor* (Oxford, 1986).

——, *Parliament under the Tudors* (Oxford, 1991).

——, 'The Marian Establishment and the Printing Press', *EHR*, ci (1986).

——, '"A Close League with the King of France": Lady Jane Grey's Proclamation in French and its Part in a Planned Betrayal', *Proceedings of the Huguenot Society*, xxv (1991).

——, 'The Function of Ceremonial in the Reign of Henry VIII', *Past and Present*, cxlii (1994).

——, *Protector Somerset: A Reassessment* (Bangor, 1994).

LOADES, D., *John Dudley, Duke of Northumberland, 1504–1553* (Oxford, 1996).

LONDON, H.S., *Royal Beasts* (East Knoyle, 1956).

MCCONICA, J., *The History of the University of Oxford,* iii (Oxford, 1986).

MACCULLOCH, D., 'Kett's Rebellion in Context', *Past and Present,* lxxxiv (1979).

——, ed., 'The *Vita Mariae Angliae Reginae* of Robert Wingfield of Brantham' (Camden Society, 4th series, xxix, 1984).

——, *Suffolk and the Tudors* (Oxford, 1986).

——, 'Bondmen under the Tudors', in *Law and Government under the Tudors,* ed. C. Cross et al. (Cambridge, 1988).

——, *Thomas Cranmer: A Life* (New Haven and London, 1996).

MACGREGOR, A., *The Late King's Goods: Collections, Possessions and Patronage of Charles I in the Light of the Commonwealth Sale Inventories* (1989).

MANNING, R.B., *Village Revolts: Social Protest and Popular Disturbances in England, 1509–1640* (Oxford, 1988).

——, *Hunters and Poachers: A Social and Cultural History of Unlawful Hunting in England, 1485–1640* (Oxford, 1993).

MILLER, H., 'Henry VIII's Unwritten Will: Grants of Lands and Honours in 1547', in E.W. Ives et al., eds, *Wealth and Power in Tudor England: Essays Presented to S.T.Bindoff* (1978).

——, *Henry VIII and the English Nobility* (Oxford, 1986).

NICHOLS, J.G., 'The Second Patent Appointing Edward Duke of Somerset Protector', *Archaeologia,* xxx (1844).

——, *A Catalogue of the Portraits of Edward VI* (1859).

ORMOND, R., ROGERS, M., and DAVIES, A., *Dictionary of English Portraiture* (4 vols, 1979).

PARKER, K.T., *The Drawings of Hans Holbein* (Oxford and London, 1945).

PARRY, G.T.R., 'Inventing "the Good Duke" of Somerset', *Journal of Ecclesiastical History,* xl (1989).

PETTEGREE, A., *Foreign Protestant Communities in Sixteenth-Century London* (Oxford, 1986).

POLLARD, A.F., *England under Protector Somerset* (1900).

von RAUME, F., *The Political History of England* (1837).

REDWORTH, G., *In Defence of the Church Catholic: The Life of Stephen Gardiner* (Oxford, 1990).

RICHARDSON, W.C., *History of the Court of Augmentations* (Baton Rouge, Louisiana, 1961).

ROSE-TROUP, F., *The Western Rebellion of 1549* (1913).

RYAN, L.V., *Roger Ascham* (Stanford, 1963).

SCARISBRICK, J.J., 'Cardinal Wolsey and the Common Weal', in *Wealth and Power in Tudor England: Essays Presented to S.T. Bindoff,* ed. E.W. Ives et al. (1978).

SCHEURWEGHS, G., 'On an Answer to the Articles of the Rebels of Cornwall and Devonshire', *British Museum Quarterly,* viii (1934).

SEYMOUR, W., *Ordeal by Ambition: An English Family in the Shadow of the Tudors* (1972).

SHAGAN, E.H., 'Protector Somerset and the 1549 Rebellions: New Sources and New Perspectives', *EHR*, cxiv (1999).

SHAW, W.A., *Three Inventories of Pictures in the Collections of Henry VIII and Edward VI* (1937).

SIL, N.P., 'Sir Anthony Denny: A Tudor Servant in Office', *Renaissance and Reformation*, new series, viii (1984).

SIMPSON, A., *The Wealth of the Gentry, 1540–1660* (Cambridge, 1961).

SLACK, P.A., 'Dearth and Social Policy in Early Modern England', *Social History of Medicine*, v (1992).

——, 'Social Policy and the Constraints of Government, 1547–58', in *The Mid-Tudor Polity, c. 1540–c.1560*, ed. J. Loach and R. Tittler (1980)

SLAVIN, A.J., 'The Fall of Lord Chancellor Wriothesley: A Study in the Politics of Conspiracy', *Albion*, vii (1975).

SPEIGHT, H.M., 'Local Government and Politics in Devon and Cornwall, 1509–49, with Special Reference to the South-Western Rebellion of 1549' (University of Sussex PhD thesis, 1991).

——, 'Local Government and the South-Western Rebellion of 1549', *Southern History*, xviii (1996).

STARKEY, D., *The Reign of Henry VIII: Personalities and Politics* (1985).

——, ed., *The English Court* (1987).

——, ed., *Henry VIII: A European Court in England* (1991).

——, 'Representation through Intimacy: a Study in the Symbolism of Monarchy and Court Office in England', in *Symbols and Sentiments*, ed. I.M. Lewis (London and New York, 1977).

STREITBERGER, W.R., 'Financing Court Entertainments, 1509–58', in *Research Opportunities in Renaissance Drama*, xxvii (1984).

STRICKLAND, A., *Lives of the Queens of England from the Norman Conquest* (8 vols, 1851).

STRONG, R., *Tudor and Jacobean Portraits* (2 vols, 1969).

——, *Lost Treasures of Britain* (1990).

——, *Artists of the Tudor Court* (1983).

——, *The Tudor and Stuart Monarchy: Pageantry, Painting and Iconography* (3 vols, Woodbridge, 1995).

SURRY, L., *The Portraits of Edward VI* (Portsmouth, 1925).

SWENSEN, P.C., 'Patronage from the Privy Chamber: Sir Anthony Denny and Religious Reform', *Journal of British Studies*, xxvii (1988).

THURLEY, S., 'Henry VIII and the Building of Hampton Court', *Architectural History*, 1988.

——, 'The Banqueting and Disguising Houses of 1527', in *Henry VIII: A European Court in England*, ed. D. Starkey (1991).

——, *The Royal Palaces of Tudor England* (New Haven and London, 1993).

TITTLER, R., and BATTLEY, S.L., 'The Local Community and the Crown in 1553: The Accession of Mary Tudor Re-visited', *Bulletin of the Institute of Historical Research*, lvii (1984).

TREVOR-ROPER, H.R., 'The Bishopric of Durham and the Capitalist Revolution', *Durham University Journal*, new series, vii (1946).

Victoria County History of Warwickshire, vol. ii (1908).

WARNEFORD, F.E., 'The Star Chamber Suits of John and Thomas Warneford', *Wiltshire Record Society*, xlviii (1992).

WESTFALL, S.R., *Patrons and Performers: Early Tudor Household Revels* (1990).

WHITAKER, E.C., *Martin Bucer and the Book of Common Prayer* (Great Wakering, 1974).

WHITING, R., *The Blind Devotion of the People: Popular Religion and the English Reformation* (Cambridge, 1989).

WILLIAMS, F., *An Index of Dedications and Commendatory Verse in English Books before 1642* (1962).

WILLIAMS, P., *The Later Tudors: England 1547–1603* (Oxford, 1995).

WOLFFE, B.P., *Henry VI* (1981).

WORDIE, J.R., 'The Chronology of English Enclosure, 1500–1914', *Economic History Review*, 2nd series, xxxvi (1983).

WORSLEY, G., 'Henry's Flying Horses', *Country Life*, clxxxv (Oct. 1991).

WRIGLEY, E.A., and SCHOFIELD, R.S., *The Population History of England, 1541–1871: A Reconstruction* (Cambridge, Mass., 1981).

YOUINGS, J., 'The South-Western Rebellion of 1549', *Southern History*, i (1979).

INDEX

Adams, Clement 14
agrarian disturbances 57, 58–69; *see also*
  Kett's rebellion
Albiac, Acasse d' 13
Alfred, king 37
Allegory of the Tudor Dynasty (attrib. de
  Heere) 186
Allen, Francis 178
Ambleteuse 91
Ames, John 63
Anabaptism 119, 124
Anglo, S. 33
Annebaut, Claude d' 16
anti-Catholicism 42, 76, 148, 187
Appleyard family 79
Arras 156
Arundel, William Fitzalan, 11th earl of 6,
  31, 32, 92, 93, 95, 109, 139, 165, 172,
  173–4
Arundell, Humphrey 70, 82, 83
Arundell, Sir John 75
Ascham, Roger 12; *Toxophilus* 12n
Ashley (Aysshley), John 15
Ashridge (fish-driver) 82
Aske, Robert 3
Askew, Anne 24n
Aston, Margaret 187
Aucher, Sir Anthony 144
Audley, Thomas, Lord 8, 10
augmentations, court of 34, 112, 141, 175,
  177

Bale, John 24, 45, 126
Barbaro, Giosafat, 'Travels to Tana and
  Persia' 15
Barkham, Berkshire 155
Barnes, Robert 126
Basire, James 188n
Bassano brothers 149
Bateman, John 153
Bath, John Bourchier, earl of 171, 178
Bath and Wells, bishop of 31
Bath and Wells, bishopric 48
Beadle, John 154n
Beaumont, John 113
Becket, Thomas 37
Becon, Thomas 42–3, 62, 180
Bedford, earl of *see* Russell, John
Bedingfield, Sir Henry 171, 175, 177
Beer, Barrett 81–2, 103

Bellin, Nicholas 145, 168
Belmain, Jean 13, 141
Bernard, George vii, xiv
Bill, William 14n
bishops, status of 31, 47, 118–21, 125–30
Blackheath 157
Bodmin, Cornwall 70, 82
Body, William 70
Boisdauphin (French ambassador) 143
Boleyn, Anne (2nd queen of Henry VIII)
  1–2, 164
Boleyn, George (brother of Anne) *see*
  Rochford, Lord
Bonner, Edmund, bishop of London 84,
  121, 125, 126
Book of Common Prayer (1549) 51–2, 65,
  182; sanctioned by parliament only 47;
  opposition to 71, 77–8, 83–4, 101, 121,
  178; revision (1552) 116, 121–4, 151, 182;
  Ridley and 119; Hooper and 119, 122;
  Bucer and 122; Princess Mary and 130
book dedications 43–6
Boulogne 52, 53, 54, 95, 107, 113
Boxley, Kent 78
Boys, Thomas 142
Brand, Robert 81
Brandenburg, marquis of 158
Brandon, Henry (brother of duke of
  Suffolk) 107n
Brereton, William 2
Bridewell palace and hospital, London 100,
  188
Brigden, Susan 23
Brinkelow, Henry 112
Bristol Mint 109
Britton, Angela viii
Bromley, Sir Thomas 17, 25
Brown, Robert 171
Browne, Sir Anthony (later Viscount
  Montagu) 17, 22–3, 29, 33, 36, 133, 178,
  187
Brunswick and Lunenburg, Otho, duke of
  144n
Bryan, Sir Francis 33
Bryan, Margaret 8, 10
Bucer, Martin: and Prayer Book 51, 122;
  De regno Christi 99; Cranmer and 117;
  De ordinatione legitima 118; and Hooper
  120; *Censura* 122–3; on bishops 126; death
  128